"*Permission to Land: Searching for Love, Home and Belonging* is a life-changing story of what it's like to grow up under the veil of bipolarity and drug abuse and to have that multi-generational pattern of abuse shape a life. Marci Brockmann shows us how she used tools she learned in therapy and through the creation of art to find her true self, heal her childhood wounds, and take control of her life to find balance, home and love."

—Sue Montalbano, LMHC

"In truth, *Permission to Land: Searching for Love, Home and Belonging* is a tumultuous journey that is in equal parts grounded and commonplace as it is unique and ephemeral. The reader bears witness to many circumstances that we have all faced at one time or another, and just like a mother, mentor, sister, or best friend, Marci Brockmann translates these experiences in a way we can come to understand the significance of our own conflicts, and our own mountains. Marci's life is a prime example of how one can not only live with their heart wide open and come out the other side but emerge with resolute grace and timeless wisdom."

—Kerry Jane Kelvas, Author and Creator of the YouTube Channel *Metanoia*.

"Marci Brockmann has written a book with a profound message. It captures the emotional component of living a life that was both traumatic and abusive. Her story speaks to everyone as it helps us heal and understand the long-range effects of abuse and the impact it has on our journey and destination. She reaches her reader in a most helpful and informative way making them feel connected to her stories and feel close to her. Her psychological knowledge comes through in her story and gives hope and empowerment to those who suffer from a history of familial mental illness. A must-read."

—Barbara Kanal, DSW

"Owning a story and loving ourselves through that process is the bravest thing that we will ever do."

—Brené Brown.

"Memories have ways of becoming independent of the reality they evoke. They can soften us against those we were deeply hurt by or they can make us resent those we once accepted and loved unconditionally."

—Azar Nafisi, <u>Reading Lolita in Tehran: A Memoir in Books</u>

"People change and things go wrong but just remember life goes on."

—Mac Miller

PERMISSION TO LAND

SEARCHING FOR LOVE, HOME & BELONGING

MARCI BROCKMANN

LIBRARY OF CONGRESS CATALOGING-IN-PUBLICATION
DATA
NAMES: Brockmann, Marci, author.
TITLE: Permission to Land: Searching for Love, Home & Belonging/
Marci Brockmann
IDENTIFIERS: ISBNPaperback: 978-1-64746-221-5
ISBN Hardback: 978-1-64746-222-2
ISBN eBook: 978-1-64746-223-9

Library of Congress Control Number: 2020906069

SUBJECTS: 1. Brockmann, Marci. 2. Family — Divorce—Shared
custody. 3. Bipolarity—Mental Illness—Addiction. 4. Parenthood—
Child rearing. 5. English teachers —Education—United States.
6. Victims of family mental illness—Emotional abuse.
7. Self-awareness—Personal growth—Journaling. 8. Dating—Love—
Romance. 9. Marriage—Remarriage. 10. Title —Permission to Land:
Searching for Love, Home & Belonging

Printed in the United States.
Book Design by Debbie O'Byrne

TABLE OF CONTENTS

ACKNOWLEDGMENTS

This book has been percolating in my brain and heart for a long time and because of the safety and love I now have in my life, I finally felt comfortable enough to face all the dragons I kept hidden in the deep cave of memory. Confronting one's dragons is a challenging, heart-wrenching process that is at once humbling and cathartic as well as painful and joyful. I have made peace with it all. This undertaking would not have been possible without the love and support of my ever-patient husband, Michael, who helped me talk out my ideas and adhere to my message; my amazing daughter, Simone and my son Ethan, who are forever my biggest champions; my wonderful editor and friend, Craig, whose insight and surgeon-like precision helped me excavate my heart more deeply in order to make my book what I had hoped it would be. I'd like to thank my sisters, my father and my stepmother for walking down memory lane with me to dust off old memories and help me find their places in the timeline of our family history.

PROLOGUE

How well do any of us know anyone?
How well do we even know ourselves?

Most people go through their day, even their whole lives, taking things as they come, living on the receiving end of life like a canoe bobbing on the current. What if instead of sitting passively in that canoe, floating along with the rocking water, just staying afloat, you could instead captain a motorboat with a strong engine that you could actively steer ahead toward the future? What would it be like to try that? It might be new to take control, especially if you haven't done it before or in a long time, but how would it feel? It might be pretty great.

Please, allow me the liberty of extending this metaphor a little. Suspend any doubt you might have about my ability to spontaneously turn a canoe into a motorboat. You spend your whole life, until this moment, passively on that canoe, then you decide to command your own strong motorboat and take control. What causes you to choose to change and do that? For everyone, I think the catalyst can be a different thing—or a series of things. It could be ongoing trauma, surviving an accident, grieving a tragic loss. It could be the birth of a baby, a big windfall, or a lucky break.

As a regular journal writer and a self-aware person, I thought that I was in control and aware of the choices I was making. But, years later, as I turned around and took the long view back over the years of my life and read my own voice from my faraway past, I saw patterns and paths that I hadn't noticed along the way, and the whispers of my own voice over more than three decades of writing finally allowed me to get to know myself more completely. Along the way, I discovered a few things that I need to share.

Through excavating my past and writing this memoir, I have told my own truth as I see it. These memories, stories, and experiences happened to me, and although they do involve other people, they are really not about those people. They are about me, the choices I made, how I behaved and thought and felt. This memoir is of my life, and because I chose to write about people without consulting them, I have changed almost all of the names of the living for their anonymity and protection. In some cases, I have conflated people or situations for ease of storytelling and brevity, but the tone, emotions, and experiences are as true to reality as I understand them to be.

We all suffer through and survive trauma, and while the details may change between each of our lives, the stories of others, what shapes and molds them into who they are is highly interesting and infinitely relatable. The pain that my familial mental illnesses, narcissism and addiction caused is particular to my experience, but millions of us share in the wounds and fears they caused. And hopefully, we also share the triumph of overcoming the pain and finding love, home and belonging for ourselves.

Although this is my story, it is also everyone's story.

Thank you for picking up this book and coming on this journey with me.

CHAPTER 1

GRIEF, LOSS, AND WHAT NEVER WOULD BE

"Some people believe holding on and hanging in there are signs of great strength. However, there are times when it takes much more strength to know when to let go and then do it."

—Ann Landers

For the final eighteen months of my mother's life, we did not speak. Not a word. We didn't have any contact. This felt as terrible as it sounds, but my mother was bipolar and a prescription drug addict, and these afflictions turned her into someone else. Where once she was capable of being kind, generous, warm, emotionally available, funny, creative, zealous in her love for me, as well as judgmental, critical, impatient, and often short-tempered, she had become something else. She was a mean, cranky, vindictive, nasty person who was terrible to be around. Drugs and addiction turned her into the worst, most unhappy version of herself.

We had a huge fight in January 2012. She said she was coming over my house to join my children and me in cookie baking after dinner. When she arrived over three hours late to find that we had baked the cookies two hours before, she lost it. Suddenly, I was a horrible daughter who was raising two spoiled, selfish brats. I tried to remain calm as she stood in my casual but carefully decorated living room and screamed at me in her shrill, drug-altered voice. The louder she became, the calmer I was in response. No one was going to behave that way in my home, the home I built out of peace and love to cradle my children and me in safety. That fight was so scary and horrible that it left my kids huddling together on the bed in my daughter's yellow, floral bedroom with the door locked, and me slamming my front door as she cursed me out from my own front lawn in the dark. This was a disaster of biblical proportions. It was a long time coming. Once I calmed my kids down, the first priority, I had the biggest stress-induced asthma attack of my life in the privacy of my own bedroom. I felt like I was wearing a corset that was getting tighter and tighter, squeezing my lungs until I could no longer breathe. Luckily, my inhalers and anti-anxiety medication are never far away.

Before this horrible night, I tried everything I could to help her find herself in the mess that her health had become. I tried privately and kindly talking to her, taking her to doctors, even staging an intervention with the family. Nothing worked. She refused to listen to any of us or acknowledge a problem. Few family members were willing to take a hard line along with me and stand up to her. So, my battle was harder than it had to be because I was the lone voice of reason in a crowd of well-meaning but cowardly others.

This time, I was taking the tough*est*-love approach and would do whatever I needed to do to help my mother, and, above all else, to protect my children. Growing up with my mother like this took a toll on me that I felt throughout my life, and I needed to shield my children from the continuation of this cycle. I didn't want them to suffer any more; it had gone too far already. Since talking to her hadn't worked because she grew so defensive that she didn't hear me at all, I decided to write her a letter so I could calmly, slowly, and succinctly craft my language to tell her precisely what needed to be said. And because it was written, she could read it, and digest it in her own time and refer to it as often as she needed. It took me a week to write the letter. I was so nervous about sending it to her and at last drawing my irrevocable line in the sand that I sent it to her best friend of over forty years to make sure I was kind and loving while also firm and clear. She read the letter and told me that it was beautiful, supportive, kind, loving and very clear about my intentions.

In the letter, I wrote that I loved her but couldn't allow her to treat us the way she was and had for a long time. I implored her to accept help. I made a promise and gave her a choice. I would be with her every day of her life, holding her hand and supporting her, if she would check into an in-patient drug rehabilitation hospital and agree to do the necessary work to change her life. We would circle her with love and support every day, and she would never be alone again. Or, if she chose to do nothing and continue along her path of self-medicating with her oxycodone/ psychotropic drug cocktail, she would never see us again. She would never see her only daughter or her grandchildren again.

It was the toughest thing I've ever had to do, but I had to try tough love to save her and remove my children and me from this toxic situation, no matter the cost to my relationship (such as it was) with my mother.

I never heard from my mother again.

I did learn from her best friend, my Aunt Marie, who agreed with how I was handling this and was working toward the same result for my mother in her own way, that my mother was beyond angry with me and thought I was 100 percent wrong. She was indignant. She could not admit she had a drug problem. She could not admit she was out of control. She dismissed everything I said, saying I was an English teacher and not a doctor. What did I know?

Of all the people in my mother's life, I was the only one to challenge her about her health and take a stand. In all fairness, she had a bitter, mean, awful mouth on her when she was under the influence, when she felt vulnerable and afraid. It was very difficult for everyone, including me, to stand up to that onslaught even if it was in her best interest. Part of me gets that. But only part of me. I always tried to please her and actively wanted to make her proud of me and love me. I think that I always knew there was something extra-sensitive or unpredictable about her and even as a child worked really hard to earn her love. Somewhere deep inside, I learned to doubt if I was a good enough daughter to be loved. When she got angry and blew up, even if it was not my fault, I felt the tension and anxiety of it deep in my bones and would do anything to cheer her up and change the energy of our interaction because when it changed and became positive, lighter and happier, I felt safe and loved. She had been so temperamental for so many years and I felt so beaten down that even though standing up to her destructive behavior was what I had to do, it really hurt me to take that action. It laid me bare and vulnerable to her defensive incursions and I really wished I had a "normal" mother who baked me cookies and hugged me without baggage and agenda.

I was also in a unique position as her only daughter and the mother of her only biological grandchildren; I was in the hot seat. Many times, she attacked me verbally and insulted me to my face when she was under the influence of the drugs, which was most of the time. She flew off the handle and screamed at me for perceived offenses. She cursed me out after my daughter was born because my newborn took my attention away from her. She made impossible demands of me and took no responsibility for her actions. Not one single time did she ever admit that she had said or done any of the hateful things she did or said. It was like they never happened, like I had imagined them. Either she really couldn't remember the events because of the drugs, or she was so deeply embarrassed by her behavior that she couldn't admit it. For her, it would be better to ignore and deny than to face any of it.

No relationship in the world is like that of a mother and her daughter. (As the mother of my daughter, I know this to be true.) Although I knew, as a mother, this was the right decision to protect my children, I felt deeply guilty as a daughter. The guilt was ever present, simmering in the background of my life. For a long time, every time the phone rang, my stomach clenched, and I held my breath until the caller ID showed me who was calling. Once or twice, it was her calling to scream at me (her best friend had warned me), so I didn't answer. Not surprisingly, she didn't leave any messages. And then nothing. Silence.

A little over a year later, in March 2013, I saw my mother in a dark, somber funeral home at my uncle's wake after his shocking and sudden death. I knew there would be a large crowd of family members and friends paying their respects and expressing their grief and empathy. I was very upset about my uncle's passing, but I was also anxious about seeing her there. I insulated myself with my cousins, who were all around my age, for protection. At some point, a group of people shifted, and I could see into the back of the room, and there was an older woman, who looked sallow and gaunt, sitting next to my stepfather. It took me a hot minute to realize that that older woman was my mother. She looked like she'd aged twenty years since I saw her last. It was truly frightening. Had I seen her on the street, without the context of this event, I would not have known it was her.

We had no contact at all, which was fine by me. I missed the mom she was when she was in a good mood and a good place. I wished I could have her back, but since I could not and life gave me *this* mom, I did not want to fight with her at all, especially at my uncle's wake. We were all grieving, and I couldn't handle it. Actually, I didn't want to have to figure out how to handle a skirmish with her there of all places. Later, at my cousin's house, where we were all gathering for solidarity and support, she stationed herself on the opposite side of the split colonial style house in their brand-new kitchen and did not *allow* my nephews or my stepfather to talk to me. If they were loyal to her, they were not to talk to me at all. That's how she wanted to play it, and they were willing to go along. I was shocked. How weak could they be? Fourth-graders know better than to submit to such coercion. I never saw my mother alive again.

In October 2013, over eighteen months after we had had the fight to end all fights, my mother, at the age of sixty-nine, died of heart failure during an afternoon nap, according to the coroner, most likely due to more than twelve years of drug abuse. Her body just gave out. She didn't suffer. It was painless and quiet.

Overwhelmed with sadness, loss, and grief, I tried to process the anger I felt toward her. She had chosen drugs over her only daughter and biological grandchildren, and now my attempt at tough love had failed utterly because she was dead. The little girl inside me was devastated and lost; the grown-up woman was angry and disappointed. I struggled with guilt over what I could not control and tried to make peace with my raging emotions. I had longed for a close mother-daughter relationship, built on trust and love. I had *craved* it.

I would never have that with my own mother, and at that moment I vowed to have that with my daughter. Together, we have worked very hard to create the *bionically* strong bond we have. We have misunderstandings and fights. Sometimes, I have to be more mom than friend, and she bristles a bit but knows everything I say is from genuine love and caring, from my fierce desire to nurture and protect her.

How could I reconcile my complicated relationship with this belligerent woman who used to be my beloved mother? I had no idea. I cried alone. I cried to my therapist. I cried with my children, my friends, my aunt. Answers were stubbornly slow in coming.

We all deal with grief in our own way. My nephew, my stepfather's grandson, had called me after the coroner left with my mother's body. He had gone to her house to visit and found her already dead in her bed. Now that she was gone and the restrictions were lifted, that side of the family was free to talk to me again. It took my mother's death for them to again include me as a member of the family. It was a very awkward and hard-to-process situation.

I was given the responsibility of picking out what she would wear into her final resting place. Walking into my mother's bedroom after so long was otherworldly. Her perfume still hung in the air. Her well-used, cream-colored terrycloth Dearfoam slippers were on the floor next to her bed. Her reading glasses were cast aside on her night table with a well-worn book of word search puzzles. The furnishings were unchanged since I had been there last; the gold-and-jewel-toned coverlet was on the bed, and the matching cornices hung above the windows, overlooking the overgrown backyard.

I remember her almost endless indecision when she was choosing the shape of those cornices. She always struggled with decisions like that. It took her no fewer than ten trips to dress stores to pick out a dress to wear to my wedding. Picking my wedding gown was quicker and more painless. It took her weeks to pick out siding for her house, only for her to second-guess the decision and not do the project.

I don't remember what I picked out for her to wear, loose black pants and a colorful flowy top of some sort, I guess, but I made sure she had those slippers on her feet. Comfort was key. I don't remember her jewelry or anything about her appearance. Jews have closed-casket funerals, but I wanted to see her one last time. She didn't look like herself. I could tell it was her, obviously, but she looked old and altered. It was hard to stand there, knowing it was the last time I would ever lay eyes on her, knowing it had been so long since she had hugged me. I placed a letter in the casket with her, one that I wrote on stationery with a beach scene, telling her how devastated I was. I needed to have the last word.

No one in the family was willing to eulogize her: not her sister, her cousins, her husband. As her only child, I was compelled to step up and give her a respectable send-off, despite our complicated relationship and the eighteen months of silence that preceded her death. For two days, in between making arrangements for her funeral and the actual burial, I pored over seventy years of family photographs and forced myself to remember the good times: the themed birthday parties, the holidays shared with family and friends, the laughter over stupid Halloween costumes, graduations, weddings, bar mitzvahs, vacations, and silliness.

I saw her as a beloved child with her parents and sister. I saw her laughing with friends, smiling with my father in good times and later with her second husband. I saw her thin and curvier. Little by little, I started to see my mother as a flawed, imperfect human being who had a dreadful disease. She suffered and endured pain and disappointment. She had ileitis, kidney stones, and Crohn's disease. She loved her family with all her heart, and when she could, she tried to make each of us feel special. My mother was never happier than when her friends and family were around her. She had been a generous, beautiful soul who became lost and couldn't find her way back. I stood in the front of the room at the funeral home and told the assembled family and friends what I knew about my mother to be true. I made it through my eulogy with grace and kindness, emphasizing who she was before her illnesses and addiction, focusing on the woman she probably always wanted to be, and trying to ensure that others' last memories of my mother would be happy ones.

The bright, cream-colored room in the funeral home was filled with the many people who came to pay their respects and say goodbye to her. I was happy there was such a good turnout. So many of her friends from years earlier came to share the grief and tell me stories about her that I never knew.

My eulogy for my mother:

Thank you all for coming here this morning as we share in our grief over the loss of my mother, Janet. Where do I begin? How do I sum up my feelings for my mother and our relationship? Over the last few days, images of our relationship have been playing in my mind like a slideshow. The sweet, loving, and nostalgic mixed together with arguments and anguish, as our lives blended together so that no one memory is completely good or bad. Everything is laced with essences of the other.

My mother was a complicated woman, who was haunted by her own issues for most of life, but she had a heart of gold. She had a generous, loving spirit, and she bathed those she loved with more warmth than one hundred suns.

My earliest memory of my mother is from when I was about four years old. I was wearing my favorite long, white and green gingham dress with the blue fabric flower on the blue-ribbon waistband, running down the sidewalk into my mother's waiting arms. She held me tightly up to her body as she walked into our house. The memory fills me an overwhelming feeling of safety and makes me realize that no matter what our relationship evolved into because of her illness, she always loved me with every cell of her being. That is what

I am trying to hold onto while letting all the other feelings go. Her love for me has allowed me to love my own children as steadfastly and intensely as I do.

When I was a little girl, she wanted to have the house in which all my friends wanted to come to play. She created a home filled the laughter of children, which was one of her favorite sounds. My friends and I would bake with her, do arts and crafts and a thousand projects. When my younger cousins were born, they would come, sometimes for weeks at a time, and join in on the fun. Some of our best memories growing up were of these times.

We used to love our shopping trips at the Walt Whitman Mall for clothes, shoes or gifts and used to make a game out of eating the chocolate truffles from the chocolatier out of their waxy paper bag. We held the luxurious chocolate between our tongues and the roofs of our mouths, relishing every bit of the creamy goodness. We felt so decadent.

My mother was a consummate party thrower. She'd stress over making everyone's favorite foods, the tiniest details like ornaments on the Chanukah tree, and tiny dreidel-shaped erasers and toys for the little children; her parties and Seders were always the hits of the holiday season. She would shower her children, grandchildren, nieces and nephews with very generous gifts because my mother loved to give people things that made them happy. She was happiest when giving to others.

To my mother, family was the most treasured gift. She loved her parents, sister, best friend Marie, aunts, cousins, grandchildren, nieces and nephews with such steadfast loyalty and devotion. She always said to me that family is the most important thing. That one should always be able to count on one's family no matter what. This was a lesson that she said she learned from my grandmother Betty and her three amazing sisters, Mattie, Sylvia and Gertie. They had learned to love this ferociously from their mother, my Great-Grand-mother Anna. So, my cousins and I grew up in a matriarchy of love and devotion. No one ever had to guess, with any of these amazing women, how they felt about you. If they loved you, you knew it without a doubt. They did everything they could to make us feel loved, treasured and protected.

From my mother, I learned some pretty invaluable lessons. Through the way she lived her life, I learned how to love and be generous with my heart, how to look at the positive side of any situation, how to do research to help make a deci-sion, creativity, flexibility, patience, resilience, independence, self-sufficiency and not to let fear stand in my way. Together, my mother and I painted our house, figured out how to lay tile and linoleum flooring, tended our vegetable and flower gardens -- although the rabbits ate most of our crops, we kept planting anyway. I learned from each of these experiences and am, in turn, teaching them to my children.

She always had projects in varying degrees of completion. Creative projects that she dedicated herself to 100 percent. For PTA fundraisers, she would organize fashion shows, write whole scripts for plays and songs to parody famous songs and movies, she designed newsletters and organized phone chains. She wanted to be involved in my education as much as possible, and her long-term commitment to the PTA was her way of doing it.

She loved to go to Atlantic City and play the slot machines and people watch and used to take frequent trips there with my grandmother and great aunts. She and Allan loved to go fishing out of Captree with their grandchildren. She loved to get together with her girlfriends or cousins and go out to dinner for a night of laughter. She loved to hang out with her grandkids, nieces, and nephews and play with them and continue the tradition of arts and crafts projects. She loved to throw parties and fill her home with the sound of laughter of her friends and family. She loved to come over to my house and play board games or bake cookies with my kids and me. My mother loved to spend time with her best friends, Marie and Tommy, talking to all hours of the night, going shopping and just being together. We spent days, long weekends, and our annual Christmas Eves with them making treasured memories as members of their extended family.

I'd like to share a funny story that I have always loved from my mother's adolescence. Somewhere around 1960, my grandparents were away on a trip, shortly after my mother got her driver's license. Mom was eager to drive, and somehow, she persuaded her younger sister, my Aunt Maggie, that they should adopt a duck for a pet. She convinced her sister that their parents would think this was the greatest idea, and they drove from Syosset to Sayville for this duck. It was a cute duckling that waddled around the house. Needless to say, my grandparents were none too pleased when they returned home but saw how in love their daughters were with this duck and let the duck stay. My grandmother even bought the duck a red leash, and they walked it around their neighborhood in Syosset. But ducks grow, so does their mess, noise and ability to climb two flights of stairs. Eventually, my grandfather couldn't stand it any longer and tried to give the duck away to a restaurant called Villa Victor because they had a lovely duck pond. He drove over, placed the duck in the pond and drove away, but the duck followed him. So, he drove back and again placed the duck in the pond, and again the duck followed him. After the third or fourth attempt at this, he finally paid a gas station attendant from across the street to hold the duck until he was out of sight, then place him in the pond with the other ducks. He then told his daughters that the duck was better off there in the nice pond with his friends. So, when I heard this story, and I was asking to take the baby chicks home from my first-grade class, my mother couldn't say no.

Toward the end, my mother's world shrank as she struggled with illness, but I know that her love and devotion to her family and friends never shrank—her heart was full of love and cherished memories. Her impact on all of our lives will never be forgotten as we will treasure our own private memories of her forever. Someone once said, "Nobody can go back and start a new beginning, but anyone can start today and make a new ending." Let's make today the day we all start anew and recommit ourselves to living the best lives we can, stay in touch between milestone events, try something new, call an old friend, let go of an old grudge. Let's pay tribute to my mother by keeping her commitment to friends and family in our hearts.

The funeral and *shiva* were hard to get through as I found myself explaining excerpts of the story of our last year or two to countless people. I was trying my best to be strong for my children, to provide them with comfort and peace, but inside I was screaming.

I was desolate and outraged that she died while all that had transpired between us was unresolved. I felt wounded. Incomplete. Shattered. I had no closure. How would I heal the emptiness and betrayal I felt after my mother chose drugs over me? I had found some measure of forgiveness through the photographs that helped me to eulogize her respectfully, but I was still aching for comfort from the woman she had been before the disease of drug addiction took her away from me— the woman she had been many years before, who genuinely loved me and was proud of me. I hadn't seen that woman in so long, it was hard to remember who she was. During the day, the distractions of life diverted my thoughts and occupied my mind, but every night, I slept with a hole in my heart.

A few weeks later, while going through her things, I found a letter she had written to me shortly before my daughter was born, twelve years earlier, while I was pregnant and before the very heavy drug abuse started. She was facing another intestinal resection surgery for her Crohn's disease and, being the hypochondriac she was, she thought she was going to die on the operating table. She didn't die then; instead, she had filed this letter away in her locked filing cabinet and had not given to me, but now I had it. In this letter, written in her unmistakably neat script handwriting on a piece of colorful paper depicting a sunset, she told me how much she loved my children and me. We were the light of her life and heart. No mother could be prouder than she was of me. I had trouble focusing on the words through the flood of tears as I read the letter over and over. This was her reaching toward me from beyond to give me the forgiveness and closure I needed. She heard me. Somehow, she led me to the letter at the moment I needed it the most.

In the six years since her death, I have come to know my mother more than I knew her in life. She was beloved and respected by many. She is missed daily, and the gifts of her spirit live on in her best friends, my family, my cousins, my children, and in me. What I learned is that we are all flawed and struggling.

Drug addiction affects more than just the addict. Its far-reaching effects change relationships and ruin lives. Friends and family are powerless and have no ability to "fix" the addiction if the addict refuses and is in denial.

We are each responsible for and capable of healing only ourselves.

We are the only ones on this planet over whom we have any control. Accepting powerlessness over others is the first step toward our own healing. We are all on our own paths, and sometimes we are lucky to have our paths merge with those we love and who can give us love in return, as well as guidance, advice, encouragement, entertainment, laughter, and hope.

Every day, we need to reach out and share our hearts and souls with those we love. Today and every day, we need to let them know how much we cherish them and the blessings they bring to our lives. Now is the time. Now is all we have. I have made it my practice to tell those whom I love that I love them every time I see them. Who knows when the last time will be? I never want to let anything important remain unsaid.

For weeks after my mother died, I was in tears. I'd be calm for a time and then flooded with sorrow all over again. Grief is not linear. I wept for the loss of my mother and the loss of the hope I had that she would get better and once again be the mother who loved me.

Alone in my house, I was sitting on my beige striped living room couch on a Sunday night. The house was eerily quiet because my children were with their father. Suddenly, I heard the upstairs toilet flush. This was not water pressure equalizing in the pipes. This was a full flush. No one else was home. At the time, I had no pets except for two finches named after characters in *To Kill a Mockingbird*: Jem Finch and Scout Finch. I felt some sort of energy come down the stairs, sweep around the house, pass through me and out the back of the house. This energy was pure, peaceful, and cold (in temperature). I had a very clear feeling that my mother flushed the toilet. Let me tell you, my mother had Crohn's disease, so if there was a household noise that I would associate with her, it was a toilet flushing. Sorry, but it's true. Before this moment, I was a hard-science atheist with zero belief in an afterlife, but that suddenly and irrevocably shifted. Despite having no explanation as to how, I was sure my mother had been there, and I had an overwhelming feeling of peace.

Several days later, I had a dream in which she was standing behind me in her bedroom in the Commack, Long Island house where I grew up. I was leaning over, resting my head on my folded arms on top of her dark, wooden dresser; she moved my dark brown hair away from the back of my neck and kissed me there lightly. I felt her move my hair and kiss me. The movement of my hair partially woke me up from sleep, and I felt the kiss on my neck. I knew she was in the room standing next to my bed. I didn't see her, but knew she was there. I smelled her perfume. I talked to her. I wasn't nervous or scared, although my heart was racing. I told her I love her and miss her and hope she is at peace.

CHAPTER 2
A PSYCHIC'S VISION

You might have strong beliefs for or against spiritualism. I honor and respect that, and I don't necessarily recommend that visiting a psychic is for everyone. I don't claim to understand exactly what happened, but this experience brought me closer to understanding my relationship with my mother and grandmother and gave me hope in the next life at a time when I was feeling empty. Truthfully, I was a little freaked out as this was something I never considered before.

One morning on my way to work I suddenly decided that I would seek a psychic to get some answers and resolution. This was a very out of character thing for me to do. My mother believed in psychic power. I did not. I had never even considered this before and had no idea whom to see. I did a Google search of "Long Island psychics" and found Dawn Joly in Smithtown and called to make an appointment. Her receptionist told me that she is normally booked at least six weeks in advance but had just had a cancellation for five o'clock that day. I took that appointment. I told her only my first name and paid with cash when I arrived. I told her nothing about myself or why I was coming to see the psychic.

She knew only my first name. There was no way she could search the Internet for information about me with the next to nothing I told her.

Dawn Joly opened the door to her inner office and ushered me in from the waiting room, with a wide sweeping arm. "Welcome, Marci. Your mother and grandmother are already here waiting for you."

I looked at her incredulously and she said, "I rarely have last-minute cancellations. Your mother arranged the five o'clock cancellation that allowed me to have this appointment available tonight because she wanted to talk to you."

My mind was already spinning. *My mother brought me here.* Really? Could this be true? I was reeling.

Dawn ushered me into her office, which had some interesting art and colorful pictures of Elvis on the walls. She asked me to make myself comfortable and sit on a light colored, leather couch across from her black leather swivel chair. There was a small glass coffee table between us, upon which sat a large tissue box. She explained her process, that she scribbled with a pencil in a steno pad as a method of channeling spirits. She went on to tell me things that my mother was telling her about my life that she would have no way of knowing. These were things that couldn't be found in a Google search, had she even had a basis for one. She told me that we are Jewish, as my mother and grandmother were sitting at a table eating bagels and lox. My grandmother was cleaning crumbs off the white tablecloth, and she and my mother were happy and together.

Dawn said she could tell that my mother was recently deceased because she was yelling, thinking that she couldn't be heard otherwise. Indeed, my mother had died six weeks prior. She told me that my mother loves me and is very proud of me and the mother I have become. She confirmed for me that it was my mother in the house with me that Sunday night flushing the toilet and in my dream. She had been trying to talk to me. Trying to ease my pain and give me some peace.

Through Dawn, my mother told me that I had to protect my kids from people who might hurt them. This is a common one. Nothing special or specific there. She said that my daughter's happiness and destiny are in the arts and that I should encourage her as much as possible in her creativity. Indeed, my daughter has always been an artist. From her toddler years, Simone was drawing with any crayon or marker she could get her hands on. Dawn said that my son is brilliant in math and that it will take him far in life. My job was to guide my children to their paths in life and keep them safe. Through Dawn, my mother said that the man I was then dating was one of my soul mates but not who I would spend my life with. She was right; we broke up shortly after the holiday season that year. She said that my nephew, who was about to get married, would be happy for a while, but eventually there would be another woman in his life. Would this be another wife? A daughter? Who knows?

The biggest revelation for me was that my mother thinks I made the right decision in not talking to her in the end, in cutting her out of our lives. Despite how hard it was for me to stop talking to her, she knows it was the right thing to do. She is proud of me for protecting my children and wishes she'd had the same strength to protect me. She said that I'm a better mother than she ever was, and that she forgives me and will love me always. By this time, I was bawling my eyes out: ugly crying, my face full of snot. Dawn asked if this all made sense to me, a fact she was able to ascertain by my intense emotional reaction. This was exactly what I so badly needed to hear. This released me from my guilt. This gave me peace and, in essence, returned my mother, the one she had been before the drug addiction, to me. There could be no greater gift to a grieving daughter.

By this point in the session, I was sobbing, with mounds of used tissues crumpled at my feet. Dawn Joly gave me closure and confirmed for me that my mother was still with me, that she is there watching over us. In this single hour, she also threw my atheism out the window and made me more spiritual, giving me the belief in life after death and the message that love is everything. What can be better than that? My own personal cosmology was permanently altered.

A few weeks later, for the first time since his death in 1994, I had a dream about my grandfather, Max. He was my maternal grandfather, and we had been very close. He was tall and had broad shoulders, dark, olive skin, very kind, brown eyes, a generous and warm heart, a penchant for corny jokes, and very soft hands. He was a competitive golfer who had been known to play in the snow with a red ball. Max worked hard in the garment industry in New York City, the founder of a women's knitwear company. He doted on me and loved me with all his heart. He died at the age of seventy-eight, after years of illnesses. According to Jewish law, any funeral had to be within twenty-four to forty-eight hours. We were waiting for this inevitable end and were prepared, so the funeral was on May 27, my twenty-sixth birthday. Not the greatest way to spend one's birthday, but I did get to spend it with my family and friends, and in some universal or elemental way, I felt that this forever connected my grandfather and me.

My lovely dream of Grandpa Max went like this. I walked into a dark room where my grandfather was waiting for me. All the walls and ceiling were covered by honey-colored wood paneling, and the floor was honey-toned wood, also. There was a large ceiling fan with palm fronds as fan blades silently whirring above, creating a cool, gentle breeze in the room. My grandfather was sitting in a wicker chair watching the Yankees on an old black-and-white television with rabbit ear antennas on top. He smiled at me, warm and welcoming, when I walked in. When Grandpa Max smiled, he smiled with his warm, brown eyes and his whole being. He extended his right hand, and as I held it with my left hand, I actually felt the precise way his soft skin and warm fingers felt in mine. The sensation of holding his manicured hand was exactly as I now remembered. He wordlessly led me around to the wicker chair next to him on his left and held my right hand in his left. We sat silently next to each other, holding hands, watching the Yankees game on that old television. We looked at each other occasionally, and I felt very calm, an enveloping peace and all-encompassing love. It was joyous and comforting and gave me a great sense of peace that I can still feel deep in my heart each time I think of it. It still brings tears to my eyes. I believe that my Grandpa Max came to visit me in this dream not only to remind me that he loves me and is still with me but also to reassure me that he also believes that I handled the situation with my mother, at what turned out to be the end of her life, the right way. I felt his love and pride. Of course, I cannot know for sure if this was my grandfather speaking, but it affected me deeply and gave me a profound sense of closure and peace.

Since my mother's death, which was years after her own parents' deaths, most of my family on that side has fractured. The only contact I have with most of them, in her generation and my own, is through social media and an occasional visit or family event. Dreams of my grandparents and my mother from the "great beyond" are comforting and soothing and remind me that I have been greatly loved.

Children can almost never give up on their parents. So, the fact that I was able to give up on or walk away from my mother and let her proceed with her drug addiction is a testament to how much I love my children. If it had been only I who was affected by her, I probably would have continued slogging away at that destructive and toxic relationship, the same as I'd been doing for more than forty years. I felt like a mama bear protecting her cubs because my children were so negatively affected by her belligerent outbursts, her selfishness, and her manipulation. During her last visit to my house, my children were cowering in Simone's room, hiding on her bed with the door locked, crying. That could not continue. I had to do something. I had to do something decisive to fix the situation. I needed to protect my kids and end the bad Jerry Springer episode that was our relationship with her at the time. I knew that ending the situation was vital for my children and their well-being.

For a long time, I harbored and sublimated an intense amount of guilt because I knew that my children were more important than anything. Regardless of whether you believe what happened in Dawn Joly's office, I *needed* to believe it so I could get the closure I needed.

My mother forgives me. My grandmother forgives me.

They insisted, from the great beyond, that what I had done was the right thing—brave and strong and good.

Chapter 3

TO THE MOON AND BACK
(50 MILLION TIMES)

"Children will not remember you for the material things you gave them but for the feeling that you cherished them."

—Richard L. Evans

My mother used to say to my children and me that she loved us *to the moon and back*. It was a phrase we all associate with her. During the week before the fifth anniversary of my mother's death, I was watching the late-afternoon news on the overhead television while donating blood at the New York Blood Center, and on screen were the words *to the moon and back*. There was some news story about the anniversary of the Apollo landing or something, but what a coincidence that that should be the text on the screen. *To the moon and back!* Exactly what my mom always said to me. *I love you to the moon and back.* As a message from the beyond. She's with me. I used to think things like this were bullshit, but now I'm listening.

After she died, I started saying this phrase to my children as a tribute to her. My son, Ethan, turned *I love you to the moon and back* into *I love you to the moon and back 50 million times.* He has always been a numbers kid. It is now something I say to them whenever we speak, and in texts it has become ILYTTMAB.

Call it a coincidence or whatever you'd like, but as I left the blood center after my donation and got into my car, I started the engine and the Johnny Mathis song *Chances Are* started to play on the audio system. This was going to be the song we picked for me to sing at her second wedding. I hadn't been listening to music at all that day. I was listening to an audiobook, *Rising Strong as a Spiritual Practice* by Brené Brown, and as a function of my Toyota Rav4's sound system, it connects automatically to my phone and the audio book starts immediately. This time, however, I felt that this was my mother making sure I heard her and knew she is always with me and loves me. She communicated this through Johnny Mathis's soothing voice, which she always loved. Love, faith, and comfort from beyond.

Grief is not linear. It doesn't diminish over time. It isn't as all-consuming, over time, but it bubbles up in unexpected ways at unpredictable times. The trick is just not to fight it. Feel it authentically. Let ourselves live with the grief and let it stand beside us. The only way out is through.

As I write this, it's the week of the sixth anniversary of my mother's death, and I'm still mourning her and the loss of what our relationship could have been. I still feel cheated out of the relationship I wanted with her, but I learned to channel that into fostering that kind of relationship with my children and stepchildren. And even my students. I want them to know me. To really know who I am, warts and all. Our beauty lies in our imperfections. That is what makes us unique and human. That's how we really know each other and how we are truly seen. I used to hide my flaws, feeling that somehow they made me less worthy of love, but I couldn't have been more wrong. I'm flawed and imperfect, and I was and am loved.

During the time my mother and I were apart, I was often alone. I was alone standing up to her. I was alone in fighting for her life, and then I felt alone in suffering with my own grief. But through the funeral and the process of sitting *shiva* in accordance with Jewish tradition, what I found was fellowship in my grief with others. I was astonished and overjoyed at the numbers and variety of friends, coworkers, and family who gathered around my children and me in our home and offered shared connection, solace, and empathy. They helped us struggle with our own grief by bearing witness to it and sharing theirs. This helped immeasurably. There are no words to describe this adequately, and to all those who showed up for me, for us, thank you from the bottom of my heart.

Eben Alexander's *Proof of Heaven: A Neurosurgeon's Journey into the Afterlife* explores this man's own journey into the beyond after death. Dr. Alexander is a neurosurgeon and, previous to his story, a hard-science atheist. He suffered from bacterial meningitis and spent a month in a coma. While he was unconscious and while his family and medical team sought answers, he was in heaven with a young girl who he felt knew him, but whom he did not know. She showed him that heaven is a place wholly embodying love that is so beautiful and comforting that our vocabulary is too limited to express it. He did eventually wake up and regain his health, and what he learned is that heaven exists, that there is some sort of life after death, and that the most important thing about life is love. Pure love. Interestingly and hauntingly enough, as it turns out, the young girl who welcomed him in heaven was an older sister who died before he was born, someone he was never told about. It was a beautifully moving journey of love and discovery of the consciousness and the human soul.

What is the take-home message here? It's a deep one. Our time on this earth is limited and precious. Living in the moment is the new phrase, but the concept is as old as the earth itself. Authentically loving the people in our lives and staying true to ourselves is the key to happiness, and not living with regret.

Stop saying *what if* and start living now.

To put this chapter of my life into focus, to make sense of the twisted, complicated nature of our mother-daughter relationship, and my relationships with the rest of my family, journaling and revisiting photo albums had the effect of my distant past reaching forward through time to clarify my behavior and reactions to others' behavior.

Stepping back into the past, through the dusty shoe boxes of family photos, my mother's photo albums with their sticky plastic pages, and my own collection of journals in plain and fancy books, on legal pads dating to the mid-1980s, allows a time traveler's view backward and forward simultaneously. By looking both ways, I traced the patterns that emerged and began to take a long view to analyze and interpret them, to hopefully discover a larger truth within them all. This memoir is my Tardis (just another metaphor for you Dr. Who fans.)

CHAPTER 4
IGNORANCE IS BLISS

Ignorance is bliss. A cliché, but true. My early childhood was mostly happy. I was not touched much by whatever misery and domestic difficulty grew in my house. We lived in an average, middle-class, suburban neighborhood on Long Island, in a lovely, white high ranch with brown shutters on a half-acre of land with lots of trees on the perimeter. The whole tract of land that our development was built on used to be a vast potato farm, and many of the huge oak trees in our yards were old enough to have been part of the farm. The oak tree in my next-door neighbor's yard had old, rusty bolts and chains embedded into it, the likely remnants of the chaining up of farm animals. As children, we used to make up stories about the animals we imagined tethered to this tree in the middle of the farm.

We had a great weeping willow tree in our backyard that I loved to climb and hide in, especially because it freaked my mother out when I did. I was friends with all the neighborhood kids. It was the 1970s, and we all played together—riding bikes and Big Wheels, playing hopscotch, jump rope, and make-believe games like store, school, and house. For a while, our games included complicated dramas based on the *Six Million Dollar Man* and the *Bionic Woman,* Steve Austin and Jamie Sommers from the hit televisions shows. The weeping willow in my backyard, which was huge, served as HQ. We'd climb the tree and have meetings with Oscar Goldman in our pretend government spy agency, and he'd send us on missions to save the world. Because it was my tree, I was usually Jamie Sommers. The other kids played the other characters. In the summer, we'd go in each other's pools and swim. I don't remember seeing any parents with us during our neighborhood escapades, but I guess they were around somewhere. Everyone got along most of the time, and we ran the neighborhood.

My parents fought a lot and hardly ever had a peaceful day together, but as I said, I was mostly oblivious. I knew it, but I didn't *know* it. When I was very little, my parents carted me around to all sorts of places—family's homes, stores, restaurants and a bunch of therapists and marriage counselor's offices. I always had crayons, coloring books, and paper to keep me entertained, and it wasn't until I was much older that I even realized where we had been. I don't think these appointments helped my parents at all. They were always fighting.

My mother had a pathological pattern with respect to these couple's therapy appointments. She was inherently narcissistic and couldn't fathom that she was in any way even partly responsible for the marital difficulties, or even her own happiness. They'd go see a new therapist and fill the doctor in on what their problems and dynamics were, and as soon as the therapist suggested that my mother wasn't a 100 percent innocent victim and that she had to take some responsibility for the state of her life and the state of her own happiness, she fired the therapist and angrily labeled him or her a quack. She refused to ever see her own culpability in anything. Whatever was wrong or making her unhappy was always someone else's fault.

My mother could never let anything go; forgiveness and resolution were never part of her vocabulary or behavior. Whenever my parents fought, my mother brought up past arguments and perceived slights, and this caused my father to defend, not only the problem at hand, but also past things that he thought were already resolved. I remember him yelling back at her and accusing her of "beating a dead horse." I think my mother always felt inadequate and undeserving of love, which made everything for her into a fight to prove her worthiness by demanding that others work hard to make her happy. My dad often walked right into her emotional traps, which always triggered angry explosions. In his defense, she set up no-win scenarios for him, and later me, so he was wrong no matter what he did.

I know that they were very concerned that their fighting was negatively affecting me as a kid and had me evaluated by at least one of their therapists. I only have vague flickers of memory of one of those meetings. I climbed up onto a scratchy, brown sofa and was asked a few questions by a friendly brown-haired man. I didn't know him, but I wasn't scared, as I answered his questions—whatever he asked. The determination of my mental health after this little meeting was that I did not know much of what was going on with my parents; I was aware of their fighting, but I was naively unaffected by it. I think this was an overly simplistic view that they wanted to believe. Sure, I was generally a happy child, but I also had a secret world inside my own head where I was scared and anxious. I played out these emotions with my stuffed animals and Barbie dolls, pretending dangerous situations and angry fighting. If anyone was paying closer attention to me, they would have seen it well before I was old enough to articulate what I was feeling.

There were times when the anger got particularly venomous and loud and I had no choice but to be aware of the arguing, the volatility, and the high anxiety in the air. I usually hid in my room. I had a spot inside my closet, I'd slide the left sliding double door open, move the stacked boxes to the side, and scrunch myself into a ball with a teddy bear or my pillow, close the door and quietly wait it out. Other times, I was oblivious. I let it roll. But I think I internalized a lot more than I admitted to anyone, including myself. I wouldn't know this or the effects of it for years.

Because I grew up with so much unpredictable volatility, anger and yelling, deep down I felt it was my fault or at least that if I was better, smarter, more caring, or better behaved then I could have prevented or made the situation better. I was and still am to a degree, physically affected by others' anger and, over time, I learned behaviors and relationship diplomacy that, in my mind, would prevent angry emotional explosions that I internalized as my fault. I carried this unhealthy, people pleasing behavior into almost every single romantic relationship of my life.

I think that what kids experience is just accepted as normal because that is all they know. Whatever they experience—the happy, the traumatic, the sad—it's all they know, so to them it's normal. It's not until they are older and see what it's like in the houses of extended family and friends that the abnormal at home starts to look abnormal.

I was mostly concerned with my artwork. I do remember drawing in class when I was very young. Everyone at my table was drawing their house, pets, cars, or something else kids draw. I, on the other hand, was very focused on drawing a pattern of yellow and white flowers like one would see on fabric or wallpaper. I was trying to create a repeating floral pattern with a pink background. I didn't have the skill yet to produce what was in my mind's eye, but this was my focus nonetheless.

My parents often slept in separate rooms, especially in the latter 1970s, from when I was about the age of eight or ten. They explained to me that my dad was a light sleeper and my mom liked to stay up late, so separate rooms made sense. What did I know? I was a kid. I accepted this. I just know that I kissed daddy good night in the guest room with its lonely twin bed and mommy in the master bedroom with a king-sized bed and the plush purple carpeting. Now that I'm a married adult, I know that this was a symptom of their deeply troubled marriage. They had nothing in common. They didn't often socialize with other couples, except for my mother's best friends or family. They never went out on date nights or talked intimately that I ever saw. They slept separately. We didn't have much of a family life, the three of us. We ate quiet dinners of takeout in front of the white plastic television. I talked with them separately, not as a family. We went on only one vacation that didn't involve visiting my maternal grandparents in Florida. My dad was always working.

There was time when I was a very little girl, probably five or six, and my grandparents were coming over very often. I think even then I noticed that my mother was in a better mood and felt better when her parents were around. I always loved and adored them and never wanted them to go home. This one night, I hid their car keys in the toaster oven and went to sleep when I was told. I was very excited and had trouble sleeping actually because I knew that when it was time for them to go, they would not know where the keys were and wouldn't be able to leave. As a child, I didn't see that they would probably just figure out eventually that I did something with them and wake me. I thought that meant that they would have to sleep over and I would get to play with them again in the morning. But, of course, they woke me and asked, "Marci, do you know where the keys went?" I sheepishly slid out of my cozy bed and dragged my small slippered feet across the floor until I got to the kitchen and opened up the toaster oven. I thought they'd be mad at me, but it turns out they thought I was just a little scamp. It was fun, and I guess I communicated to them effectively enough that I didn't want them to leave because all I have are warm memories of that time.

I was very close with my maternal grandparents, Betty and Max. Betty was a warm and nurturing caretaker, wonderful mother and grandmother. She loved her children fiercely, but loved me, the first grandchild, and then Stephen and Sarah, the younger grandchildren, just as fiercely. When I was a little girl, Grandma regularly took me for lunch at a Howard Johnson's restaurant near her home in Syosset. We would sit in a booth and eat lunch, just the two of us. I felt so special and grown up as she lavished all her attention on me. We'd play a game that she made up where we would pretend to be married ladies with small children and we'd have a conversation about what our lives were like.

Grandma would say with melodramatic exasperation, "My husband works such long hours that when he gets home he is so tired. He has no clue what I put up with all day from my kids. They wear me out!"

I'd reply, "Husbands don't know how hard it is to be home all day with the kids while trying to clean the house."

Grandma would roll her eyes and agree, and then continue. "These children drain all my energy as they are always asking me questions about everything."

"I can't wait until mine are old enough to help out around the house," I said, feigning the voice of a fed-up housewife even though I was only about eight years old. For the game, which lasted the whole lunch, we kept this overly dramatic conversation going.

After every meal, we ordered Swiss chocolate almond ice cream, which was served in fancy glass dishes, and as gross as it sounds, we would eat the ice cream and spit out the almonds into our napkins. It was a competition, and we counted the almonds when we were when done. The one with the most almonds won. Won what? Nothing. It was just a game. If people looked at us curiously, I never noticed.

Grandma took me on shopping trips to the mall several times a year, and we spent the entire day picking out clothes for me. I would try everything on while she sat outside the fitting room and watched me model if for her. She would decide if she liked the outfit or not and whatever we liked, she bought and while I was sheepish about her spending so much money, she was not. It was so much fun! We just cut off all the tags before we took the clothing inside so grandpa wouldn't see. Despite owning his own company in the garment industry in New York City, he didn't really know the retail prices of things, and this was their way to avoid arguments. I got lots of great clothes, so I wasn't about to intervene.

As the eldest of her three sisters, Grandma was the matriarch of the family. After years of watching and taking care of her younger sisters while their mother, my great grandmother Anna, was working, she was the first married and the first to have children.

I have always loved the story of how my grandparents got together. My grandmother lived with her parents and sisters in a Brooklyn tenement apartment building with one shared bathroom on each floor and one phone shared by the entire building. Betty had heard the new boy, Max, who lived upstairs, talk on the phone in the hallway. She could tell that he was smart, and she liked the way he looked. She wanted to go out with him and had a hunch that they would get along well, but girls did not ever ask boys out in those days, so she had to engineer a plan. Her youngest sister, Gertie, was having trouble in math, so Betty told her to go upstairs and ask the new boy, Max, for help but not to bring her book. Betty knew that Max would need to see the math problems to be able to help Gertie, so he would have to come down to their apartment. While Gertie was upstairs talking to Max, Betty told her mother that if the boy from upstairs asked her to the movies for Saturday night, she had to say yes. Great-grandma Anna evidently agreed.

A few minutes later, Max came into the apartment behind Gertie to help her with math, and Betty flirted with him. Just as predicted, a few minutes later, Max said, "I suppose your mother wouldn't let you come to the movies with me Saturday night." Without missing a beat, Betty shouted across the apartment, "Ma, can I go to the movies with the boy from upstairs on Saturday?" And then the rehearsed reply can from the other room: "All right. You can go." As of that next Saturday, they were a couple. The date had gone well for a grand total of twenty-five cents for two movie tickets and two trolley fares. If they skipped the trolley, they could get ice cream for their walk home.

Grandpa Max was the patriarch of the family and was always there whenever anyone needed advice or a bit of wisdom. He had a great sense of humor as well, with an infectious laugh that filled up any room. He and grandma steered the helm of the family ship as it weathered many storms over the years. He was an avid golfer—he even played in the snow with a colored ball. He loved music and sometimes played electric guitar and would let me play with it, even though I didn't know how to actually play it. He said, "respect the instrument," and he let me play it. We watched golf and baseball together, which I never pretended to like, but I put up with because I wanted to spend time with him. To make up for watching endless hours of boring golf on T.V., he would also eagerly watch Barbra Streisand in *Funny Girl* or *A Star Is Born* with me.

My mother was very happy with our extended family around. My maternal grandparents were over often, along with my mother's cousins and aunts, who were my grandmother's sisters. If they weren't coming to my grandmother's or our house, we were going to their house. Great Aunt Gertie had gatherings in her home in Queens often in those days. There was always a ton of food: bagels, cream cheese, Nova Scotia lox, kugel, potato latkes, roasted chicken, and tons of rugalach and other desserts. Jewish families, much like Italian families, equate food with love. I also remember a lot of laughing, card games, and a kindly old man, whose name I think was Moshe, who would play piano with me. Moshe was seventy years old if he was a day, and I think he was dating the mother of one of my great uncles.

My grandmother and her three sisters were of the first generation born in America to Russian immigrant parents who escaped from early-twentieth-century pogroms. They were always extremely close, and they filled their hearts with one another and each other's families. To them, being close with each other was not an option. They were taught by their mother from the old country that family was the most import-ant thing because she had always grieved leaving her family of origin behind. My mother and her cousins, the children of my grandmother and her three sisters, raised their families to feel the same way. They nurtured all of us with love, anxiety, worry, and an open heart of generosity that is unparalleled in this world we live in. I was lucky to be nurtured by them and taught to love with my full and open heart by being loved by theirs.

Holidays were always something very special that I looked forward to all year. Mostly, we all got together in my grand-mother's house, as she was the family matriarch, and celebrated Passover Seders, Rosh Hashanah new year celebrations, and Yom Kippur break fast with food, noisy conversation, and the loving hearts of the growing family. Thanksgiving and Hanukkah were also spent together in a loving embrace of family. Smells of cooking matzoh ball soup and delicious brisket were always abundant and joyful. Once my grandma no longer wanted to handle hosting the holidays herself, the gatherings shifted to my mother's house or to my Aunt

Maggie's house in New Jersey. Most often, they were at my mother's, I think, because it was easier for my grandmother to not have to travel so far.

My mother lived for holiday celebrations with the family. No matter how foul her mood had been or how she was feeling, she always was able to muster happiness, excitement, and peace if she knew her family was coming. She'd spend days preparing the traditional foods that we all loved—she made the best brisket and matzoh ball soup, although her latkes always were tinged green (from the chlorophyll being exposed to light after the potatoes were chopped). She catered to the specific tastes and dietary needs of each of us. She seemed to genuinely like to accommodate. When I think of holidays, I think of family. When I think of holidays, I think of specific foods and the warmth and deliciousness that filled our lives.

My grandmother Betty was famous for pouring herself a Johnny Walker on the rocks, taking a sip or two and then leaving the glass somewhere and forgetting where. I would come along, find her glass, and down her drink. I liked scotch, still do. Johnny Walker has helped me through some very stressful times as a grown up. During these frequent get togethers in the 1970s, throughout my very youngest childhood, all my relatives thought I was the quietest, most well-behaved little girl because I would fall asleep almost anywhere. But the reality was that I was drunk and passed out. I was three, four and five years old and a scotch connoisseur.

Aunt Gertie's dog, Charlie Brown, a huge, lumbering chocolate Labrador, would stand guard as I slept on the guestroom bed with its mustard colored coverlet until the adults were finished socializing. Charlie Brown was not my only canine bodyguard. My grandmother's dog, a black and white toy fox terrier with a long narrow snout named Buttons, who did not like anyone (including my grandfather), would stand guard as I napped on my grandparents' bed in their fancy black and white bedroom, or sit near me as I played in their den. Once, he ate an entire box of sixty-four crayons and vomited in technicolor all over their brand-new brown tweed carpeting. My grandfather was pissed off. This dog growled at everyone and bared his teeth at the slightest provocation. To get him to go out when he didn't want to, one would have to wear quilted oven mitts to pull him out from under the bed to avoid lacerations.

Mom was extremely close to her best friends, Aunt Marie and Uncle Tom. They met when they lived across the hall from one another in the garden apartments when they first got married. Coincidentally, these were the same garden apartments, on the same street, in which my first husband and I lived before we got married. Aunt Marie and Uncle Tom have two sons, Joseph and Will, who are about my age. We kids were all raised as cousins. We played all sorts of games, competitive and imaginative ones, but the imaginative ones were our favorites.

Joseph and I assembled elaborate haunted houses for Halloween in the basement of my parents' high ranch house, we played school and house. We staged a pretend wedding ceremony after my Aunt Maggie's wedding in 1974, using my mother's bridesmaid's blue and white floral bouquet. I wore my night gown with a flower crown of matching flowers in my hair, and Joseph wore a pair of my pajamas and a brown cape trimmed in orange fringe from a witch costume that I had in my closet from the previous Halloween. We liked to joke, as we got older, that we were each other's first spouses. Joseph, his younger brother, Will, and I were very close as kids, spending weeks at a time together at our houses over the summers. Once we were middle school and high school age, we drifted apart, as our interests and social lives were vastly different. But we still saw each other and hung out when our parents got together. Our mothers would stay up all night talking, so we knew that these get-togethers were always going to be sleepovers.

One summer day in 1977 or so, when we were about eight or nine years old, Joseph and I decided to make a playhouse out of the large cardboard box that his mother's brand-new dishwasher came in. We had it all planned out. We would cut open a door, cut squares in two of the walls for windows. I made curtains from scrap blue and white gingham fabric and stapled them over the edges of the windows and made window boxes for the outside with extra cardboard. Then, with the paint that Uncle Tom said we could use, we painted the exterior and interior walls of the house and made it look very pretty. This started out according to plan, but somewhere between the window cutouts that were too large and the multiple coats of paint that made the cardboard box very soggy, the whole wet, sticky, smelly house collapsed in on us, covering us with gobs of yellow paint. The worst part was that we took the can of paint from the wrong side of the basement. What we used was oil-based, not latex. The only way to clean us off was with turpentine; water and soap would not cut it. That night, our mothers showered each of us (in two different bathrooms) with a disgusting combination of soap and turpentine and scrubbed us clean. We all had red eyes and were coughing from the fumes of this awful concoction. It was an experience we will never forget.

My mother always had big Hanukkah parties for our family, all her grandchildren, the nieces and the nephews. She went hog-wild buying gifts for everybody that she knew they would love and decorated a fake fichus tree in her living room to be a Hanukkah tree. She made pretty handmade ornaments with all our pictures on them and potato pancakes, brisket, and matzoh ball soup. The table was beautifully set with her quirky Hanukkah dishes, flowers, and blue plastic dreidels, and there would be little bundles of gold foil wrapped, Hanukkah gelt on everybody's plate.

Christmas, when I was little, was spent with Aunt Marie's family. We were adopted into their loud, passionate, Italian

Catholic family and enjoyed delicious food and festivities with them. Inevitably, someone's cousin or boyfriend would disappear for a bit and arrive sometime later disguised as Santa. I knew that Santa was not real. I was told flat-out that Santa was not a real person but instead was a lovely, magical myth and a symbol of hope and generosity. My parents asked me to not ruin this fantasy for my friends or cousins, who were Christian, and I happily complied. Somehow, even in my child-like mind, I felt superior that I knew the truth and they were being misled. I looked at them like I was a wizened grown-up who derived pleasure from their innocent belief in St. Nick.

Once I was married to my first husband and established my own household, we still split our time on holidays, but now we had three families to divide our time among. I think that we quickly realized that three Thanksgivings in one day was kind of an impossibility; we can't all be Lorelai Gilmore. And the worst part was that we made nobody happy, least of all us. The tradition evolved into certain holidays being shared with certain people, so there was some predictability and less anxiety and traffic.

When I got married, because my mother-in-law was a half-Jewish and half-Protestant and my father-in-law was raised as an Orthodox Jew, we celebrated a hybrid Christmas/Hanukkah with them in their home. This was always a lavish affair with all the Christmas trimmings plus a beautiful, antique silver Hanukkiah, fabulous food, candles, and mountains of holiday gifts.

Despite all of my emptiness and loneliness and my quest to fill my life with love and connection that ran me ragged for years, family and holiday touchstones have always been extremely important for me. No matter the stress in my relationships with my parents, the holidays always pulled me closer to family and the undeniable, unbreakable bonds we all share.

My social life was not that social in later elementary school. I wasn't invited to many parties. There were a few girls who invited me, and the rest of the class, to their birthday parties, and I was happy to be included but also knew that the only reason I was being invited was because they invited everyone. I had sleepover birthday parties for quite a few years in a row with friends in my elementary school class—girls I knew from dance or gymnastics and my neighborhood. Birthday parties were always a big affair, with decorations, games, lots of food and snacks, swimming, sleep over games like Truth or Dare, and M&M fights, from which we were still finding M&Ms months later. My mother used to love it when there was a party to plan or I had friends over. She would perk up, step into her June Cleaver costume and for that little sliver of time she was the consummate mother and housewife. She took pride in how others, even children, perceived her and the parties she hosted. It made her feel good about herself. I know that she loved me and wanted me to have a nice party, but she also wanted to be seen as the one who threw the nice party.

When I was a very little girl, we ate dinner together in the kitchen as a family. In the corner of the kitchen, perched on the corner of the beige rectangular, Formica table was a small white, plastic television with rabbit ear antennae. Every night during dinner, we watched television, many episodes of our favorite shows: *All in the Family, MASH, The Jeffersons*. As I got older and my parents drifted further apart, we ate fewer meals together and my mother cooked less often; we ate takeout instead. After a while, despite my mom being a great cook, she didn't cook much unless we were having company. If company was coming, she put on her June Cleaver and cooked up a storm. That definitely portrayed a false impression of what our domestic life was like. From the outside, we looked like a perfect little family. If only visitors knew what happened when they left.

I clearly remember, when I was about ten years old, going with my father to a Honda dealer to pick up a car that he had bought, and from there we were going to the Long Island Railroad station in Huntington to pick my mother up. He was going to surprise her with this brand-new mint green Honda Accord. He was so excited. I knew this was not going to go well and slid down low in the back seat. This was a small car, and my mother—who was 5-foot-10—would not fit in the car comfortably. It was also a manual transmission, and she couldn't drive that kind of car. When she was shown the car in the parking lot at the train station, I saw the look on her face—the rage, disappointment, confusion, anger—and I wanted to melt into the backseat and disappear. Somehow, my father couldn't predict this reaction or didn't care that she would be angry because he worked hard and wanted this car. Either way, it was the same result. I wanted to vanish into the mint green velour backseat.

My dad once gave my mother a gift, I think it was jewelry, and what woman doesn't like the gift of jewelry? My dad was excited about the gift—I think he thought he would make her happy with it. I don't remember if it was for an occasion or just because, but he couldn't find wrapping paper in the house, so he wrapped it in plain, brown paper. What's the big deal, right? Well, that plain brown paper was the cause of a huge fight between them. Maybe this was part of another argument they were having, I don't know, but she was furious that the present was wrapped in offensive plain brown paper. I don't know what kind of jewelry was in the box, all I know is that I was in the corner of the dining room putting an album on the stereo when this started, and as she screamed, I edged my way out until I was safely in my room with the door closed.

They had their issues and were not a very good match as a couple. Both the new car purchase and the offensively wrapped gift of the jewelry unfairly garnered the same reaction from my mother. As a child and an adult, I know that a major purchase like a car should be discussed with both partners in a marriage and, at the very least, the type of car should fit both people. I was shocked that my father stepped into that one and angry at him for being so stubborn or naïve to cause another volcanic eruption. I somehow felt that he should play her game and appease her to avoid setting her off, as I had learned to do. I didn't want to have to deal with her being angry because of his mistake.

The jewelry incident was just cruel on her part. Rarely did the thought count with her. It was the end product or the presentation that mattered and from her point of view, if you knew her and loved her, you should know that. I remember her screaming, "if you really loved me and paid attention, you'd know what I want." She was overly sensitive and expected those who loved her to read her mind and know what she wanted and how she felt—that somehow because we loved her, we should know what she wanted. And the converse was also true, if we didn't know what she wanted then we didn't love her enough.

This was impossible to deal with. It was a lose-lose situation for everyone around her. She had high standards for other people's behavior but not her own, so she was constantly disappointed because no one could ever live up to her expectations. No one was a mind reader, so we all got it wrong most of the time, and she unfortunately felt unloved or unappreciated as an extension of her disappointment.

Even as a kid I knew that this was not going to turn out well. Even though what she was saying was wrong and unfair, the way she explained her reasoning made it seem logical and acceptable. She was high maintenance, very sensitive about her figure and size, and she carried around a lot of body shame, which caused her to dress in ways to hide what she saw as her flaws. She was so sensitive and hard to handle; I think that I just gave in to her and never called her on any of her behavior because it was easier to just go with the flow. In my head, I must have asked myself, a thousand times, why does she get to act this way? Why do I have to put up with it and be the mature one?

This became my M.O. for the longest time—keep the peace, apologize for whatever addled her in an effort to keep things calm, do whatever I could do to make others happy and happy with me. Avoid drama and yelling and disappointing others, especially Mom, at all costs. I am non-confrontational and hate arguing. I don't like when decisions that should be easy to make wind up as tense as hostage negotiations and as a result, I tend to do some quick research and make quick and sometimes hasty decisions. Most of the time this has worked out reasonably well, but not always.

The one vacation we took as a three-member family was to Niagara Falls. My father and I saw the typical tourist sights and tried to make the best of what turned out to be a disappointing trip. I don't think my mother ever joined us for any activities before dinnertime. She slept all day in the small hotel room. I remember leaving the hotel room and pacing the navy-blue carpeted corridor as my parents were arguing over my mother's sloth-like behavior. Dad felt that she was ignoring us. The situation had several sides for me. If she was going to be in a good mood and try to enjoy herself with her husband and daughter, then I wanted her to come sightseeing with us. If she was going to sulk and complain then I wanted to just go with my dad. In my memory, she joined us for the next several days of tourist activities, and I have a few pictures of this trip that bring back memories of me, sporting a jaunty side ponytail, with my mother trying to be happy. I don't have many pictures of me with my mother when I was a child, so I treasure these.

From my mother, I got my creativity. She loved needlepoint and used to drag me to needlepoint stores to pick out canvases and yarn. I don't think there are stores like this anymore, but in the 1970s, you could find them. She made so many pieces and gave them away as gifts. She was good at quilling, which is the art of twirling paper around a stick and then shaping the curled paper into designs. She wrote parodies of songs for various events she was involved in organizing with the PTA of my elementary school—they staged elaborate fashion shows with themes from iconic movies like *The Wizard of Oz*.

We did art projects together; painted, drew, made pom-poms. She taught me to sew by hand and with a sewing machine and do needlepoint. Twice, she showed me how to knit, but that didn't stick. We even worked together to put down a brand-new sheet vinyl floor in the main hallway of the house and paint rooms. We planted gardens of colorful flowers and vegetables for our meals. She was very creative and had a keen eye for detail. Every year, she handmade my Halloween costumes, dance and twirling costumes, and encouraged creativity in me.

I remember a story she liked to tell about finger painting with me. She bought rolls of white finger-painting paper and rolled it out on the kitchen table, dressed me in a smock, which was an old dress shirt of my dad's that I wore backward, and put bowls of different-colored paints out in front of me. She told me to dip my fingers in the paint and create whatever I wanted on the big, blank paper. I just silently stared at her. She nudged me to try it. Still, I stared at her. She looked at me encouragingly, and I cautiously dipped one index finger into the red paint, saw that my finger got dirty, and I made a scrunched-up face. Then I wiped the finger on my smock and refused to finger paint. My mother, in an effort to encourage me to try again, put all her fingers in the paint and made large swirls on the big paper, smiling encouragingly. I was unmoved. Too messy for me. It was not evident at that moment that one day I would be a painter.

Despite my resistance to that entreaty by my mother, and despite the obvious strife in our house, I felt loved. It was my normal. I was an only child and lived a great deal of the time in my own head, a place I've grown comfortable. I was an active reader, watched some TV, played with my friends, and had different names for all my stuffed animals. I had the generic cats, bears, and dogs, but I also loved the exotic stuffed animals like cows, chickens, dinosaurs, and my favorite, giraffes. I kept them all lined up on my bed against the light blue wall of my room and talked to them all every day. I gave them names and voices and loved them so much that they had the prime real estate on the bed; I slept on less than half of the twin sized mattress.

One day, my father walked into the guest room to find me lying on my back underneath my brown Formica kid-sized table that I used for crafts. I was painting the underside of the tabletop, pretending to be Michelangelo painting the Sistine Chapel, but I called it the *Sixteenth* Chapel. If my dad was shocked or surprised by this, I don't know. I don't remember my reaction to him, but I was very focused on my task and was happy. When recounting this sometime later, he was surprised that I had any idea what the Sistine Chapel was.

CHAPTER 5
PARENTING MYSELF

My mother was a sickly child. She had rheumatic fever and spent almost a year in bed with only her immediate family as company. She got used to adults and never felt comfortable with kids her own age. She was painfully shy around new people and avoided most situations where she would be with people whom she perceived as smarter, more educated or more anything than she was. This limited her world, reinforcing her lack of self-esteem, and isolating self-talk reinforced her own inner dialogue. Or so I imagine. I never got to talk to her about any of this. This is my assessment based on what I know and what I've seen. My mother and I never talked about these things in-depth; in her state, I'm not even sure she could access her feelings to this degree. It's fallen to me, as her daughter, as her witness, as someone who loved her in life and misses her presence, to make sense of what often seemed senseless. There's a fuller story to her, even now, years after she's gone.

When I was a small child, she had ileitis—we now know it as Crohn's disease. Late one night, I heard commotion from outside my bedroom. I woke up to find my grandparents at the house, and my dad was letting the EMTs in to take my mother to the hospital. She had had some sort of intestinal abscess that had erupted, and she needed immediate emergency surgery to survive. I peered into the darkened master bedroom to see her writhing in the bed, moaning in pain. I was scared that she was going to die. For more than two weeks, she was in the hospital and I was allowed to see her only once. When I did get to see her, I was so excited and climbed into her hospital bed with her and played with the bed controls, raising and lowering the head of the bed and eating her lunch off her bed table. My very tall mother weighed only about 110 pounds and was grotesquely skinny, as she had lost more than fifty pounds in a very short time. I think her sickliness as a child and her life-threatening illness as a young adult are what contributed to her hypochondriasis as an older person. She was used to being sick, so even when she wasn't, she looked for all the ways that she *could* be sick. Every sniffle could send her to the doctor. I think this set her up for a lifetime of obsession about her health—or, really, obsession with illnesses. As a middle-aged woman, she became a full-blown hypochondriac. Being sick also meant that she could remain in the center of everyone's thoughts and care. She got waited on and catered to, and I'm sure that that felt comfortable and safe for her. It's really not surprising that she would want to perpetuate that.

During the time my mother was in the hospital, I stayed with my maternal grandparents, Betty and Max. Each morning, Grandma Betty made me oatmeal with honey and milk. She sat with me in her yellow-and-kelly-green kitchen with white, lacy curtains on the bay window surrounding the kitchen table and told me stories like Rapunzel and Cinderella while I ate. She gave the characters unique voices and was very dramatic in her renditions. To this day, whenever I eat oatmeal, I recall that kitchen and special time with her. It brings tears to my eyes and I feel her love wash over me.

During this time at my grandparent's house, I developed a fever. As a child, I normally ran very high fevers—103 to 105 degrees, what would be perilous for others, were kind of normal for me. My grandmother was very nervous about this, but I was aware enough and mature enough to tell her what to do. I dutifully took my baby aspirin and told her that my pediatrician, Dr. Schwartz, had instructed my mother to put me in a tepid water bath to lower my body temperature. Although I hated this and it was torturously uncomfortable, I insisted that grandma do this, so she did. I took the awful bath, my fever was reduced, I slept and ate and rested in my pink room at grandma's, and all was well.

I remember being praised by my grandmother to my grandfather and then again to my mother over the telephone, and I felt proud of myself. I had known what to do, given the instructions, and endured it for my own good.

As an adult looking back, I see that I was really the only knowledgeable adult and I was a kid. These early moments were the beginning of me seeking approval and praise from others and I quickly learned to behave in whatever way necessary to earn the praise. If others were happy with me then I was happy with me. My self-esteem came from external sources.

I was parenting myself from a very young age, which really set me up for a lifetime of unhealthy behaviors that would characterize my lifelong relationship with my mother. I became a people pleaser—a trait I would carry throughout my life, in every situation with every boyfriend, with every friend, with every teacher, with every boss. I rarely really respected my own needs or said how I actually felt because that was secondary to making people like me, to making sure a situation and everyone who was involved remained calm. As the pleaser and the diplomat, I became, in my mind, the person who selflessly does what she thinks the other person wants, tries to predict what they want her to do, who does whatever she can do to conform to her perception of what will make the person love her, be proud of her, make any situation better, easier, smoother, more peaceful, more consistent. I needed to please them to make them like me so I would like myself and feel I was worthy of love.

It was not until I was able to be free of those relationships and their inherent power struggles and inequities that I was even remotely able to do the same with my mother. And, as we know, it didn't happen until after she died. That's very sad.

It isn't a surprise that in my relationships—with boys, friends, and my parents—that I sublimated what Marci wanted. I didn't say when I didn't like something unless it was emergent. I went along with things, and I allowed people's opinions to sway me. This is not to say that I was a total pushover or that I don't know my own mind, because I did and I do, but I thought I was doing the right thing for my relationships. Relationships require compromise; therefore, I should compromise on everything.

What I didn't realize at the time was that I was losing or ignoring all of my boundaries and my sense of self, so the person that they were in a relationship with wasn't actually me but some incarnation of me that I fabricated to try to please them. Then they would be confused because they were not actually in a relationship with the real me, just the fake me, who did not actually exist. At some point, I was resentful because I didn't get to be the real me or even get to know her. And, consequently, I was lost in those relationships. Because here's the truth: I didn't have them in the first place.

Chapter 6
Some Dads Are Daddies

My relationship with my dad was great when I was a little girl. Our relationship was much less drama-filled than the one with my mother. Dad worked a lot. He wasn't around much during the week but was always around on the weekends.

We had so many things that were just ours. We used to do this acrobatic trick that would freak out anyone watching, especially my mother and maternal grandmother, which I have to admit was part of its charm. It went like this: My dad would lie down in the main hallway near the kitchen doorway and I would get ready by standing at the far end of the long hallway in front of my bedroom. He'd count down and I'd run headlong toward him and then spring into the air and somehow land with my hands on his hands in the air above him and my feet on his knees. It does bear to note that I was a very skinny child, so my father was in no danger. Whoever was there watching, my mother, aunt or grandmother, would scream in fear that we would get hurt, but dad and I kept doing it to egg them on.

My father and I used to go on errands together on Saturday mornings. Each week, it was a competition to see how many mundane things we could complete in shorter and shorter periods of time. We had a great time even if we were buying milk, dropping clothes at a dry cleaner, or going to the post office. We would marvel at how much we could get done in one afternoon. We reveled in our productivity. We enjoyed picnics at Sunken Meadow State Park with our miniature schnauzer, Candy, and played catch or Frisbee in the warm sunshine. Every winter, Dad took me into New York City to Rockefeller Center to go ice skating.

After I watched the Olympics in 1976, I got the popular Dorothy Hamill haircut and I had fantasies about being a figure skater. I don't know how it all came about, but in my fifth-grade year, I started to take figure-skating lessons. The town next to mine had a skating rink, and at five a.m. my dad would get me up and we would drive in the dark over to the skating rink. It was cold and eerie being at this huge rink so early in the morning. I'd skate my lesson, we would have breakfast at IHOP, and then afterward Dad brought me to school. I don't know if we did this once a week or more often than that, because it didn't last that long. Not too long into my figure-skating dream, my skating teacher taught me how to take off into a single axel. She was very detailed and specific about how I leaned my body, where my center of gravity would be and how my feet should be positioned. I was so excited because with this move, I was going to start to feel like a real figure skater.

But then she said, "Marci, we are about to run out of time so I can't teach you to land the axel until the next lesson. The foot and leg positions are complicated, and I'd like to spot you through the first tries. So, don't try this on your own," she said sternly. In between, I was not supposed to practice the jumping at all.

Was she crazy? What ten-year-old has the willpower to not try it?

I went to open skate the next day to practice and tried the axel. I skated around in a wide circle, shifting my weight the way I was taught, followed my center of gravity, twisted and leaped up in the air in my first-ever single axel. At this point, time stopped while I was mid-spin and I remembered that I was never taught how to land on the ice and realized why this was not a good idea. So, I panicked and landed in a heap of icy limbs, breaking my arm in two places. Despite the fact that I could have gone back to skating lessons after my arm healed, I never did. I still can skate pretty well but can't do anything fancy at all. And I never did learn to do an axel.

My father took me places, paid attention to me, played games with me and had patience with so many things and I knew that he loved me. I never doubted that ever. Not until I was a teenager. When I was a freshman in high school my parents separated and for six months, I didn't hear from him at all and during those six months I questioned everything I ever thought I knew about him and his feelings for me. I completely stopped trusting him.

The rest of my childhood continued as you'd expect. Typical suburban girl in the 1970s and early 1980s. I joined a Girl Scout troop for a few years and learned that I don't like camping. Girl Scout tents are not watertight and when girls are cold and dirty, they act very badly. After a few very soggy camping trips, some sewing lessons, and a few Christmas caroling events, I quit Girl Scouts.

I lived in my own creative world dominated by my imaginative play. I convinced my friends to play restaurant and dance party with me and we staged the Miss America pageant in my basement. We went through all phases of the typical beauty pageant competition. The talent portion was always singing—we'd lip-sync with 45s on my parents' stereo. My favorite song to sing was Barbra Streisand's *A Woman in Love.* We used our imaginations, a lot of makeup, and some costumes to make this come alive. I also drew, painted, did ceramics, wrote, and lived a whole universe away sometimes in my own creative world.

As a child, I had plenty of friends in my neighborhood and at school, and I felt accepted and part of school life for the most part. There were always events like parades, carnivals, book fairs, costume contests and parties. But underneath, in a place I didn't like to visit or acknowledge, let alone let anyone else know about, there was an ever present, deep sense of anxiety and unease. It was like I was subliminally aware of something shaking the bedrock of my life. Every year, from fourth grade to sometime in middle school, I missed quite a few days of school because of anxiety—deep anxiety that I couldn't verbalize that affected my gastrointestinal system, making me severely constipated and causing a great deal of pain. My mother insisted on my drinking extra water and tortuously gave me suppositories and enemas to get my system moving again. Little did I know that this unspoken, deep-level anxiety would plague me off and on throughout my life.

We all have moments of feeling excluded, unwanted, and judged. I was not athletic and did not like team sports. Gym class was a special torment because of this. Whenever kids were to pick teams for kickball, volleyball, or field hockey, the teams would fight over who got stuck with me. Not who got to have me on their team but who got stuck with me. My hand-eye coordination was that of a blind slug, and I knew it. I didn't really blame them for not wanting me on their team. I knew I was a liability. But it hurt. Years later, when I turned forty, I was diagnosed with an advanced cataract in my right eye and part of the intense testing my ophthalmologist conducted he figured out that my eyes have never worked together the way they are supposed to. The norm is the eyes work together and merge what they each see into one image. My eyes don't work together that way, but my brain learned to compensate. My lack of hand eye coordination is biological. Not being picked for teams and teased about it was the emotional fallout that diminished my self-esteem for years.

CHAPTER 7
DON'T LET ANYTHING GET IN YOUR WAY

"Never, never, never give up."

—Winston Churchill

The summer between sixth and seventh grade was when I first got a taste of my personal power to excel when I commit myself to something. When musical instruments were introduced in fourth and fifth grades in elementary school, I must have not been paying attention, but by the end of sixth grade, when I saw my next door neighbor with her shiny, silver flute I decided that I wanted to learn to play the flute too and play with the middle school band. My friends were already playing their instruments for two years and had a huge head start. Somehow, my mother persuaded the director of the music department and the seventh-grade band director to let me audition for band in early September, when the next school year was to begin. I think that the band instructor agreed to this but dismissed it, thinking that I'd flake out and not show up or that I wouldn't be able to play. But flake out

I did not. My parents got me a private flute tutor, who came once a week to teach me to play. I took this very seriously and practiced over an hour every single day the whole summer. Lauren taught me everything from basic fingering and reading music to keeping time and to break down difficult parts of a piece to master them. Lauren wrote a special version of *Color My World* for me to play for my audition, and I was thoroughly prepared.

The day of the audition, my mother drove me to the middle school where I would be attending school as an incoming seventh grader. The school was huge, so much larger than my elementary school that I wondered how I would ever learn my way around. I walked into the musty band room, with all the metal folding chairs neatly arranged in rows on the graduated floor. The director, Mr. Piccolo, shook my hand, and I sat down and took out my flute. While I was setting up, he was at his desk rummaging through papers and seemed to be barely paying attention to me. I was very nervous. I had been practicing and knew I was ready, but I hadn't ever played in front of anyone before. I took a deep breath, held up my flute and began to play. By the time I got a few lines in, the director stopped his paperwork and was paying complete attention to me. He was surprised.

From his desk, he asked, "Can you play scales?"

I nodded and meekly said, "Yes."

"Play a C major scale," he said obviously testing me. I played the C major scale perfectly. He raised his eyebrows. "Now, how about a G major scale?" he asked. I played that one perfectly as well. Each scale he asked me to play, D, A, and E major, I knew them all. He was impressed. I could see it on his face. I was so damn proud of myself.

"How did you learn all that in two months?" he asked. "Kids your age have been learning for a year or two."

"I had a private tutor and I practice for hours every day," I answered.

Not only was he pleased to offer me membership in the band, but he also told me that I was going to be first chair. This meant that not only was I good enough to be in the band, but I was the best flute player. I remained first chair for seventh and eighth grades.

I learned that when I want something badly enough and put in the time, there is no stopping me. I will succeed. I will do it.

Seventh grade was a blur. I loved school and changing classes and teachers. There was so much more freedom when we weren't stuck in the same classroom all day. I had some great friends, and we were inseparable. Melanie and Risa became the sisters I never had. I was always with one or both of them. School was safe, social and full of things I loved—learning, band, friends, and boys.

At this point, I was slowly starting to be invited to boy-girl parties where hormonal kids eager to experiment and act grown up would play *Spin the Bottle* or *Seven Minutes in Heaven*. I was too shy to play and did everything I could to avoid playing, even if it meant going upstairs to hang out with the kids' mothers or looking for the bathroom and never coming back. I was terrified to kiss a boy and I was terrified to not kiss a boy. I wanted to be included in the fun and feel like I really fit in, but I just wasn't ready for this next step.

This was the year of my first crush. Matthew lived close enough that I was able to bike to his house to play basketball with him or video games on his Atari system. We would laugh and talk, although I have no idea what we talked about. He had dreamy dark brown eyes and the sweetest smile I had ever seen. I tried to conform to be the kind of girl I thought he would like, just as my grandmother told me to do. I wanted him to kiss me. I wanted to be his girlfriend, and I was taking my grandmother's advice—like what the boy likes so he sees how much he likes being with you. Hence, the basketball and video games. These were not things that I would have chosen to spend time doing unless there was a cute boy involved. When we hung out together, we were both very comfortable and our conversations were fluid and filled with laughter. I thought he felt exactly the way I did.

In June, when his birthday came around, I baked him a cake and walked the ten or twelve blocks over to his house, balancing the cake on my nervous hands, to give it to him. I was hoping for some sort of confirmation that he liked me the way I liked him, but I when arrived at his house with the cake, our mutual friend Lila was already there with her arms around him. Turns out, he asked her out that afternoon and I had no choice but to give Matthew the cake and eat it with him and Lila. Grandma's advice put me in the friend zone, before I even knew what the friend zone was, as one of the guys. Lila was a cheerleader, wore short skirts, was very pretty and feminine. Matthew liked her. Of course, he did. I was disappointed, but I did not let it get to me. What I did decide was not to listen to my grandmother's advice about boys.

One day in eighth grade, I was walking downstairs in my school on my way to the cafeteria to meet my friends for lunch, when out of the blue, I was pushed down the stairs. Someone pushed me from behind, and I stumbled all the way down, unable to grab a handrail or stop my fall. When I landed in a heap at the bottom of the concrete and tile staircase, I limped my way to the nurse's office, reported the incident and got a lot of ice. I didn't break anything, luckily, but I did gain a collection of purple bruises. Witnesses reported that a boy, named Peter, pushed me down the stairs. I was not friends with this boy at all; I hardly knew him. He thought that a great, surefire way to get my attention and get me to like me back was to push me down the stairs. When he returned from his several-day suspension, my best friend, Melanie, asked him what he was thinking. He confessed sheepishly that he liked me, and that he made a very bad choice. I wondered what the hell was wrong with him; if he treated a girl he liked in this way, then how the hell would he treat an enemy?

Later that spring, I was the victim of another boy's scary lack of boundaries. His name was Ryan, he was tall, skinny and had straggly blond hair that stuck out from under the tan leather cowboy hat he wore to school every day. Ryan lived in my neighborhood, so he was on my bus to and from school, but he got on and off after I did every day. Suddenly Ryan, who I never voluntarily spoke to, started to sit behind me and quietly say things to me in a creepy, sarcastic, scary voice.

"Aren't you a pretty girl?" he'd say in a creepy voice. Or, in a sarcastic tone he'd say, "Gee, I'd love to date you. You're so pretty. Will you go out with me?"

The things he said were not bad, it was the way he said them that creeped me out. I did my best to ignore him. He never got a rise out of me. I never got visibly angry. I did tell him to leave me alone, and I moved to a different seat on the bus, but he followed me to the new seat. Other kids would get out of his way to make it easier for him to bully me. They didn't want to be his next victim and their silence paved his way to continue. In the 1980s, bus drivers did not seem to get involved in student behavior and things escalated.

One morning, he smeared green, lime-flavored lip balm into my hair and mushed it all up. The nurse at school couldn't get it out, so I had to wear my hair in a ponytail that day to cover it up. I reported him, but no one in the administration did anything.

A few days later, he got off the bus at my stop and walked about ten feet behind me all the way to my house. He was calling after me, saying the same things he was saying on the bus in that same creepy, scary voice. I was terrified. Without adult supervision, there was no telling what this boy would be capable of doing. When I got to my house, I cut across the lawn and took off running, struggled with my lock, but got it open and went inside. There was no one else home, and I needed Ryan to be gone. I grabbed the cordless phone and yelled at him through screen door, "Get off my property and leave me alone or I'm calling the police!" I held up the phone and dramatically dialed 9-1-1 with my index finger slowly pressing the buttons in mid-air so he could plainly see. Before I could complete the call, he was gone. He never bothered me again, and as far as I know, he didn't get in any trouble at school, either.

I had found some assertive power I didn't know I had.

CHAPTER 8
A FAMILY TORN APART

*"Family is supposed to be our safe haven. Very often,
it's the place where we find the deepest heartache."*

—Iyanla Vanzant

I n the autumn of my freshman year in high school, after a
particularly fun day performing with the marching band
at a football game on a gorgeous crisp day, I returned
home to find my parents waiting for me in the living room.
As I removed the rest of my itchy, forest green marching band
uniform, I heard them say we needed a family meeting. This
was not wholly unusual, as we had had family meetings from
time to time. I felt so great that day that even a family meeting couldn't dampen my mood, but they looked so serious.
I was almost laughing at the seriousness. What they told me
seemed like a relief at the time, but little did I know that it
would irrevocably change everything about my family and
my relationship with my parents.

They told me that they were separating and getting a
divorce. They told me that my father was moving out—that

day, in fact—and that I would still see him all the time. I was relieved. I had an inkling something like this was coming despite not even verbalizing it to myself. They couldn't believe how well I took the news. No tears. No protests. They had been sleeping in separate rooms for years, which I knew was not normal. My friends' parents and grandparents shared a bed.

They fought all the time, and not just verbal fights. My mother would make it physical by throwing pillow and full glasses of water at my father. It may have gone further than that physically, but that was all I saw. They were both obviously miserable, and because of that, I was miserable, too. The tension in the house was so thick it could be cut with a chainsaw and when I was alone and quiet and not distracted by school and my own social life, I was anxious and always felt like I was unsafely teetering on a precipice.

When I had been in elementary school, several years in a row, my parents offered to send me to sleep away camp and no matter how wonderful they made it sound or how enticing it was to think about—all that freedom, escaping the tension in the house, meeting new friends and trying new things—I didn't go because deep down inside I was afraid that I'd have nothing to come back to. That somehow without me around my parents' marriage would implode and my family would cease to exist. I felt that by staying home I could keep an eye on them.

This separation and whatever happened next, would have to be better than that.

So, I thought.

My dad had already rented an apartment in Queens and had already moved all his things there. How had I missed that? He left soon after that last family meeting, and it was just my mother, our miniature schnauzer, Candy, and me in the house. My life, over the next six months, was covered by a dark shadow. I wasn't allowed to tell anyone that my father left, and my parents were divorcing except for my best friend,

Melanie. Melanie's parents were in the middle of an awful divorce, so I knew she would understand everything I was thinking and feeling. She was shocked because to her, from the outside, she thought my parents were happy and everything was great. My mother put on her June Cleaver sensibility when my friends were around. That was so convincing that I sometimes believed it as well. Everyone she knew believed that she was happy, that she and my dad had a great marriage.

My mother would not let me tell my grandparents. She was embarrassed that her husband left her. We lied to my grandparents and told them my father was doing a lot of traveling for business. Her embarrassment and need for secrecy left me isolated and miserable and cut me off emotionally from my grandparents, with whom I was so close. I wanted to tell them, to be able to receive comfort from them and help me make sense of this, but I was sworn to secrecy.

My father, who had promised to see me all the time before he left our home, disappeared from my life for quite a few months. We had little or no contact at all. I hardly saw him, and I felt abandoned and alone. I was hurt and angry with him for leaving me and for leaving me alone with my mother. There was no buffer between us anymore. I know that their marriage was not happy, and their separate bedrooms and the total lack of conversation were obvious clues, even for me. But I was the kid. I was the one who was supposed to be loved unconditionally and always taken care of. It wasn't working out that way. Any sense of security, trust or safety I had felt before was now gone and I was left to pick up the pieces by myself. I had the impression that he was off building a new life for himself, settling into his new apartment and looking for a girlfriend and that all of that was more important to him than I was.

In the many heartfelt conversations I had with my father while writing this book, I learned a different version of the story. After my dad left, he said he often called the house to talk to me when he knew I would be home, but my mother would tell him I wasn't home or not answer the phone at all and tell him later that the phone was broken or had been shut off. (This makes no sense to me, but I can't exactly ask her for her side of the story.) He told me that he wrote me letters, many of which he kept photocopies of and showed me recently, but I had never received those letters. My guess now, as I try to piece all of this together, is that my mom was angry at him for leaving her and was punishing him. Never mind that she was hurting me by keeping my father away from me.

This separation caused my mother to fall into a downward spiral that she never wholly recovered from. She was depressed and rarely left her bedroom. Her bipolarity blossomed and tortured us both because her lows lasted so painfully long. She hid in her room, always a bag of *Doritos* and a two-liter bottle of Diet Coke on her bedside table.

As a college student in a photography class, years later, my assignment was to create a photographic portrait of someone in my family without them actually being in the picture. The idea was to tell a visual still life story of a person. I staged that scene to represent my mother – her bedroom, blankets messed up, open Dorito bag on the bed with chips strewn all over, a 2-liter bottle of Diet Coke on the night table next to a glass, all illuminated by the blue glow of the television screen. It was the truth. That was my mother when no one else was around. I never showed her that photograph or even told her about the project or the 'A' I earned because I knew she would be hurt and embarrassed and because of that, I imagined that she would be angry at me.

I was left to fend for myself. I was my own parent and got myself to school, ate whatever was in the refrigerator or ate takeout. She was pitiful. I loved her and wanted to make it better for her. I didn't know that it wasn't my job to make it better for her. It was her job to make it better for me and for herself. Her insistence on secrecy plunged us both into loneliness and made the whole situation worse than it had to be.

Mom used me as her therapist instead of finding one herself and confided in me when she should have talked to a friend her own age. There were things she told me about their marriage that I should have never been privy to. She told me all about the content of their fights, the words they said to each other and the names they called one another. She more than indelicately told me about how my father didn't make her feel feminine and attractive and about their dissatisfying sex life. She complained incessantly about how disappointing her marriage had been and how angry she was that he left us. It was always that he left *us*, not that he had left *her*. She needed me to hate him and be angry with him, too, and to take her side exclusively.

I became her caretaker and was barely able to take care of myself at fourteen years old.

It was around this age that I started keeping a journal. I had read about a person who wrote in a journal for most of her life, and after years and years of writing she had a huge pile of journal books. I romanticized the notion of personal writing and began in a lovely hard-covered book. Now, almost forty years later, I have a large pile of journal books locked in a Rubbermaid storage box under a table in my art studio. Someday, when I am very old or gone, people will read them and learn that I was once a silly girl with a quirky and romantic sense of the world. They will also learn that I research everything and overthink constantly. When I started writing every day, I learned quickly that it is cathartic. I wrote about everything but mostly about the boys who I liked and my parents' unfortunate marriage. I could figure anything out if I wrote about it enough.

By this time, I was writing in my journals every night before bed, but now I was also writing poetry and short stories and drawing. This was a way to be creative and make sense of my internal life of thoughts and ideas. I have always had an active internal dialogue, and because I was an only child and figured out early on that I couldn't really talk to my parents about much of anything, I resorted to my interior thoughts and writing for solace. Dad was always busy. He always worked several jobs to make enough money to support us and when he was home, before he moved out, he was exhausted. My mom was always stressed, felt her life was very hard, that she had a lot to put up with; Her reactions to everything were volatile and unpredictable. Given the same exact situation, she could react in any number of ways, so I was never able to get to know her. I know that my children know me and based on my consistency as a parent they can safely predict how I will react to something or what my opinion of that thing will be. There is a deep comfort in that for anyone, especially a child – to know one's own parent well enough to securely and reasonably predict her responses. In this light, I never knew my mother and even more sadly, I don't think she ever really knew herself.

Despite whatever I was going through at the time, my journal always gave me someone to talk to, to voice my frustrations and fears, to report the happenings and experiences of my life. I tried very hard to makes sense of my relationships, figure out my parents and my connections to them, school, friends, jobs, career plans, and with a lot of focused self-reflection, I tried to figure out myself. Sometimes I felt that I was not good enough—not smart enough, pretty enough, worthy enough—to be happy and feel secure. I would write to try to figure out why I felt that way and how to feel better about myself. I had to figure out things on my own, and journaling gave me a leg up. Journaling helped a great deal. There were even times when I was totally engrossed in the emotionality of what I was writing about that I wasn't aware of what I was writing. Only after reading it, once I was done writing it, was I able to figure out how I was feeling. Then, with some distance, I could look back and start to see patterns in my thoughts and behaviors. Reading my own words was sometimes as if I were reading the writing of a stranger.

This whole excavation into my journals from more than three decades, in order to write this memoir, has been eye-opening. As I read, some of it came back to me. The more difficult and torturous times came back quite easily, but at least half of the experiences I wrote about and the people I had all these things to say about are just phantoms to me. I don't remember the vast majority of them at all. How important could they have been? Why did I let them consume so much of my brainpower and have control over my thoughts and self-esteem? My life turned inward and largely existed inside my own mind. My internal dialogue and my journal were my primary modes of expressing myself.

I shared a great deal of these ideas and feelings with Melanie and her older sisters as I spent a great deal of time at their house being a *de facto* part of their family. They lived in a huge house with a curving staircase that led upstairs that was comfortable and inviting, and I felt like I was at home there. There was no tension in her house – all was peaceful. Her family was fun, effusive with their feelings, and included me in almost all they did together. Melanie and I were like sisters, and I treasured our friendship. It was a closeness like none other I had experienced in my life and I was grateful.

As I write this now, I wonder if I unfairly leaned on her and her family in those years because I felt that I had no one else I could confide in, not only because these familial problems are hard to talk about but also because of the secrecy my mother imposed on me.

In between all these very difficult, grown up issues, I was in high school trying to live a normal life, whatever that was. My friends had different homes, different families, and different situations to deal with, and everyone was just doing the best that they could. I took some pride in my schoolwork and really loved learning new ideas. I wanted to make my teachers proud, but I had a hole inside me that ached to be filled. I tried to fill it with my friendships, school activities, and with the quest to find a boyfriend. My friends and I went out whenever we could on double dates, group outings, movies, bowling, restaurants. Sometimes our parents knew where we were. Sometimes they didn't. Occasionally, Melanie and I would lie to our parents and tell them we were at each other's houses for sleepovers. Her parents trusted her, and my mom was asleep at the wheel, I could have gotten away with anything. With our alibies intact, we went out with boys in Babylon or Dix Hills, drove around, drank and made out with them in their cars. We were normal teenagers, and in secret we drank and smoked, experimented with weed. We never tried any illegal substances stronger than that. Nancy Reagan scared us off anything stronger.

I was driven to find a boyfriend, and in retrospect, I think that boys must have sensed my desperation, which made me gullible and vulnerable to the lines teenage boys give teenage girls to get their attention and try to get into their pants. A lot of boys got my attention, and I dated many of them. Most of them were quite convincing of their feelings for me and their interest in a relationship, but when they discovered there was a limit to what they were going to get from me, the truth of their lack of interest or actual availability would come out. I kept falling for new guys' fickle, teenage behavior. Even as a teen, I was looking for love and commitment. I was looking for something that a teenage boy is incapable of giving. I wanted someone to pay attention to me, hold me, and reassure me that I was going to be all right.

Eventually, after a long time of keeping up the charade of secrecy, my mother told her parents and the rest of the family about the divorce. I don't know how they reacted or if they admonished her for her secrecy or felt wounded by it: all things I would have felt. I was not present for those conversations. I just knew the veil of secrecy had been lifted, which seemed like a great thing.

Finally, we could all talk about this and I wouldn't be virtually alone with my feelings. But in reality, what this meant was that my mother and the rest of the family would begin bashing my father in front of me.

I faced an unending onslaught of attacks on my father by my mother and her allies. Few of them had the discipline and sensitivity to not share their negative opinions of him in front of me or directly to me. I was told that my father was selfish and had abandoned my mother and me and that I was better off without him. They told me that he was a horrible husband and father; That he had cleaned out their bank account and left my mother penniless with a mortgage and bills to pay, with a daughter to raise. I was told that he and his lawyer were greedy assholes trying to sell the house from under us and leave my mother, and me by extension, without anything.

I was hurt and confused by all of it and without him around to defend himself or give me his side of the story, I was left to attempt to figure it out alone. Being an empath and being a self-aware teenager, I was very susceptible to their negative accusations against him and thus started to believe them. He had disappeared completely for six months, what was I to think? How else could it go? There was some truth to what they said, even if it was colored more darkly than the actual truth.

Through my mother's tutelage, I began to resent my father for all the reasons she told me I should, some of which were actually true. All these feelings felt awful. Over the years of their separation, leading to their divorce several years later, in 1988, over and over I heard stories about his hurtful, mean behavior that portrayed my mother and I as the victim of his abuse. Supposedly, he broke into the house—his former marital residence—and had the locks changed twice, filed for custody of me when I was over seventeen years old. Those and so many other stories blended together into an awful, stinking pile of manipulation from all sides. I didn't know who to trust.

I trusted that I would always be physically safe, but I did not trust that I would always be emotionally safe. My own emotions were a minefield of confusion. I still needed my parents, but they were consumed by their own lives and emotional minefields. I felt that I didn't have anyone in my own family to turn to or take care of me. I was adrift and trying desperately to make sense of it all.

I wanted to see a therapist. Melanie and her sisters went to one, and I thought that sounded like the greatest thing in the world. A trained adult I could confide in and who would not judge me or take offense to anything I said would help me learn how to figure out myself and my small little world.

My mother was only too happy to make this happen. We found Susan, who seemed nice enough. I thought that maybe I could open up to her. Unfortunately, my mother insisted on being in the room with me when I spoke to Susan, which was 100 percent wrong. Mom told the Susan that we were so close there was nothing that I couldn't say in front of her. I couldn't contradict my mother in front of her, or I'd face the wrath of her judgment and disappointment when we left. I couldn't say how I really felt, either, because that would be seen as a betrayal and then I'd face it from her when we left. She would never accept that I had any problems with her behavior as it would be seen as betrayal and I needed her now more than ever. I sat there mute about many of the things I was freaked out by in my daily life. I was able to talk about some things relating to my father, because my mother liked my complaints about my dad, but there was a lot I wasn't sharing. I was gagged by my mother's presence. Eventually, we stopped going because the therapist said I was not ready to talk.

Why didn't this so-called trained professional ask my mother to leave? It seems the most obvious thing to me now. But she didn't, so therapy then was a waste of time.

Since then, I have spent many years of my late adolescent and adult life in therapy – a journey that has taught me that it's not a waste of time when done right. In fact, the amazing therapists whom I have seen have helped me wade through unhealthy, dysfunctional behaviors that I learned to help me cope with my deep insecurities, fears, and anxiety and helped me find the strength and tools within myself to create a happy life for myself. It's not an easy process, by any stretch of the imagination, but it is one that is worthwhile and meaningful.

CHAPTER 9
REFUSING TO BE SHY

"Shyness is nice, but shyness can stop you from doing all the things in life that you'd like to."

—Steven Morrissey

I was generally a shy person. Many people have a hard time believing that, but it is true. I had my close friends, and with them I could be my silly self. Like most teenage girls, I was nervous around new people and especially boys. I had some serious trust issues, but I also felt that being shy was a liability. I felt that people didn't respect shy people. My mother told me stories about how shy she had been as a young person and all the experiences that being shy kept her from enjoying. I didn't want that for myself. Certainly, being shy was not going to get me noticed or get me any friends or boyfriends, so I decided that I wasn't going to be shy anymore. It wasn't working for me. It sounds impossible, right? But that is literally what I did. I just *decided* to not be shy anymore. Honestly, I just decided.

When a situation presented itself where my normal reaction would be to stay quiet or hide in plain sight on the outside of the group, I forced myself into the center. I forced myself to make an introduction to someone new, or make a joke, or just interject my ideas. If I embarrassed myself or people didn't like what I said or didn't laugh at my joke, the world would not end. I would not get swallowed up in the earth. Life would continue pretty much as it had before. The first time I put this to the test was during my freshman year of high school. I was in the hallway after school with a group of kids I had recently met, and we were making posters to advertise the school's drama production. They were all joking around and laughing. The old me would not have said anything, just would have laughed along with them. The new me decided to jump in the middle of the conversation and joke around with them all. I don't remember what I said, but they laughed at my joke. They accepted what I said and felt like I belonged.

I had tested the waters and felt buoyed by them.

The amazing part of this is that it worked. It really did. Of course, I had self-doubt and second-guessed myself, but I still put myself out there. With this newfound freedom from shyness, I decided that I would audition for the high school musical production. I picked a song, *Someone to Watch Over Me*, the Linda Ronstadt version, and learned it thoroughly. I practiced it over and over, rewinding the cassette to the beginning so I could copy Ronstadt's phrasing and intonation exactly. I really could sing this song well—her songs would be my *go-to* songs to sing in my future, but I didn't know that then.

When my name was called to audition, I was so nervous as I walked into the almost empty chorus room. All the teachers, who were directing the musical, were in the room: Mrs. Buono, Mrs. Stefffens, Mr. Kastrinos and Mr. Weinsoff. I was a fixture in the music department because of band, marching band, and playing flute with the orchestra, but I hadn't sung for any of them before. This felt very different because I was being judged. That's what auditions are. Because of my nerves, I didn't do a fabulous job; I choked a bit. I was disappointed with my performance during the audition, but I made it into the chorus. For that, I was elated!

Staying after school with all my new friends, learning dances and music, blocking and cues was a great way to make new friends, learn new things and keep me out of my house. During musical season, which lasts quite a few months during the winter and early spring of a school year, I was rarely home before five or six in the evening, and that suited me fine. I was able to stay out of my mother's way and not have to worry that whatever I was doing was going to be up for her judgment or approval. School-sanctioned events were perfect ways to get some freedom. Each year, for all four years of high school, I was involved with the musical productions: *Bye Bye Birdie, Oklahoma, Hello Dolly,* and *Oliver.*

Those were among the best experiences of my young life, reinforcing the lessons I had learned along the way and giving me freedom to be me.

CHAPTER 10
CRUSHED IN ELEVENTH-GRADE

"Let's face it. No kid in high school feels as though they fit in."

—Stephen King

Before I started high school, I had met a girl who was going into tenth grade and was in band, and she told me horror stories about how mean and grouchy the band director was. She went on and on about how he tormented students and made their lives miserable by forcing them to march in the school's marching band. He was the only band director for the high school, so if we wanted to play, we had no choice but to be in his class. This made me extra nervous to start high school, but when September started, I found that the band director, Mr. Brasch, was demanding but warm, kind, and caring. He insisted that we learn our parts and practice so that the whole band would be better, which is reasonable and part of his job. I found that I wanted to learn my part to please him and myself. His famous saying was, "You are only as good as your last performance." So, no matter how well you played yesterday, you have to keep it up and not rest on your laurels. If you suck today, it doesn't matter if you were good last night. People will only remember that you sucked today. I took that to heart and have carried that forward throughout my life. It is one the foundational mantras of my strong work ethic.

As it turned out, marching band, which may have been mandatory, was also actually a lot of fun. We practiced for a week in August before school even started so that we would be ready to perform when the football games started a few weeks later. The hard part was learning the marching formations and drills so that when we got our music, we could play and march at the same time. Each day, we took over the large, black asphalt parking lot in the back of the school and lined up in evenly spaced rows on lines that were painted on the lot to resemble the hash marks on the football field. Depending on the coordinate, or space we each were in the formation, we had specific directions. It took a little time to get used to, but if we all did what we were supposed to do with snappy turns and high knees, then the formations we created on the field would be pretty for the audience to watch.

I loved being a part of such a highly choreographed group, and the challenge of marching and playing well simultaneously was very exciting. Saturday afternoon home football games were fun. Crisp autumn air. Crowds of excited teens and families all loudly cheering for their team. Playing music and marching with my friends. Time away from home and all the drama.

Over time, Mr. Brasch became my one of my most trusted confidants and allies. I found him easy to talk to and spilled everything about my parents' divorce, my dad leaving, his lies, my mother's depression, etc. ... all of it. He listened. He didn't offer too much advice because what was there to say? From his professional standpoint, he was not concerned that I'd hurt myself or that I was in immediate danger, but he did know that I needed to talk. He let me talk, and he listened. I became a fixture in the music wing. I was there hanging out in the office, with or without the teachers, during free periods or hiding out in a practice room, with or without my flute. Mr. Brasch nicknamed me the "Band Aid," which was a good name for me. I helped out when I was in the band office, and I was a bit of a klutz. The name fit both ways.

More than twenty years later, I was sitting at my hall duty post near the front-side entrance of the Long Island public high school where I teach, and I saw Mr. Brasch walking down the hallway toward me. I hadn't seen him since my mother's second wedding in 1992, and here it was more than twenty years later, and he was in my school walking toward me. We recognized one another right away, said hellos and hugged. Then the obvious question, we both asked: What are you doing here? I told him that I teach English here and have since 1995. He retired from teaching full time and now works as a local liaison overseeing student band teachers who are students at the Crane School of Music at SUNY Potsdam. He was there at school that day to observe and meet with a current student band teacher. We made plans to meet up after school at the Starbucks across the street the following week when he would be there next.

Starbucks, no matter where in the country you are, all look the same and always have such an energetic vibe. Maybe it's the caffeine. Maybe it's the comfy chairs and the gas fireplace. Peter Brasch was already there when I arrived, sitting at a round table by the wall of windows on the long side of the cafe, and his bright smile reminded me of all those years ago when he was my school ally and confidant. I bought myself a coffee and joined him at the table.

We spent the next two hours catching each other up on our lives. He and his lovely wife had hosted annual end-of-the-year parties at their house on the south shore. Their home was big and beautiful and right on the water overlooking the Great South Bay, with a sprawling yard that was perfect for the huge, loud parties they generously hosted for us all every year. Because of these parties, we got to know his two daughters as well. I asked about them, and so much time had gone by that these adorable little girls were now grown up professional women. I told him all about my life, my circuitous career trajectory that led me to teaching, my divorce and two amazing children, and my mother's death. He was engaged and interested, as always, and we easily and comfortably talked like old friends.

I thanked him for his kindness and caring all those years earlier when I was his student and in an awful place emotionally. In some very meaningful ways, he kept me sane with all that was going on at home. Having a teacher like that to trust can make all the difference to a kid. I told him that I strive every day to be a teacher like he was/ is, and to make my students feel important, cared about, and cherished. It was a lovely afternoon. We exchanged cellphone numbers and email addresses and promised to meet up again. So far, we haven't because life gets so busy and takes our attention in a million different directions. The teenaged me was grateful for Mr. Peter Brasch. I don't know where he is today, but he will always have a place in my heart.

I think that Peter Brasch and I were brought back together so that I could say thank you, so that I could see how far I had come. Was my mother responsible for our meeting up after all these years, so that I could have that full circle closure? I'll never know. I like to think so.

Joseph was tall, blond, and athletic. He was the guy that every girl had a crush on, and I was no exception. He was polite and friendly, and he seemed to be friends with everyone. We sat near each other in Mrs. Simmons's first period English class and had been partnered together to work on an essay. We worked diligently in class and talked pretty easily, but I wouldn't say we were friends or even friends with the same people. That night, Joe called me at home to ask me a question about the essay for English. We chatted briefly as I answered his question, and then I was aware that he suddenly seemed a little awkward. Then he blurted out that he liked me, and he asked me to go to the movies with him Friday night. I was instantly elated and couldn't believe that he liked me. I, of course, said yes, and we agreed to talk about the details in English the next day.

The next day as I got dressed, I tried to do my hair extra nicely and chose an outfit that I felt beautiful wearing. I was eager to make a good impression and make Joe glad that he asked me out. I wanted to make sure that I was perceived as worthy. I wanted to believe it myself. When I walked toward our first-period English class, I saw Joe standing with his older brother, John, who was a senior and a circle of their jock friends. Cautiously, I walked toward them; a group of athletic boys was more than a little intimidating. As I got closer and they saw me coming, they started to whisper loudly enough to be heard. I took a deep breath and walked over to Joe and said something innocuous and noncommittal like, "It was nice talking to you on the phone last night." He replied, "I didn't call you last night. That was my brother," and laughing, almost spitting out his drink, he turned away from me back toward his friends. They all laughed at me.

I was crushed. Mortified. Of course, he didn't like me. Of course, he didn't ask me out. Now they were all laughing at me. I tried to tell myself that it didn't matter. It's not like I was friends with them or should care what they thought. None of my friends knew that I thought Joe had called, so no one would talk about it with me and I could just sweep it under the rug and let it go. But it still hurt. And obviously, since I'm writing about it thirty-five years later, I really felt stung.

Mrs. Simmons knew that I was upset. She was so intuitive that she read it on my face and asked me to stay after class to make sure I was all right. I was touched to know that she cared so much. We talked often after class, about all sorts of things. I easily confided in her about what happened with Joe and the laughing. She said some comforting words, I don't remember specifically what, but I did feel a little better.

In my journals, I proclaimed to myself that Mrs. Elizabeth Simmons was my favorite teacher. With her caring, empathic manner, she connected with me, and I'm sure with other students as well. She was a great English teacher and generated in-depth discussions about characters and the conflicts they faced in the literature that we read. She loved words and showed us how the right word can communicate the specific idea that you want to express. We did extensive vocabulary study in her class, and I improved a great deal as a writer. She is one of teachers upon whose example I have modeled my own teaching practice.

In eleventh-grade English, with Mrs. Simmons, I read *The Crucible*, by Arthur Miller for the first time. It is a grim play about the evils of human nature and the lengths we will go to protect ourselves and get revenge on those of whom we are jealous or afraid. The plight of not being believed and of being suspected of things when one is innocent is something I related to. Honesty in the face of corruption. Utter helplessness. All themes of the play and in my life. Little did I know then that I would spend more than twenty years with John and Elizabeth Proctor, as I have taught this play every year of my entire teaching career as a high school English teacher. I have become friends with John Proctor and feel the full weight of his suffering; annually, I am dreadfully sorry that I can't arrange a better ending for him by the end of Act Four.

The Great Gatsby is another novel from junior year that enthralled me. I never had patience for Daisy's vacuousness or Jordan's dishonesty, but Jay Gatsby's extraordinary gift for hope is something we share, as I have always kept my eyes looking forward, waiting to try again to succeed or meet a goal. I also connected with Nick Carraway as the loyal confidant and true friend. Nick worked hard, wanted to make it in an honest way, genuinely cared about Jay Gatsby and was the only one at his friend's funeral. The only one to care. Nick was isolated because he was a deep thinker and pondered what made the others tick. I think he lost some semblance of his own direction during the fictional summer of 1922, as I also felt like I was lost and had less direction than I craved.

To me, Nick Carraway and John Proctor had similar sensibilities about them that I felt I understood. Atticus Finch, from *To Kill a Mockingbird*, which I had read in tenth grade, became my moral compass. There have been many times in my life when I've asked myself "What would Atticus do?" when trying to solve a problem or make a decision. Scout's impression of her father was that he was the staunchly moral protector of not only the Finch family but also the town of Maycomb and those with limited power. Atticus was the beacon of light, and I respect him.

No one asked me to Junior Prom, and it didn't even occur to me that I could have asked someone or gone solo. Instead, I was going to get something to eat and go bowling the few friends of mine who didn't go, either. We had it all planned out, but when I asked my mom about going, she gave me one of her smooth guilt trips. "Do whatever you want," she'd say in her flat, depressed voice. Each time she did this, which was often in this period of our lives, I interpreted it as *go and leave me, you ungrateful, selfish good for nothing*. On junior prom night, I didn't go out with my friends. I stayed home and cleaned every nook and cranny of the house, while silently seething about having to stay home. I martyred myself cleaning because I thought it would make her happy and make her happy with me. Meanwhile, she ignored me and watched television all night.

Now that I am much older and have had more life experience as a mom, I think I can make some sense of these guilt trips. Sometime in my thirties, I had a conversation with my mother about these guilt trips and how much I felt I missed with my friends during my last few years of high school. My mother was confused by this and didn't remember guilt tripping me at all. According to her, when she said, "do whatever you want," she meant it literally—*do whatever you want*. She didn't care if I was home or not. She didn't care what I did at all. She was so consumed with herself and her own depression and lack of control over her life that she was completely unconcerned with what I was doing.

Which interpretation am I better off with? The one where she guilt-tripped me to stay home so she wouldn't have to be alone or the one where she didn't care at all what I did?

My mother was so inwardly consumed, especially during these days of her divorce. According to my journal, during the week of May 24th, 1985, she visited her lawyer three times to prepare legal documents concerning my parents' separation. The way I see it is this: My mother hadn't gone to college, she had no formal training in anything, and had never held a full-time job. So, because of her lack of financial independence, she was freaking out.

Now that I think about it, some of her fights with me over grades, cleaning the house, or over who paid for pizza at college might have been an over-compensation for those times when I didn't really enter her thoughts at all. That somehow because she was yelling at me over something she felt she should be concerned about, she was proving to herself that she was a good mother because mothers are concerned and yell about things. That may be over-simplistic, but it makes sense to me.

This is not to say that I always was angry and resentful toward my mother when I was a teen. There were times that we had fun together. We would go get our hair done or go shopping at the mall and have fun browsing or maybe actually buying something. We always bought a small wax bag of chocolate truffles, which were our favorite. Three alternating layers of dark and milk chocolate in a bite-sized cube. We would put one in our mouths and push it up to the roof of our mouths with our tongues, let the chocolate melt to slowly enjoy the velvety goodness.

The trouble with her unpredictable moodiness, which is what I called her bipolarity before I had ever heard of the word bipolar, was that I never knew which mother I'd wake up to, Cruella De Vil or Mary Poppins. I usually went to sleep before she did as she also suffered from insomnia and sometimes, she'd still be awake when I arose for school. On these mornings she could be happy and, although she was tired, she was loving and sweet. Other mornings, she might scowl at everything and bite my head off for turning on a light or making too much noise in the bathroom with the blow dryer.

She could change moods on a dime, and many times I would do anything to avoid going home like joining clubs and being involved in every production and musical group. One day my mother came home quite a while after I got home. I had made ravioli for us for dinner, but I wasn't a very good cook and burned some sauce in the bottom of the pot. The ravioli tasted fine, but there was burnt sauce on the bottom of the pot, and she flipped out. She stormed out of the kitchen into her bedroom and slammed the door which ricocheted back open again from the force. I walked down the hall toward her room and out of the blue she screamed at me, "You better not make any plans for next weekend. You will stay home and for once in your life help me around this house. I'm sick and tired of doing everything myself. Unless I ask for help no one pays any attention to me! Everything is a mess and I am sick and tired of doing it all myself!"

I had no idea what had happened and felt blindsided. She had had a problem with a PTA committee she was on, but that surely wasn't enough to cause this explosion. In my journal I guessed that the pressure of being a single mom, the pressure of her venomous and turbulent divorce and the sense of chaos she felt in her life was wearing on her. I was probably very close to hitting a bull's eye on that guess, but I also internalized this rage as somehow my fault and wrote,

What in G-d's name brought this on? I understand she got upset about the burnt pot, but I apologized and promised to never do that again. I will do everything I can to prevent it from occurring again. I just don't understand what is wrong with her. She flips out all the time lately at the slightest thing I do. I can't handle the tension I am feeling all the time. The tension is so thick you could scoop it with a spoon. Can this all be because of me? I'll just have to be more understanding and listen to her and try to understand what she is going through. Maybe there is something I can do to make her feel better? I hate feeling afraid and anxious being near her because I am afraid that she will blow up at me, or just blow up in general. I will try to talk to her later when she calms down. Hopefully, she will calm down soon because the tension is going to kill me one way or another.

I saw the real issues, she was scared, lonely, and overwhelmed, but I also took it personally and heaped the blame, or at least the responsibility of a solution onto my own shoulders. I realize now that sure my mother was pissed about me not doing the chores I was supposed to do and annoyed that I burnt the pot, but she didn't have to rehash the last argument we had about me not remembering to put chemicals in the pool that had been settled weeks ago. She saw patterns in behavior and one thing always reminded her of ten other things that she threw in my face every chance she got. I saw her do this with my father when they fought when I was little. It wasn't fair to him and it certainly wasn't fair to me.

I know that the underlying real problems were much larger than either of those minute things that typical moms and teenagers squabble over. It's easier to yell and scream about vacuuming and pots than it is to admit to one's self that you are terrified and afraid to be alone.

Mom was always worried about money, which was a real concern, and some days I would come home to find her surrounded by brightly colored shopping bags from stores in the mall stuffed with clothing, shoes and purses and it looked like she bought out all the stores. Other days, she'd still be in her dirty nightgown, her hair all rumpled and askew, and she'd be scowling about money with such ferocity she might have been about to apply for food stamps.

To earn a little money, I got a job at Meat Farms as a cashier. My mother said she was proud of me for getting the job on my own. The store was close enough to my house for me to walk if I had to since I didn't have a driver's license, but my mom said that she could also drive me if she was around. I liked having a job with responsibilities. The store was always freezing, with the air conditioning blasting arctic temperatures, but I learned the register quickly and was good at my job. My manager, an older, dad-type man with brown hair and glasses, liked me and gave me more hours. I was a reliable employee with a great work ethic, and I was very courteous to the customers. I got along with my co-workers well, too. I liked my independent working self.

We had a fight one day, during a summer thunderstorm, about some household chores that I said I would do but didn't get to. I felt that her major flip out was very over the top considering we were talking about some dusting and vacuuming. Our heated conversation ate up the time I had allotted to get to work and I asked her for a ride to work and she refused to drive me. She was angry and in one of those hair trigger low moods when even the slightest thing could set her off. She was already furious and me asking for a ride was the straw that broke the camel's back. I tried to get my shift covered that afternoon, but couldn't, so I walked in the rain all the way to work.

Deep down I loved her, and I knew she loved me, but her depression, anger, and unpredictable moods were too much for me to handle. I felt like I was losing myself and, despite being frustrated by her, I was afraid of losing her. I wasn't nearly ready to be without my mother, and because I was not getting along with my dad at all during this time, I was horrified that if something happened to my mother, I'd have to go live with him. At this point in my life, that whole scenario terrified me.

The unpredictable tone of my household and the constant stress and tension had a huge effect on me and my relationships with my friends. As I read through my journals from that spring and summer, I'm struck with the swiftness I changed my mind about things. One day, I would be spitting mad at a friend, for not calling me when they said they would or for not sitting with me at lunch and then next day all would be forgotten. One week, I would be all jazzed about one boy, and the next week, no mention of him but lots of talk about someone else. I was fickle and changeable, but I was also quite self-aware and introspective. I wrote, "I have a great flaw in my personality, I'm too easily swayed by other peoples' opinions on many things. I'm very gullible. If someone I 'like' tells me something—I can't help it—I always believe him. I can't help it. I always fall into the same trap. I only notice the continuance of the pattern after the fact. But, maybe now that I'm aware that this negative pattern exists, I can do something constructive to change it or break it."

I was so starved for love and affection that I ate up any attention I got from boys, even if they did not have the best intentions. Little did I know that breaking myself of this would take three more decades, a lot of therapy, meditation and journaling.

CHAPTER 11
A VERY CLOSE CALL

"The first time you fall in love it changes you forever."

—Nicholas Sparks

During 1985, my junior year of high school, I met a sophomore boy, Danny. Danny was very tall, super cute, and very funny. I was in the cast of the musical, and he was on stage crew, so we were around each other all the time. Danny flirted with me every day, and I really liked him and flirted back. This was the first time that I experienced what it was like to really have a boy like me a *lot* and to really like him back. Turned out that he lived not too far from me, within easy biking distance, which was the measurement of choice since we didn't have cars or driver's licenses. Danny and I talked on the phone every night, even though we saw each other at rehearsals every day. We told each other private, secret things we never told anyone else before. We were both suffering through domestic dramas from things our parents were doing. The actual events were different, but the resulting stress and anxiety we felt as a result were similar. We bonded over that and a mutual sexual attraction that neither of us ever felt before.

Once the school musical was over and we had more time on our hands, we enjoyed the spring biking to each other's houses and taking walks while holding hands and sharing our deepest and darkest secrets. We went out on some dates, but what I clearly remember as that spring unfolded into summer was falling in love with him. I could feel it sliding through my body and brain like a warm, inviting blanket. Danny reciprocated my feelings, and we started to experiment sexually. Very slowly. Lots of making out and heavy petting, as they used to say in my parents' day. We were growing so close, and I thought we were falling for each other, mutually. Then, just when I thought we were on the same page, he told me that he also really liked a girl named Julie in his grade at school. I didn't know Julie, but I hated her.

We had lots of back and forth talking and letter writing and crying (both of us). He had ambivalent feelings toward the other girl just as we were getting together. He was candid about that and had a hard time choosing between us. I put up with his teenage boy player attitude because I was so starved for any sort of positive attention. I settled for scraps, because I really felt I loved him, but I was losing my patience with his game, and I started seriously thinking about ending it with him, despite how devastated I would have been. Danny didn't want this, but this may have been what tipped the scale in my favor. By June, after lots of flirting and annoying ambivalence, we pushed Julie out of his life and he declared that he was all mine.

School was over for the summer break and we both had a ton of time to spend together when we weren't working at our respective jobs. Once, he came over so we could be alone and have my house to ourselves when my mother was going into the city for her one day a week job working at my grandfather's showroom in the garment district. We spent the day in my bed in each other's arms, like the shy teenagers that we were. We weren't ready to go all the way yet, though.

We said our *I love yous* at some point that I unfortunately do not remember, and strangely enough, I didn't write about it (but I wrote about so many other irrelevant things; why, I don't know). What is very vivid for me was our curiosity and awkward eagerness with respect to exploring physical intimacy and every inch of each other's bodies. It seemed like we were moving toward the big event very slowly, but it probably wasn't slow at all. During June, each time we saw each other, we'd go a little further and a litter further. Touching and being touched more and more by each other's hungry, nervous, extremely excited hands. We felt safe. We felt loved. It was a beautiful unfolding of our physical intimacy. We experienced everything for the first time together and in his waterbed in his parent's basement, we premeditatively lost our virginities. It was exactly what we both wanted and were planning for. It wasn't great, if you know what I mean. We had no idea what we were doing. The first time is rarely great for girls.

Over the next few months, we got better at it. As most people do. But as teenagers, we were not always as careful as we should have been, and later that fall, I didn't get my period when I thought I was supposed to. I panicked. I loved him, but at seventeen I was not ready to be a mother. He was only sixteen and not ready to be a father. I did not want to be pregnant. I was scared to death and told no one anything. I wrote about it feverishly in my journal, but that was only essentially talking to myself. It was great to get my feelings out, but that gave me no solace or advice. My reasoning was not logical, but my plan was to stress by body out so that if I was pregnant, I would miscarry, and it would all be over. I exercised like a fiend, didn't eat well, didn't get enough sleep, I carried heavy things and worked my body hard. I didn't get my period. I didn't feel any PMS only ever-present anxiety.

I went to the drug store and bought a basket full of pregnancy tests, sneaked them into my house and hid them in the shower of the basement bathroom so my mother wouldn't find them. She was clueless and needed to stay that way. I took the pregnancy tests—all of them over the next couple of days and every single one came out negative. This was the 1985, and I wasn't sure of the accuracy of any of them. The results were always not pregnant, but why was I not getting my period? I eventually told Danny, and he obviously freaked out. His reaction was exactly like mine. We agreed: We didn't want a baby. I told him about all the negative tests, but that I still wasn't getting my period. He was so upset that he stopped talking to me and essentially broke up with me. I was now single, without the boy whom I loved and who may have gotten me pregnant. I was barely paying attention to school and my best friend, Melanie, whom I finally confided in, suggested I tell my mother. This was like walking into the dragon's cave unarmed hoping to get at the treasure he was guarding. I was terrified, but I had no choice and needed someone to help me. I was desperate, so I braved it.

I spent the whole day quietly circling my mother, terrified to tell her. I kept trying to figure out how to start, what exactly to say. When I told my mother, in my scared, little voice, she demanded to know who the prospective father was. This was an absurd question because I thought she knew very well that I had been dating Danny for months, up until very recently. From my perspective so many years later, I think that she was still so involved with her own life that she didn't notice what I was doing at all. To her, it may not have been obvious who I was dating.

Since it was nighttime and all the stores where we could buy another pregnancy test were closed, we had to sit on this news overnight. The plan was to take another home test in the morning and make an appointment with a gynecologist for an exam and official test. I had never been to a gynecologist before, so this was a new thing to be nervous over. But, as Mother Nature is a crazy bitch with her own agenda, I got my period the next morning. Whew! Not pregnant! What a huge relief! Turns out, that all the stress I was forcing up on myself to bring on a miscarriage was keeping me from getting my period. Plus, all the anxiety wasn't helping, either. I called Melanie to tell her the good news. Then I called Danny and he was relieved, but we didn't get back together. In fact, by the end of the next week, he had a new girlfriend and had moved on. This almost pregnancy had been a very close call with a very big, life-altering oops. Although I was heartbroken that Danny suddenly had a new girlfriend, I was so relieved that I wasn't pregnant that I more easily than expected just let it all go.

Despite the frenzy I felt to fill the loneliness and all the schoolgirl fantasies I recorded in my journals, I had only the one real boyfriend, and more of our attachment happened before we actually got together. Our actual relationship only lasted about ten weeks, and after that he quickly moved on to another girl.

Teenage boys can be players. I think even the most upfront boys are/or have the potential to be. Kids are naive and trying to figure out the treacherous minefield of love, sex, and romance. Danny did love me, as he confirmed years later, but he was so screwed up without viable relationship models himself and had no idea what he was doing. He was trying to make himself feel good in an adult world full of complicated family issues. In the end, our heartbreak could have been much worse. Luckily, because there was no pregnancy, we were able to walk away and try to assuage our feelings another day in different ways.

My mother took out her frustrations on me and was, at times, unreasonable. I was always anxious, wanting to please her, needing her to be kind and loving, needing her to be somewhat predictable. She never was predictable. My father was a ghost. I rarely, if ever saw him. Part of that was due to his selfish involvement exclusively with his own life that was very far removed from me and our past life as a family, and part of that was because I was pushing him away because I didn't trust him and also because not pushing him away would have been disloyal to my mother.

I think that that is why I grew up being a people pleaser. It's part of my core personality to want others to be happy, but the anxiety I feel when people I love aren't happy is not normal. Other people's unhappiness, expressed frustration, or sadness makes me feel upset, nervous, and anxious and quite a bit guilty despite the fact that I cognitively know that most of the time, what is bothering them is *not* my fault and I bear no responsibility for its existence or its solution.

I still feel what I feel. The difference in my life now is that I feel these things, acknowledge them, but then let go. I don't feel the need to get involved, mix in and fix it, like I used to, but this new behavior of *laissez-faire* was very difficult for me to achieve. I thank my wonderful therapist for that, because it was only through hours of digging at the root of this behavior and seeing how it did not serve me that I was finally able to let it go.

CHAPTER 12
THE BIG SECRET

"Secrets tear you apart."

—Mitch Albom, <u>For One More Day</u>

My father and I had a distant relationship for a very long time, pretty much starting when he separated from my mother. After the initial six months of absolute silence between us, when I started to let him into my life little by little, when he would ask, he would come over and take me out to dinner. Each of these daddy-dates was pre-arranged. The easy spontaneity of our previous father-daughter relationship was gone. We used to be so silly and fun together. Now it was different. We would talk while we ate, but it was awkward and stilted between us as we quickly ran out of things to say. I didn't feel like I could trust him because he had said he wasn't leaving me, and yet, to me, that is exactly what it felt like he did. Plus, my mother's negativity toward him was inside my own head. There was no escaping that yet.

It felt like I was dating my father. They were bad, uncomfortable dates. We would sit in his navy-blue Buick Century and listen to music because conversation felt forced. Suddenly, there was a fixed amount of time to be with him, and our manner was so formal. I had no idea how to be with this version of my father and I knew that although my mother let me go out and see him, because she was so angry and hurt by him, I felt pressured to have a bad time. Somehow, I thought that if I had a good time with him that meant I was being disloyal to my mother. I'm not sure if she purposely made me feel this way or if I took it upon myself in empathy for her pain, or fear of her outbursts. She sometimes even pumped me for information upon my return home, so if I had fun, I'd have to lie to her about it. It was an awful position to be in.

I felt like I was less concerned about my own feelings than I was about managing or being sensitive to the feelings and needs of my parents.

My dad was holding back from me, even while I know now that he was eager to be a part of my life. In figuring out how to rebuild his own life, he lost sight of how to be a father to me. It didn't diminish his desire to be a good father, but it completely got in the way. He had tactical maneuvers to make with respect to his divorce and felt that he couldn't really tell me the truly big things that were going on in his life. I felt that he had things he wanted to say, but couldn't, and at the time, I had no idea what or why. I remember thinking that all I wanted was to sit on a couch and watch television with him. It didn't matter what we watched, but I yearned for us to be relaxed with each other again and not be pressured to talk. But he couldn't come into the house anymore and I had no idea where he lived. I knew it was in Queens somewhere, but didn't have an address, nor was I ever invited there. It was separate from my world and everything I knew, and he wanted it that way.

Many times, when I would try to call him, he wouldn't be at home. I'd leave a message on his answering machine, and sometimes it would be days or even weeks before he would call me back. It was the 1980s and all we had were landline phones and analog answering machines, which made keeping in touch much more of a challenge than it is today. I felt that between our dinner dates, which didn't even happen once a week, I was abandoned by him. I wondered what would happen if I was sick or in trouble. What if I needed my father to help me immediately? He wasn't there or available. Quite a bit of my mother's loudly shared resentful distortions about him began to seem true in my eyes. In all the time he lived in the apartment in Queens, I never saw it or was invited there. It seemed to me that he had a secret life I was not allowed to be part of. I felt that I could no longer trust either of my parents to consider anything from my point of view or to be there for me. I couldn't even trust that what they told me was true. It was obvious, even for teenaged me, the they each were operating solely according to their own secret agenda. I felt scared, lonely and alone.

Early spring of my junior year of high school, my father picked me up and we drove to one of the local colleges for a college fair. We walked around, talked with college representatives, and collected literature. It was a nice day, and because of my excitement by the prospect of being able to go away to college to live on my own in a dorm and learn all sorts of new things, I was happy and time with my father was easy. We had an external focus and plenty to talk about. I didn't know what I wanted to study or what I wanted to do with my life, but I knew that leaving home and moving somewhere far away sounded deliciously liberating and my dad had been to college and was helping me get there.

After the college fair, my father suddenly seemed nervous and said that he had something to tell me. I don't remember the course of the conversation and what exactly was said by either of us, but the upshot was that he had a girlfriend, named Kay, whom he had been dating since February of 1984. It was now May of 1985.

He was living with her.

She had two daughters, six and nine years younger than me, and for the first time in his life he was happy. I was glad he was happy, but I was overwhelmed by the whole situation. I thought he was living in a yellow apartment in Queens that he hated. I had felt badly that he hated his apartment, but as it turns out, he didn't live there anymore, and hadn't in more than a year. He just kept a phone and an answering machine there, and I was just finding out. I knew he had been holding something back, but I had no idea that it was this big. He had kept all this from me for so long because his lawyer didn't want my mother and her lawyer to know. He had lied to his daughter because it was better for his court case.

I was crushed, but didn't know how to process any of it, so I held all that close to the vest and let my curiosity about all of this guide me through the rest of the night.

My father wanted us to have dinner with Kay that night, and I agreed. It was awkward, but I was curious, so I went with it. We had dinner at a Japanese restaurant called Sapporo. It was the kind of restaurant where you sat in booths sunken into the floor and had to remove your shoes before you sat down. The servers wore kimonos and the music was soft, authentic Japanese melodies. I had sushi for the first time. I had been curious about sushi since Molly Ringwald's character in *The Breakfast Club* ate sushi as her lunch. It was gorgeous—colorful and interestingly shaped. I loved the different dishes for soup and soy sauce, the pickled ginger on the side, the delicious ginger dressing on the salad and that I got to eat it all with chopsticks. During dinner, Kay was being playful, and she tickled my feet through my socks and startled me. I jumped suddenly and kicked the table up with my knees. The china cups of Japanese tea jostled and spilled over. Tea everywhere. It was funny and memorable.

I don't remember anything else about that dinner, except that it was weird, but nice, to be more included in my father's life.

From there, we went back to their house in Great Neck and I got to see where they lived. It was a lovely ranch-style house with a long porch on the front that was hidden by large, green shrubs on the corner of a tree-lined street. Sometime later, Kay's daughters, Beth and Jill, arrived home from a night out with their father. I was meeting my future stepsisters and, despite my only learning of their existence that very day, they had known about me for a long time. My dad told them all about me, secretly took them to see me at various events at my high school. They secretly saw me perform in concerts and in school musicals. I never suspected my father was not there alone because they always sat separately and hid themselves from me. Their enthusiasm to meet me was infectious. They were over-the-moon excited to meet me and were utterly adorable.

I was trying to stay afloat and treading water, going with the flow.

Of course, I wondered why it had taken him so long to tell me about Kay and her daughters. Why had he kept this all from me? Why did he still have me calling him at his Queens apartment when he no longer lived there? This was still many years before mobile phones were common, so landlines and answering machines were all we had. I was full of questions and curiosity.

Beth and Jill and I went into Jill's room to talk. They eagerly wanted to show me their rooms and things. We wound up playing a version of *The Dating Game*; it was exactly like the television show, except the bachelors were stuffed animals. I was the unsuspecting bachelorette on the show looking for a date. Behind a partition hid my potential dates—all stuffed animals—whose personas were being supplied in cute, manly voices created by little girls. After my various questions, the winning bachelor was a small, pink pig named Kurt, who wore a jaunty black-and-white striped shirt. To this day, just the mention of Kurt and his stiped shirt evokes laughter from all three of us.

When my mother found out about Kay and the girls, she was irate. How could my father have lied to us both about where he was living and with whom he was living? She repeatedly and loudly told me how I should feel about this. It all started with the same refrain. How dare he?

How dare he…

1. Be in a serious relationship and not tell his daughter?

2. Let me call and leave messages on an answering machine in an apartment where he no longer lived?

3. Get involved in the day-to-day lives of Beth and Jill, taking them to various activities in their lives, attending their school functions, going on vacation with them, taking them to ballet class, while at the same time not doing any of those things with me and not including me in any of it?

I came to believe my mother was right. How dare he? I might have taken longer to figure all that out without her and eventually come up with the same list. Maybe. But this secret hurt me a great deal. I had been left out and abandoned by him after he promised that he wouldn't do that very thing. While I was missing and needing my father, he was helping Kay raise her children.

Mom was never one to keep her opinion to herself, so why start now? She should have kept her mouth shut and let me process this myself, but she didn't operate that way. She was only concerned about her own feelings and how she could use this to torture my father and get a better settlement from him.

To me, it now proved that my father was just as secretive as my mother, and I was alone to find my own way. They each obviously had their own lives and plans that didn't include me.

For a long time, my relationship with my dad was distant because I didn't know how to deal with his new life and new family. He was very busy working to pay for all his new responsibilities and his old ones, plus huge legal bills. I sort of get it now. Then, I did not. I liked my father's new family, but I resented the whole situation, how it was kept from me, how I now had to share my father with all of them—or feel like I was losing him because of them. I felt cast aside. Adrift. Sadly, it was a feeling I would experience as a recurring theme in my future. My father went on vacations to exotic places with his new family that I wasn't invited to attend, he drove them to ballet lessons and attended their school functions. He, Kay and the girls celebrated holidays as a happy family with Kay's extended family and I was not part of it.

I felt utterly abandoned by him as he left me alone with my mother who had become increasingly depressed and volatile. She was angry 24/7 and often took it out on me because I was the only one there. And while I still thought that my mother was somewhat interested in my life at times, I don't think she could see past her own misery and fear.

My parents' divorce was being run by their unscrupulous lawyers, who instigated more fights between my parents than were actually there. Their divorce was going on for way too many years. My dad did vindictive things. Mom fought back and did some crappy things. He fought back again. It wore on. It was a bloody battle of legal bullshit that kept escalating as my parents even tried to weaponize me to use against each other.

The only winners in these skirmishes and the long, torturous war were the lawyers. What my parents paid in legal fees between 1983 and 1988 could have paid for me to complete college through my Ph.D. at Harvard five times over. As an adult now, I feel badly for them that they were so blinded by mutual hatred and bullied by greedy lawyers. As the kid in the middle of their fight, I wanted to get as far away from them both as I could. Geneseo would be the perfect place to go. It was a beautiful college campus and was a glorious, nine-hour drive from Long Island.

CHAPTER 13
SENIOR PROM DISASTER

"I can't believe seven guys said no!"

—Melanie, (my high school best friend.)

During the spring of my senior year, everyone was buzzing about prom. I was no different. Melanie and I, and a few other friends, were going to share a limousine. Melanie had a steady boyfriend who graduated the year before and was going to escort her to prom. Our other friends were either dating someone who would be their prom date or quickly figured out who they were going to prom with. No one asked me. I had crushes on two guys, and when it became clear to me that if I didn't ask them, they weren't going to ask me, I braved it and asked them. Both said no. They had dates already or weren't going to prom. Time was fleeting. I had a dress already. I had purchased a beautiful white, strapless gown covered in tiny, bright-red polka dots. The front of the top had a stiff, up-standing ruffle hiding my deep cleavage and was styled like a 1950s gown. I loved it and felt like a million bucks in it. I put my share of the limo deposit down. I was ready but didn't have a date. I wish I had had someone in my life to tell me to just go myself with my friends. I would have had a better time.

In the end, I asked seven—yes, SEVEN—guys to go to prom with me and all seven said no. Devastating! Seven nos. That has to be some kind of record. The day of the seventh rejection, I was sitting in the band room getting my flute and music out when a bandmate, a guy who was friends with one of my rejectors, said that he didn't have a date, either, and if I wanted, we could go together. A pity date. Great. But I had nothing but humility left and said yes.

We went together. We took the obligatory pictures together for posterity, and he matched his tie to my dress. But we didn't sit together, didn't eat together, didn't dance together. It was like I was there alone anyway. Prom was at the Crest Hollow Country Club, where my Sweet 16 had been two years prior; it was the most gorgeous setting I could have imagined for prom and could have been a magical night. Instead, it was disappointing, and drama filled. Between all my friends, couples broke up, someone's date left early, someone's date was flirting with someone who was not his date, someone sneaked in alcohol and vomited in the restroom. It was not memorable for anything fun.

We hoped our after-prom plans would be better. We had planned to go into the city and try to get into a club. We were smart enough to know that to have a shot at getting in we would have to ditch our prom attire and put on club clothes. We changed and the limo drove us into the city. We saw hundreds of high schoolers in their prom clothes in line outside clubs, obviously not getting in. We chose one club and walked right up, and without hesitation or even being carded, we got in.

We were on Cloud 9. I remember it being dark, there were neon lights around the dance floor, and the music was LOUD! But other than that, I can't say I remember anything. All in all, my opinion about prom was *meh*. It was more exciting picking out my dress and getting my hair done up. I could have done that and just gone to dinner locally with my best friends and had a better time. And spent a LOT less money. The only other thing I remember very clearly was my pity date made a pass at me in the limo. He assumed that a prom date meant he was going to get lucky. Boy, was he wrong!

Chapter 14
College Freedom and the Liberty to Explore

"I ran away to find myself."

—Jillian Linares

Going nine hours away from home for college was a godsend. After the preview that orientation provided, I was chomping at the bit, totally eager to leave for college. I was so far away that I wasn't going to see anyone in my family for months at a time. There was no internet and smartphones were only fictional, so it was postal mail or landline phones for communication only, and that suited me just fine. I was grateful for the distance that would be between my parents and me.

I had never been away from home before, so I went hog-wild with the freedom. I got to choose what I did, when I did it, and with whom I did it. Or didn't do it. It was great. I loved my classes and was excited to discuss big ideas in class and have professors care about my opinions and ideas. I dove headfirst into my freedom, made new friends and wildly flirted with boys and exerted my sexual liberty. It was a blast, but it was also dizzying and disorienting.

I felt a bit like an overwound clock.

My roommates and I settled into our tripled dorm room in the only all-girls dorm on campus. Our room in Steuben Hall was on the first floor, adjacent to the front doors of the building, so anytime anyone didn't have her key, she knocked on our window for us to let her in. This got annoying and old very quickly. Because our window was right there next to the main entrance, when the curtains or blinds were open, our room was like an aquarium. Our room was called The Fishbowl. I made lots of friends in my dorm and we had a great time socializing—parties, small chat sessions, study groups, dorm meetings.

This was the year that I discovered *The Color Purple*, by Alice Walker. I identified with Celie's struggle as she came from the worst of all possible circumstances, starved of real love (except for the love she and her sister shared), and through kindness, patience, perseverance, and a little luck, she was able to build a life full of love, safety, and meaning through her own determination and the compassion and help of other strong women. It was a page-turning novel that I tore through and finished reading the last pages with tears streaming from my eyes. As I sat in the campus movie theater and watched the movie for the first time, I saw my Celie come to life with Whoopi Goldberg and I cried my way through the entire thing. Each year, for at least the past decade, I get to share this novel and the film with students. I love sharing literature that I love with kids and help them understand Celie's world and how she felt. Her experience enriches our own.

I sang first soprano in choir in Geneseo. I love the camaraderie of a music group, everyone collaborating on a piece of music, following the director to create something beautiful. Even the feel of the breath resonating in my chest as I sing is such a pleasure. Singing with that group was a great experience. Our director, whom we lovingly called Doc, had such supreme control over the group; with the flick of a hand or even a finger, he could change the dynamic level of the music. Amazing. I remember being so nervous to sing for him as he tested us all individually to make sure we knew our part, and the supreme nervousness as I tried out for a solo in my first concert there. I didn't get the solo, but I did get into a smaller, all-female chamber singing group.

I was able to take voice lessons as a class for all three of my semesters at Geneseo. A professor, who was an opera singer and who had written books about the physical mechanics of singing, taught me exactly how the sound is made in the body and how to get the best sound by raising the soft palette and visualizing a golf-ball-sized space in my mouth as I prepared to sing. It works every time to create a whole, round sound. This is really where I learned how to make my voice beautiful and, really, that I could. That was a revelation. We learned to sing in other languages, such as Italian, French, German, and Spanish, which was so much fun. I still remember performing the songs that had been assigned each week, after I had labored over learning them in that small room with four other students, the professor, a baby grand piano and the accompanist. The first couple of times, I was nervous, then that melted away because we were really learning from one another without judgment.

I loved singing with these groups—it was great fun being part of a musical collaboration like these and the directors had such control over everything that we sang, dynamics and articulation, and we all become close for those semesters. It was always such a wonderful experience.

Despite all this singing, I was an English Literature major since I've always loved writing and reading. Getting lost in a book has always been one of my favorite things. I was in a novel class my first semester and we were reading *Moll Flanders* by Daniel Defoe, which is about a woman who led a difficult life because she was abandoned and abused by the people in her life. The lecture and discussion got me keyed up. This professor loved it when students debated with each other, and he often said controversial things to spark debate and argument. One day, I got so enraged at what the boy sitting behind me was saying that I could feel my blood boiling and couldn't contain myself. Before I could stop myself, I had turned around in my chair and was yelling at this boy. We were arguing like we were the only ones in the room. A couple of minutes later, someone else in the class joined us and it was at this point that I realized we were in class. I blushed and sheepishly slid back into my chair. Instead of being upset, the professor was thrilled. I was relieved because I totally loved it.

I loved my 19th-century American literature class, which was taught by a very hunky professor who regaled us with very interesting facts about Emerson, Melville, Hawthorne, Thoreau and so many others. He lit a fire in my belly. I was amazed at how thoroughly these authors (and many others) could connect to my own human experience and guide me forward, if I listened (or read) carefully enough. At the time, freshman year, I was awakened by the transcendental essayist Ralph Waldo Emerson. In *Self-Reliance*, I learned that I could delve into a deeper spiritual experience through introspection and listening to my intuition—I could learn to understand my own self by looking into my own soul and feeling my own connection to nature. I began to see that by closely listening to my own heart, I could figure out what brought meaning and peace to my life and develop a vision for my own future. I realize now that even though this seemed like a revelation to me at the time, this was something I had been doing for myself for years through my journal writing. Only now, because of Emerson, I had a new sense of clarity and purpose with my journaling.

To the eighteen-year-old Marci, R.W. Emerson seemed to be saying that she was strong enough and capable enough to be the commander of her own ship, that she wasn't doomed to be bandied around by others' whims. She could navigate her life herself. As I dug more deeply within myself, I found the strength to compartmentalize my emotions and my life so I could move forward in my life and begin to thrive instead of being bandied around like Moll Flanders had. Literature was reaching forward through time and helping me find my way.

I think that this was where the literature professor and writer in me were born.

Often, I happily stayed after class to chat about these ideas with my professor, who was as equally turned on by the transcendentalists. In high school, I had written a paper about H.D. Thoreau and his collection of essays called *Walden* that so thoroughly examined his sojourn into the woods, and I compared it with my own life, so much that my twelfth-grade English teacher accused me of plagiarism. She had not seen this level of sophistication in my writing in my previous essays and did not see how it was possible that I had written my paper. Gee, thanks! Ever hear of growth? Maybe she was that good of a teacher and she taught me some great stuff that I actually used? Maybe Thoreau lit a fire in me that I ran with? Maybe all of the above. When I produced all my pre-writing work (nothing was digital then, but I saved all my notes, notecards and previous handwritten drafts in a folder), she rescinded her accusation and gave me the *A* I deserved. This memory is with me every time I read a paper from a student that shows a leap in thought and sophistication. I know that unpredictable growth is possible and that students need to be given the benefit of the doubt. Now with the internet, of course, I can determine the authenticity and originality of a student's writing on the spot.

One of my favorite classes my first year in college was a class in theater set design. We got to design sets and lighting schemes for plays and build models. It was great fun. The first day, I sat next to a guy named Kyle, who was two years ahead of me in school. Kyle was funny and cool with his floppy brown hair, and he invited me to hang out with him and his friends. They were all wonderful, quirky people, and very soon they became my new family. Everyone had baggage of their own and together we found acceptance, community, and love. We were all together all the time. We encouraged each other to try new things, to be creative, to be better people. We played games, listened to music, drank a lot, smoked a lot of pot. It was college. This is what people did. This was the first time I felt completely free to live and love the way I wanted to and be completely safe to do so.

Besides my friendship with Melanie in high school, I had no idea that this type of friendship was possible.

The southeast corner of the second floor of the student union building was our central hangout spot. We called it The Office. As in, "I'll meet you at *The Office* after class." We also referred to ourselves as *office*, so it was personified as well. As in, "that guy over there seems like he'd be so *office*. We should invite him over." It was within the warm and safe embrace of this new family that I met my best friend, Tim, with whom I have been friends with ever since, and Kendra, who was also from Long Island like Tim and I were. There were so many wonderful, outgoing, creative, kind people who for one reason or another were living with emotional scars. I felt right at home.

I also met Michael, a young man who, as it turns out, would factor into my future happiness in a much larger, more significant way than either of us could have ever predicted.

One of our responsibilities in the theater design class was to help build the set for the musical *Pippin,* which was being produced that fall. I loved that show. Everyone was assigned a job to do. The atmosphere was creative, loud, and fun. I loved it! My job was to glue Styrofoam bricks together to build the castle turrets, and one Saturday I sat on the floor of the stage for hours gluing these bricks together using a caulking gun filled with construction adhesive. This shit was sticky and strong.

At some point, I tried to stand up and couldn't. I was sitting with my legs crossed in front of me, I pushed up from the wooden floor of the stage with my palms and couldn't move at all. I straightened my legs and tried to wiggle free. No luck. I called some friends over, and several guys tried to pull me up by my arms. Still nothing. I had glued my ass to the stage with construction adhesive. More people came over and were trying to come up with a solution to free me from the stage. Someone thought to use a wide chisel or scraper to separate me from the floor, but we were afraid it would cut through my jeans and cut me.

The only way out of this predicament was to take off my pants. So that is what I did. I stretched my legs out and lay down on the stage floor to unzip my jeans and wiggle my way out of my pants. I needed help because I had no leverage. Luckily, the style was to wear longer shirts that we tied at the waist, so I untied my shirt and had enough material to cover my undies, thus exposing less of me to the theater full of people. Once I was out of my jeans, it was much easier to pull them free from the stage with a tug. Some fragments of wood from the floor were still stuck to my jeans, but I could put them back on again and I was free from my bondage.

It was hysterical and is still a story I regale students with each year. Students want to know if I was embarrassed to take my pants off in front of everyone, and the answer is really no. I don't know why, except that I had no choice. Either take my pants off or stay there forever.

One of the guys who helped me off with my pants and free myself from the stage, as everyone gathered around and stared, was also in the theater design class and friends with Kyle. Mark was from a tiny town in the middle of upstate New York, somewhere I had never heard of before. Mark and I had a lot in common because of our many shared interests, and we got along famously. Mark was also a freshman and was majoring in physics. Actually, his major was video games and drinking, but he dabbled in physics.

Mark was a disaster for me in many ways. We dated for two and a half years, which was about two and half years longer than it should have lasted. In that time, he crashed his car, nearly killing us both on Route 17; he cheated on me with anyone in a skirt and denied it while succeeding in making me feel foolish and guilty for not trusting him; he drank and smoked all the time and failed out of college twice. The worst of it was that the entire time that he was in a supposedly committed relationship with me and sleeping around on the side, he was actually in a relationship with a girl from back home with whom he went to high school but I didn't know this until quite a while later.

Mark failed out of Geneseo after our first semester, and we maintained a relationship long distance while he was home and I was at college. His parents and sister loved me and I them, so I would fly across the state to Rockland County to stay with them for a weekend every few weeks. His parents were warm, kind and loving, and they generously offered me their guest room any time I came to visit and included me in all the family activities. We cooked together, watched movies together, and occasionally celebrated the Jewish holidays together. They even came down to Long Island in 1987 to have Thanksgiving dinner with my dad and Kay's side of the family. Everyone met, and although I was very nervous about how it would go, everyone got along and had a lovely time. I have no actual memory of this event, but I wrote about in my journal, so it must have happened.

Mark and I had a turbulent relationship. We were both young and passionate people and tended to overreact to things. Mark was very selfish and in retrospect was narcissistic, although I had never heard that word at the time. He wanted everything that happened to be the way he wanted, including whatever I did. I flirted with and dated several guys behind his back, and he never knew. I felt only slightly guilty about this at the time because I knew it wasn't right between us and I didn't completely trust him even though I had no direct evidence that I shouldn't. Just sneaking suspicions that I didn't trust or heed. I don't have any direct memories of this but wrote about it extensively in my journals. I was not happy and often thought about breaking up with him but kept putting it off because I didn't want to lose his parents. I knew that if and when we broke up, my time with them would be over, and I didn't want to never see them again. They were so easy to talk to and be with, there was no strife or emotional manipulation or anger. It was just love and acceptance. I also wasn't their kid, so the expectations were different, and the emotionality was less intimate. There was nothing to get in the way of peace.

CHAPTER 15
A NEW BEGINNING

*"Take the first step in faith. You don't have to see
the whole staircase, just take the first step."*

—Martin Luther King Jr.

During my junior year of college, things with my parents were warming up and I wanted to be able to get home more often, now and then, as well as be closer to Mark and his family, I transferred to SUNY New Paltz, which was about six hours closer to Long Island than Geneseo.

I rented an apartment off campus in the upper floors of an old Victorian house on Chestnut Street, in which the downstairs was occupied by an architectural company. Mark would come over often and spend time with me because New Paltz was relatively close to his parents' house. Mark had officially failed out of Geneseo for the second time and was not allowed to go back, so he was now going to community college and working. During his free time, he'd visit me. It was kind of a nice arrangement. I had the independence of a college student and the warmth from Mark's family.

Cathleen and I became very fast friends; she lived across the hall from me and we shared a bathroom and a kitchen. Cathleen was from the Syracuse area, where her parents and younger sisters lived. Cathleen and I got along famously. We were both English majors, and we had a lot to talk about. We were both boy crazy and had boyfriends, but she seemed more focused on the future than I was. She taught me to make apple pie from scratch. We spent a lot of time together, and she even took me home to visit her paternal grandparents, who lived about twenty minutes from campus and our apartment. Her grandparents, warm and welcoming, were a very old-fashioned Italian couple who made us delicious Sunday dinners and entertained us with charming conversations. Her grandfather tried to test me once on the real names of pastas and was impressed that I knew that capellini is the real name for angel hair pasta.

It's funny what one remembers.

At New Paltz, I was still an English major, but now I added a fine-arts minor concentrating in photography. As such, we had to take art classes in color, design, drawing, painting—the basics. The visual art classes—painting and drawing—taught me how to make every color on the color wheel and blend colors to mix very subtle differences in pigment, hue, depth, and brightness. I learned how to look at things and draw what I saw, not what I thought I saw or not what my mind took for granted. I drew arrangements of fruit, or images from photographs, and live nude models, which was always a little awkward but fun and exhilarating. I don't know how they stood there for so long still while we literally scrutinized every wrinkle and fold and hair and shadow.

I think that early training seeped into my body under my skin, deep where I couldn't find it. And then, when I needed to paint again in my forties and figure out life through the end of a paintbrush, it was all there waiting for me—every last articulated lesson. I am grateful for that early training. Once, I got to actually take the photography classes to learn more about composition, depth of field, and color saturation—black and white versus color, what an image says and how it communicates a depth of meaning or a variety of meanings from the photographer to the audience or the watcher. I realized I've spent my whole life looking at things as an artist. Now, with a variety of media to choose from and with which to express it, I reconnected the disconnect between what I could imagine and what I actually have the skill to produce.

CHAPTER 16
CAUGHT IN THE ACT

O ne day, I came home to my apartment early from class because I didn't feel well. I was excited to see Mark's car in my driveway and ran upstairs to see him, suddenly not feeling so sick. I opened my bedroom door to find him naked on my bed in the middle of having sex with a girl I had never seen before. He was actually inside her when I walked into my own bedroom.

I screamed, "Holy shit! What the fuck is going on?" and stood there frozen in the doorway staring straight ahead at their naked bodies as they jumped up. As Mark extracted himself from between her legs and tried to jump up, he shouted, "Oh my god, Marci! You're home early," and he grabbed for his pants.

"Obviously," I said. "I'm home. What the fuck are you doing in my bed?" My eyes were taking in the whole situation and shifted to her. "Who is this girl?"

The girl stood there with her brown stringy hair sticking up at all angles and was strangely calm. She said nothing but was slowly pulling on her jeans. Mark was freaking out.

"I didn't expect you home for another hour. I was just... I was just..." his voice trailed off as he tried to explain what could not be explained away.

This time, there was no denying it—he had been literally caught with his pants down.

"What the fuck are you doing with her in my bed? You're such a fucking prick! I trusted you and loved you!" and continued to hurl a stream of insults and curses at him that would have made a longshoreman blush. By now, he was still scrambling to get dressed and I was rushing around my bedroom picking up his stuff and literally threw his clothes, shoes, his cassette tapes, and his VCR out the second-floor window onto the gravel driveway. Carol, the naked girl with the stringy hair, as it turned out, was his high school girlfriend.

"What are you so upset about?" Carol asked. "It's just sex!"

"What do you mean it's just sex?" I asked. "I thought we were in a committed relationship.

"I don't know why you are so upset. I don't get upset when he fucks any of the other girls in his life. I do the same thing."

"Wait! What?" I asked so shocked that what she was saying wasn't registering. What was she saying?

She continued, "I've known about you the whole time you've been together. It's OK."

"There have been other girls the whole time? What?" I stammered. Carol thought I was overreacting, and she was somehow OK with it all and tried to calm me down.

"It was just sex," she said again.

"*What?!?!?!*" I shouted, really losing grip on reality. I couldn't even deal with her. I just wanted them both out of my apartment and my life forever and immediately. (Yes, I immediately threw out those bedsheets! Ewwww!). Years later, through the wonders of Facebook, I found out they got married and had three kids. Whatever. You have to wonder what that relationship is at its core. Some people grow up, I guess. But some don't.

This experience, the whole, crazy two and half years of his drama, drinking, drugs and expulsions from college and the explosive breakup left me shaken and doubting everything.

Each time I had suspected the worst from him, he convinced me I was crazy. How could I have been so blind? How could I have accepted his lies and been blindsided and gaslighted by him for so long?

I had a hard time understanding how people I trusted could lie to me so convincingly and could be so secretive and devious. I had been gaslighted by a classic narcissist. He had taken every one of my suspicions of his betrayals and lies and turned them around, so I doubted myself and felt guilty for suspecting him in the first place. This felt familiar to me as his behavior and how he treated me was similar to my mother's. I fell prey to another gaslighter.

No matter how I felt victimized by his plentiful lies, I had played my own part. I stayed in the relationship because I needed to feel the security of having a boyfriend and I wanted to maintain my closeness with his family, (who for their part didn't know about his high school girlfriend, either). My flirtations and dates with other guys were symptoms that I wasn't happy or getting my needs met and that I knew that our relationship was beyond repair. I'm not excusing my behavior—what I did was hurtful, too, but I was young and feeling lost and this was how it was.

I was done with relationships and sort of went off the deep end. Being newly single and without the need for hiding in the shadows, I started dating young men at college and enjoying my sexual liberty with them. I was on the pill and wasn't embarrassed by my own sexuality or my ability to buy my own condoms. I went on dates with guys I met in class, at the movies, at the local mall where I had a part time job at a clothing store. I wasn't making lasting relationships; I was experiencing my life and what it was like to be in my early twenties and free. Cathleen, my roommate, was single, too, and we double dated and together we enjoyed being young and free.

I realized that I was attractive and flirtatious, and that I had a sexual energy that attracted young men to me, but I had insulated my heart and wasn't letting anyone in.

As a student at SUNY New Paltz, I read the college paper, *The Oracle*, every week. One week in the fall of my junior year, I noticed that the issue of the paper I was reading was *full* of typos. Every paragraph of every column of every page was riddled with errors in spelling, punctuation, and grammar. It was a disgrace. The future teacher in me came out that day and I underlined or circled every single error in the paper in thin, red magic marker and then brought it to the newspaper offices to show the editor. I had no goal here except to show them this disgrace and shame them into fixing it.

I spoke to Bruce, the editor in chief, and showed him what I had done. His reaction was a silent, wry smile and a pause. He appreciated my pointing this all out to him, but the paper was run by volunteers only and they were very short-staffed. He asked me if I wanted to do something about it, and when I said "sure," he put me to work right then and there. That first night at the paper, I learned how to typeset, print out, cut up, paste up and produce a newspaper on the cheap. This was before digital publishing, and it was all done by hand. It was time-consuming and so much fun. I stayed with Bruce and the tiny staff all night long until the morning, when the paper was ready to be driven to Poughkeepsie to the printer.

Bruce and the staff were very surprised I stayed all night to work and enjoyed the work. By sunrise the next morning, as we were leaving, they had made me production manager.

For the next two years, this would be my job—to manage the typesetters, coordinate advertising, and produce the paper every week. I learned how to manage a staff, how to create and manage a production schedule, how to creatively lay out the paper and do paste up, how to do graphic design on the early desktop Apple Macs. (This was the first time I used a computer mouse, and I thought it was one of the greatest inventions on the planet. I know, I'm a geek!) Becoming proficient in computer graphic design at the paper creating advertisements would help me get a job in computer graphic design a few years later. Working at the *Oracle* also made me an expert at all-nighters, as we didn't go to bed at all Wednesday nights because we went to press Thursday mornings. It was rough but fun!

For a short while, I dated Bruce, who was a graduate student. He was Wolfman Jack-type hairy with long, black wild hair and a full-face beard. I've never liked facial hair on men, but Bruce was an exception. It suited his wild nature. We worked side by side at the paper, and this led to a flirtation that led to drinks at a bar, which in turn, led to a hot night at his house. He lived in a huge, old mansion with an undetermined number of people, several miles from campus in a town called Modena. This crazy house was known as the Modena Madhouse, and a madhouse it was. They had wild parties almost weekly with two bands, scores of loud people, tons of beer and booze and weed and lord knows what else. The atmosphere was carefree and hedonistic—exactly what I was looking for. I liked Bruce's irreverent style, his deep-thinking, chain-smoking-Pall-Malls style of speaking extemporaneously, as if with his ideas he could change the world.

I have a very clear memory of driving to his house one late afternoon in the pouring rain. When I arrived at the Modena

Madhouse, feeling very free and happy, it was very quiet and there were only a few cars in the long dirt driveway.

When I arrived at the Modena Madhouse, feeling very free and happy, it was very quiet and there were only a few cars in the long dirt driveway. I let myself in and was hit by a very distinctive smell. A housemate of Bruce's, a young guy I didn't know well, was sitting on the ancient, brown couch in the living room and on the coffee table in front of him was a *huge* pile of marijuana. Three quarters of the table was piled six to eight inches high with big nuggets of weed. Alongside this pile was a triple beam balance, the type found in science labs, and a big box of baggies. It took only a second for me to figure out what was going on there.

I found Bruce in the kitchen cooking us an early dinner. He was completely unfazed by what was going on in the living room, as if that happened all the time. I guess I was naïve. I was willing to smoke it but had never purchased weed directly or seen anything quite like that. I was uncomfortable imagining a police bust, thinking that I would be dragged in as a bystander or accomplice. I ate dinner with Bruce, but I think that that was the last time I ever went to the Modena Madhouse. I continued to see Bruce, but we went out to bars or hung out at my place. And, of course, I saw him at the paper.

By the end of that semester, Bruce and I were over anyway. I ended it once I began to realize that the deep-thinking extemporaneous style of his was his only style. He was capable of only one song, and I wanted a whole album or a whole music library. I was bored and moved on. He was very angry, and we fought, but when I'm done, I'm done. Once I close my heart, I cement it over. I'm still that way. I have a lot of patience and empathy for people and will give them the benefit of the doubt for longer than I should, but once I've gotten to my breaking point, I'm done. That's it. Over.

During this semester at college, I shared a literature class with a casual friend named Kent. Kent had a beard and scruffy hair and wore a tan, long trench coat to complete his beatnik poet look. Each day before our shared class, he would meet me outside of our classroom and give me a cup of coffee that he always bought for me. One day, I found him sitting on the floor with his legs bent, knees pulled up to his chest, his head resting on his knees. I walked over, knelt in front of him, wrapped my arms around him and whispered something completely lewd and pornographic into his ear, just for the fun of it. At this point, I have no idea what I actually said, but it was scandalously pornographic. We both looked at each other and while my arms were around his shoulders, I realized that it was not Kent. Wow! I had just said whatever it was to a complete stranger! Quickly, I ticked off my options for a response. I opted for humorous and irreverent. I said, "Hi! My name is Marci, and you now have a great story to tell your friends. Lovely to meet you." I stood up and went inside my class. And, curiously, I never did see that Kent look-a-like guy again.

Every year, I retell this story to my students. Stories like these humanize me to them and I sincerely believe that they help us form a strong bond in which they feel safe not only to learn, but also to confide in me and share pieces of themselves. This is a dynamic that I treasure and one that makes my career so vitally important to me.

CHAPTER 17
PING PONG BALL

*"Even if we all want you here, you don't
belong until you decide you do."*

—Stephenie Meyer, The Host

By late 1988 or early 1989, my parents had sold the marital residence in Commack, in which I grew up, without telling me. I never got to say goodbye to the house or gather my things out of it. They were discarded or boxed, stored and moved as my mother moved in with Alan, her boyfriend, whom she had been dating since the summer of 1986.

Living in an off-campus apartment in New Paltz, I still went back to Long Island during school breaks, for holidays and vacations, but for the last two years of college breaks, I bounced between my father's home and my mother's. I had been given a room in each house, and I did my best to feel comfortable. I had a private room with its own bathroom at my father and Kay's house, which I enjoyed. I could spend time with the family and have my privacy. We had fun together playing games or watching TV, going to movies, playing at the park diagonally across the street with the model trains and swings. It did cause me stress, the going back and forth, but I rarely, if ever, said anything. I never wanted to stir the pot or make people feel awkward or upset. I always sublimated my own feelings and did my best to be a team player.

At family dinners, we all—Dad, Kay, Beth, Jill, and I—sat around their dining room table and played word games while we ate dinner cooked by the housekeeper. One of the word games involved trying to come up with a two-food combination that would be the most disgusting. My answer was always hot fudge and anchovies. Or we'd play the sentence game. This was played as follows: One person would start to build a sentence with one word, and as it was each person's turn in a clockwise fashion, one more word was added to the sentence after repeating all that had been added previously. The sentences we built were hysterical. Here's one:

> *The airplane swooped precariously into Sylvia's embroidered clams while she talked to elves who sideswiped elephants aquatically; meanwhile Elvis undulated lovingly while roosters perpetrated 4,000 crimes.*

When I went east to my mother's, I had my own room in Alan's big colonial-style house as did his oldest daughter and his son. I never really felt comfortable with either of them, despite us all being thrown together in the house and at holidays. Any feeling of family was always forced and fake as I tried to go with the flow for my mother's sake.

One evening, I had just taken a shower and went down to the kitchen wearing a floor length, terrycloth bathrobe with my hair wrapped turban-style in a towel. Alan's son was sitting on the couch in the adjacent den and called me into the room on my way back upstairs. We were virtual strangers living in the same house because our parents were living together, and he propositioned me. I don't remember his exact words, but it was some lascivious comment about us hooking up since we were in the same house and our bedrooms were down the hall from each other. I told him to drop dead. Then I went upstairs and told my mother, who was horrified. She told Alan, who then talked to his son. It never happened again, but I also tried to steer clear of situations where we would be alone in the same room. Forever, I would be creeped out by him.

My room was comfortable in that house, for the most part. The soft gray bedding on my bed was new, but the furniture was mine from when I was growing up, so it was familiar. I had lots of memories of getting dressed and talking to myself in the full-length mirror that was attached to the dark brown wooden dresser, that had been passed down to me from my Aunt Maggie's bedroom in her parents' house in Syosset.

It was good that I had two places where I was welcome, that I had somewhere to go when my stress level was high, and I needed a break from my parents' new extended families. For a long time, I felt like I didn't really belong in either family's world. My father had moved into Kay's house that she bought with her first husband; my mother moved into Alan's house that he bought with his late wife.

I was the only tie between my father and mother, the only evidence that they had ever been together. The only one without a permanent home. I felt lost in the shuffle and didn't know where I belonged.

In my father's world I felt like his stepdaughter, less a part of the family than everyone else. They all had a head start, a history of a few years, that I missed out on and I felt like I could never catch up. In my heart, I knew my father loved me, but his behavior didn't make me feel it. I felt that his words were empty and hollow, to a degree. I don't know what I wanted him to do to prove his love to me. He had made a place for my in his life physically, I was now included or at least invited to all holiday celebrations, I had a nice room in their house. He was paying for my college education and my off-campus apartment. I'm not sure if my feelings were caused by anything new or current; I think that I was still reeling from my adolescence, his lies and my teenage feelings of abandonment that were never accounted for or resolved. It was all still hanging there in a dark closet of memories.

Things with my mother were somewhat the same and yet different. I was still reeling from the pain of my teenage years with her and her lies and manipulation, but she was doing even less than my dad to make amends and prove her love for me, and yet somehow I was easier on her. I felt that because of her instability mentally, and her constant victimization of herself that she needed me to baby her more and not give her grief. I was afraid of her outbursts and avoided anything that I thought would trigger her. Again, I paid more attention to her needs, side-stepping her irrational emotionality and giving her thousands of free passes to be hurtful to and dismissive of me, while I felt ignored and obligated to swallow my own feelings. I resented her for me doing this. I was angry that she continually got special treatment for being a narcissistic, hair trigger sensitive bitch and everyone, meaning, I, had to deal with it. Nothing I said or did was going to change this.

Once my father and Kay got married, holidays were then split between the two households. I resented having to split my time between two homes more than thirty-five miles apart, but I didn't want to be excluded from anything. I didn't want to miss anything. So much of my life was spent looking for connection and longing to feel intricately and irrevocably part of something larger than myself and holidays, when everyone was together, were the perfect times to store up those connections. So, I split my time between the two families.

Sometimes, there were disappointments on both sides because I missed portions of the holidays that they wish to share with me, while I was either in transit or at the other's household. I did my best.

I started to see a therapist during this period of my life who told me I had two choices with regards to my parents. I could decide to not accept their behavior and cut ties with them. He said it was OK to do this if I felt strongly that it would be the best for me. But I also had another choice. I could accept that my parents were flawed human beings who, try as they might, were doing the best they knew how to do with the knowledge and tools available to them. In that acceptance, I might be able to forgive their humanity, and my own, and figure out how to carve out a relationship with them that would give me some part of what I needed. If I could do that, then I could have them and the little that I needed and maybe, over time, forget the rest.

This was amazing advice. Clear. Fair. Reasonable. Mature. Psychologically healthy. Pivotal. It helped me immeasurably then as it did when my mother died in 2013 and again in the winter of 2019-2020 when I shared an early draft of this book with my father and we hashed out a lot of old issues and pain to reach a new place of understanding, acceptance, and forgiveness. It was a process of many days and many tears, but well worth it.

In 1988, my father and Kay married just weeks after his divorce from my mother was finally legal. It took my parents a full five years to wade through the legal muck and mire fueled by their slimy lawyers. Even though the divorce was final, and they were both moving on, it would take years and years for them to get over it, if they ever did. I'm still carrying around internal battle wounds and always will. They cause me significantly less aggravation and heartache than ever before, but they are not gone.

Dad and Kay had a lovely outdoor September wedding at their home in Great Neck surrounded by family and loving friends. There was a big white tent in the backyard with twinkly white lights; we all bought new dresses. It was a beautiful ceremony, full of love and emotion. We girls stood under the chuppah, along with Kay's siblings, to witness the union of two people very much in love. I broke down in hysterical sobs, doubling over with so much emotion that I nearly swooned. I'm not sure exactly why their wedding affected me so deeply, and what caused that dramatic reaction, but I all I can say is that I've always been a deeply feeling person with ready access to buckets of tears for any and almost all occasions. On that day, I gained a stepmom, two stepsisters, and a whole new family with whom I would develop a deep and loving attachment over the next several decades.

Spending time with them all, celebrating holidays, sharing vacations—these have been touchstones of security and happiness in my life.

My sisters, Beth and Jill, are six and ten years younger than I am, and when we were children, this was a huge age gap. When I met them as a junior in high school, they were both in elementary school; when I was in college, they were in middle school, and so it goes. By the time I was in graduate school to become a teacher, which was in my mid-twenties, Jill was a junior in high school.

As a teenager, I grew to love Beth and Jill. I had always wanted siblings, and now I had two sisters. I was jealous of their very close bond, which I didn't understand completely, not having any natural siblings myself. Sometimes they'd argue with each other and they'd each try to get me to be on their side. We would have secret meetings in one or the other's room, excluding the other one, like she didn't know what was going on. It was childish and messy and always left someone crying and feeling terrible. I didn't know how to navigate this sisterly drama and often got caught in the middle when they inevitably reconciled. After a while, I stayed clear of those treacherous mud piles because they were a losing situation for me. In some ways, I think they were competing with one another for my attention. I was the shiny new toy in their lives – the mysterious, older sister they had just recently met.

During these years, our relationship was mostly long distance except for holidays and family get-togethers. We were always happy to see one another, and I was very curious about what was going in their lives. Somehow because I was the oldest daughter and because of the situation in my family when I was going away to school, I was jealous of them. It seemed to me that they got my father's attention every day because he lived with them, and I got the leftovers. They were younger and went on exotic trips with our parents that I was not invited to and couldn't have attended anyway because of my college academic schedule. Later, when I was married with a child and they were in college and studying abroad in Spain, I was jealous because traveling abroad wasn't even thought of when I was in college. I didn't even know that was a thing. I felt that they enjoyed and benefitted more from their college experiences than I did. It was childish to be jealous of them, and I let it get in the way of our relationships, but that is where my head was at the time.

Over time, we all matured. They got jobs, went to graduate school, and started their careers. Then they each fell in love and got married. I was honored to be in their wedding parties as they had been in mine. Then, in time they started building families, and we got to know each other as grown up women and mothers and our relationships stabilized, growing in depth and breadth. As adults, we have all grown closer. We confide in one another and love each other very much. I treasure the closeness we share and that our children are deeply rooted in each other's lives. All our children are also quite far apart in ages and therefore life experiences, but I hope that they always love each other as a family and will one day be closer as they, too, start to share common experiences.

Social media and communication apps have helped us all share more with each other on a daily or almost daily basis. We have a WhatsApp group, just the three of us, so we can share pictures, jokes, and daily experiences. As working moms, albeit in different stages, we are all very busy, and apps like this and texting groups like this really help me feel much more connected to them than ever before. And if I have learned anything about myself after all these years, it is that I crave connection, love, and belonging.

Each summer at the lake house in Connecticut and many Februarys in Florida, as well as Passovers, Rosh Hashanahs, Yom Kippurs, and Thanksgivings in New York, we share special times together with our extended family, our parents, spouses, and children. Sometimes we go out to eat at our favorite Chinese buffets, to Japanese restaurants, to Broadway shows, or blueberry picking. We bring with us loving chaos, silliness, and lots of laughter. To me, though, the best times, the most lovingly memorable times, are the simple ones. Hours spent lakeside reading companionably, talking about the family of ducks that visit us almost daily, griping about politics, playing silly word games amid peals of laughter and silliness. Late-night conversations about whatever is on our minds or worrying us touch a chord in me that brings tears to my eyes as I write this. These are the times I cherish.

We are very fortunate to have had some memorable trips together as a family. We have traveled to St. Thomas and St. John, and to Jamaica where we stayed for a week and shared neighboring rooms in a resort or a large house. These trips are a blessing, and I know how very fortunate we are to have had the time and family resources to go.

I think that we are still learning about each other and growing up together now as forty and fifty-somethings—and if we didn't do it as kids, we are certainly doing it as adults.

In May of 1989, my mom and I were not speaking to each other for an extended time. I have no idea what the fight was about specifically, but with my mother and I it could have been anything that caused me to ping pong myself out of her house again and into my father's. My grandmother Betty, my mother's mother, and I had lunch together prior to my birthday, and she was unusually distant, but I ignored it. She lived one town over from my father at the time and drove me to my dad's after lunch. Before we said goodbye, she said, "I know your birthday is coming in two weeks, and I want you to know that I am not buying you a birthday present. You are fighting with your mother, and I don't think you deserve a present." I have no idea what I said to this. My mouth must have been agape at this judgmental remark.

Wow! Now I didn't care about the present. Honestly, I didn't. But *deserve* implies that I'm not *worthy* of the love that a present represents. Deserve is judgment. She was judging me about an argument in which she wasn't involved and was none of her business.

This showed me another example of someone who said they'd love me unconditionally forever but didn't really mean it. Both of my parents, and now my grandma, were on the list of people I could not really trust and yet, whom I loved with all my heart and needed in my life. Mom and Grandma were both from another generation and limited in the same way. They were cut from the same cloth and could not see what I saw. My grandmother never saw my mother's problematic mental health or later her drug addiction and was probably one of her chief enablers and trigger points. It stands to reason that they both disappointed me in the same way.

CHAPTER 18
BUILDING A LIFE

"Your life does not get better by chance.
It gets better by change."

—Jim Rohn

S tarting a real job right after graduation was important
to me because I wanted to be financially independent as
quickly as possible so that I wasn't chained to my parents
any longer than I need to be. Several months before graduation I sent out dozens of résumés and began the job hunt in
earnest. I graduated from college with a job and stubbornly
decided to sublet a bedroom (without a lease) in an apartment with a female graduate student and semi-professional
photographer named Gail and stay in Westchester instead of
coming home to live in either of my parent's houses on Long
Island. I didn't consult them at all because I didn't want to
hear their opinions, and they were both upset. They wanted
me home or at least closer.

My mother was much more upset than my dad, and she
became angry, judgmental and nitpicky. Always being the

paranoid kind of person who worried far more than she should have about all the dangerous things that could happen and the frightening what-ifs that kept her paralyzed and stagnant, she tried to rain on my parade and lecture me about all the potential things that could go wrong with my plan and our relationships suffered. I stayed away more and more. It was too hard to be around her, as she was increasingly prone to mood swings and never hesitated to judge my every move. As a twenty-two-year-old, I wanted no part of this dynamic. I was making responsible decisions and was prepared to take care of myself. I'm sure, now that I have had the benefit of decades of distance from this and two young adult children, that she was missing me and in her own way grieving the passing of my childhood that she may have felt she missed parts of in the midst of her depressed, emotional haze. She didn't ever successfully communicate that to me and I could be wrong, but I don't think so.

Immediately after graduation, I landed a job at Random House publishing in New York City. I was so excited to be a city girl and have a real grown-up job in the publishing world, which seemed so exciting. I was working in the catalog department at Random House, which was as good a place to start as any, and my office mate, Delia, and I shared the same birthday. We became friendly; she helped me figure out where the best deli was, and I was settling in well, getting used to the commute and my new routine. Then, without warning, six weeks into my publishing career, Random House disbanded my whole department for some unknown reason, and I was without a job. Didn't they know six weeks prior that this was going to happen? Why hire me in the first place? I was pissed off, frustrated, and unemployed.

Coincidentally, my housemate, Gail and I were squabbling and getting on each other's nerves. I was not in a very good place emotionally, having not dealt with my swirling amorphous cloud of emotions and I don't think I was very nice to her, or considerate of her home and her feelings. She was an innocent bystander and got caught in the cross hairs of my emotional maelstrom and my loss of income. I moved out.

I decided to leave and go live with my Aunt Maggie, Uncle Isaac and my young cousins, Stephen and Sarah, in New Jersey. They offered their spare room to me to give me the distance I so badly wanted from Long Island. There, I got a job as an assistant manager at men's clothing store in their local mall, which was owned by the same corporation as the clothing store I worked in in Poughkeepsie during college. Aunt Maggie and Uncle Isaac were generous and gracious to let me live with them while I attempted to figure out my life.

I loved living with them and being a part of their routine and hanging out with my first cousins, Stephen and Sarah, who were fourteen and sixteen years younger. My work hours were long and most often at night, but we had family dinners when I wasn't working, and I got to spend a great deal of time playing with the kids, whom I always loved. At their bedtime, I would often climb into one or the other's bed and read bedtime stories. I cherished this time with them. They were so young, and this wonderful time was so short that they don't remember it, but I do. I love them, and now they are both married with kids and successful careers. I am so glad that they are so happy.

As the assistant manager of the store in Secaucus, New Jersey, I worked long hours for not a lot of money, but it was a job. Retail is all about establishing relationships; most jobs are, actually. I oversaw a small sales team consisting of high school and college students, and helped to manage everything from sales, to merchandising and inventory management. I loved it and was great at it. I am personable and I easily established relationships with customers, who frequented our store, and happily worked long hours to be good at my job. Because it was a men's clothing store and most of our customers were men, not surprisingly, it was a great place to find dates. And flirting with the customers was not only fun, but usually increased our sales.

One of my repeat customers was an attractive man named Jake. He was rugged and tall and had a very self-assured air about him, and he reminded me of a young Sam Elliott. They had the same look about them and the same husky voice. I guessed that Jake was in his early thirties. He liked me—that was obvious in the way he looked at me, flirted with me and kept coming into the store. One evening while trying on a leather jacket, he asked me out. I happily said yes and thought nothing about the ten-year age difference.

On our first date, he took me to a steak house near the mall where I worked. He was very gentlemanly and pulled out my chair, looked me right in the eyes when he talked, and listened intently to me. The simple action of eye contact and attention made me feel important, like I was the only woman in the world. I liked him very much right away. He told me all about his short marriage when he was *way too young for such things* after he and his high school sweetheart got pregnant; he had a teenage daughter only a few years younger than me. These facts of his life were distant and had nothing to do with me. I was only concerned with the here and how. I wasn't making any plans.

Jake worked as a bodyguard for the Phillip Morris Corporation and wasn't allowed to tell whom he actually worked for; that was private information requiring a security clearance. Because of his job as a bodyguard, he always wore a gun strapped in a holster under his arm and always wore a blazer or jacket of some kind. He felt he always needed to be prepared, even off-duty. I felt like I was dating James Bond, and I felt safe, protected, and very attracted to him. His permanent residence was in Pennsylvania, but long term, while working this current job, his employer paid for him to live at the Embassy Suites Hotel adjacent to my mall. It was a very easy jump from our table at the steak house to the couch in his hotel room. He was a very sexy man and knew just how to touch a woman.

Jake was very manly and strong. He knew exactly the way to hold me and touch me that would simply melt me and make me feel infinitely desirable. He put his hand on the small of my back, firmly pulling me toward him and his other hand at the back of my neck, fingers entwined in my hair as he kissed me deeply and passionately. This was the first time I felt like I had been made love to properly. He was older and knew how to make me feel sexy and bring me to a frenzy. He liked me to kneel on the couch in his hotel room that was against a window that had a great view of the sparkling lights of the city below and he'd nuzzle me from behind, kissing my neck and sending shivers down my back. It was thrilling.

We started to see each other regularly, and I developed feelings for him. I know he felt protective of me. This was the fall of 1990 and the first gulf war was all anyone could talk about. Jake kept pushing me to buy a gun and let him take me to his gun club and teach me to shoot. I refused, saying that I was a lifelong klutz who cut herself slicing bagels, and there was no way I was going to buy a gun. He was satisfied by me allowing him to put a tire iron under the driver's seat in my car in case I needed to defend myself against a carjacking. I couldn't imagine klutzy me bludgeoning someone who tried to hurt me. Regardless of how ridiculous this all felt, it was nice to have someone put so much thought and concern into my safety.

During this time, dating Jake and my long work hours, I was home at weird, late times. I know that my Aunt Maggie was not happy with me or my strange late hours. She and my uncle worked a lot and had little kids. I, selfishly, was only thinking about myself, and despite her protestations and worrying about my safety, I didn't change my ways. I knew it was putting a strain on our relationship and I felt guilty and anxious about that. I thought the solution was for me to move out, and I started to formulate a plan.

The district manager, Maria, whom I worked under, was very impressed by me, and we became quite friendly. Maria asked me to work temporarily at the store in New Brunswick, further south in New Jersey, to help her clean up a store that was left a mess by the previous manager, who had recently been fired. She let me stay with her at her house, which was closer to New Brunswick, on nights I worked late, and she promoted me to acting manager. I was in charge of hiring new staff, re-merchandising the entire store and righting the ship, so to speak. After a few weeks, things were running smoothly, but instead of keeping me on as manager at that store, she moved me to a store in Paramus, in northern New Jersey, to get that store back on track again after its manager was fired for doing drugs in the storeroom. Off to Paramus I went, again living full time at my aunt's house.

Once the Paramus store was cleaned up and doing well again, Maria hired another young woman as the permanent manager for the Paramus store and moved me back to the Secaucus store as assistant manager. I was quite pissed off, actually. I had been bounced around from store to store, cleaning up the messes of others, but was being passed over for a promotion or a raise and found myself back where I started. I was missing family events and time with my limited number of friends because of my hours and dedication to a job where I felt underpaid and underappreciated. It was bullshit.

I was eager to not overstay my welcome at my aunt's house. I wanted a new job but was confused about what I wanted to do. I took stock of my talents and decided to try to get a computer graphic art job, parlaying my computer design skills learned as production manager of *The Oracle*. In a short time, I had landed a job designing advertising for a direct-mail advertising agency in Westbury, New York, on Long Island between my parents' homes. Back to Long Island I went and back to my ping-ponging between my dad's house and my mom's. Because I was back on Long Island, my wild fling with Jake was over. This wasn't the love affair of our lives and didn't warrant a long-distance relationship. I don't know how it ended officially. We just drifted apart, but the boost to my self-esteem and my burgeoning awareness of how I deserved to be treated by a man were my very important take home prizes.

At first, I loved my new job. It was creative, and I worked with some very fun people. We worked weird hours, 11 a.m. to 9 p.m., and the office was about halfway between each of my parents' homes. It made it hard to have dinner with anyone, except on weekends, but the pay was better than retail and the hours more consistent and workers were friendly. I quickly established a healthier routine for myself. I joined a gym with branches near both parents' houses and went every single day before work. I brought my work clothes to the gym, showering and changing there.

After work, I went home or out drinking out with my new work friends. We were the only people we knew with these weird hours, so we hung around each other a lot. It was great for about six months. I liked the work well enough, could sleep until about eight in the morning, leisurely go to the gym to work out, then go to work, and after work if I went out, I could stay out late because I didn't have to be at work until eleven the next morning. If need be, I could skip the gym and sleep in. It was nice. We used to frequent a bar in Huntington called The Wagon Wheel, and on Tuesday nights we listened to a cover band called Three Men and a Dentist. They were guys in their thirties who had other jobs and just had this band on the side for small gigs like this. As you can imagine, Tuesday nights in Huntington didn't draw a big crowd, so our regular presence was noticed, and we soon became friendly with the guys in the band.

It was at The Wagon Wheel where I met Chuck, who was a recent criminal justice graduate from SUNY Farmingdale who lived in the area. With his dark brown, tousled hair and soulful brown eyes, he was sort of a young Robert Pattinson type (of course, I could make no such association at the time because Robert Pattinson was five years old). He was adorable, and we soon started to see each other. We double-dated with a work friend of mine from Greenlawn who was dating one of Chuck's friends. As Chuck and I got to know one another, he told me that his mother had died of leukemia a few years prior and his father hastily remarried to a woman he hated and who made him feel like a guest in his own home. I felt badly for him and felt that I could relate, in a sense.

One day in the summer of 1991, Chuck and I went bar-hopping in Greenwich Village. I drove my car and we blasted tunes by The Doors with the windows and the sunroof open. It seemed like the ultimate freedom. We were young and free and a day like this, full of fun, seemed in order. We parked near 10th Street. Walking arm in arm in the sunshine, we stopped spontaneously at booths of street artists and sunglass sellers, wherever suited our fancy. I bought a tribal necklace on a strand of leather and cool round John Lennon-type sunglasses. We decided to have one drink in each establishment we passed and soak up all the ambiance we could. At the third place, Chuck excused himself to use the rest room and returned with a joint that he bought off some guy in the men's room. I didn't realize how shady and dangerous this was at the time. We were young and free and stupid.

We walked outside and sat on a wooden and wrought iron bench in a little garden between two three- or four-story buildings on the same street as the bar, and we lit up. We smoked the joint and in a few minutes were very stoned. We were laughing and giggling over nothing and enjoying the warm sun and soft breezes. Ignorant of everything else going on around us, we passed out. Right there on a bench in the city. For hours.

Anything could have happened.

I woke up in the dark, realizing we were still on that bench in the Village. I wasn't in my bed as I imagined before my eyes opened. Chuck was still asleep, but I suddenly felt too vulnerable sitting out in the open as we were. I woke Chuck, and we stumbled to my car, and I locked us both in. I knew enough not to drive in my state, so I put the keys in the ignition to listen to music for a while. We both passed out again, and when I woke up this time it was about 2 a.m. and my car battery was dead. The radio had drained it. I walked across the street to an all-night bodega and called AAA to come jump start my car. After several hours, we were on our way home. I dropped Chuck off at his house, went home to my mother's house and crawled into bed. I think I was silent enough and no one noticed that I didn't come in until almost dawn.

The next day, in my car, I found Chuck's wallet and, tucked safely inside, his driver's license. Turns out his name wasn't Chuck, it was Daniel. He wasn't twenty-three; he was eighteen. And he didn't just graduate college, he just graduated from high school. I drove to his house to return his wallet to him and tell him off. Once I got there, I learned the truth about the most disturbing lie of all. The woman who I was introduced to as his stepmother was his actual mother, who had never been seriously sick in her life and obviously didn't die from leukemia. She was healthy and strong and had a liar for a son. Needless to say, I never saw Chuck/ Daniel again. He called me about a year later, confessing that he had a drug problem and had been in rehab. He was calling me to apologize as part of his twelve-step program. I accepted his apology and wished him a happy life.

After that, I decided I needed a new beginning. I stopped hanging out with my current friends. They weren't going anywhere, and I wanted different hours and to stop hanging out so often in bars. I changed jobs again. I became a portrait photographer and managed a photo studio that had two locations—one in Melville and one in New Hyde Park—and I bounced between them. I put my photography minor and my short stint as an assistant to a wedding photographer in college to good use. As with other things, I liked this at first. No two days were the same, and I got to use another talent of mine. I took pictures of people and pets for all sorts of occasions. It was fun but limiting. There were no coworkers to talk to, except for the one or two who worked the photograph printing side of the store, and there was no room for advancement. I quickly got bored and restless and began to look for a new job—a career that would hold my interest with a future.

CHAPTER 19
PAMELA AND SAM

"It's never too late to become who you want to be. I hope you live a life that you're proud of, and if you find that you're not, I hope you have the strength to start over."

—F. Scott Fitzgerald

While I was job hunting, I decided that I wanted to meet new people and make new friends, so I took myself out to see bands I liked at local pubs and bought myself a beer. I was dating myself. It was liberating and fun. I met guys, talked to them, and entertained myself. If I really liked a guy, I'd give him my number. If I didn't really like the guy, I'd tell him my name was Pamela Courson. It was a little test of mine. Pamela Courson was the common-law wife of Jim Morrison, the lead singer of The Doors. Only one guy in all the time I played this game ever figured out who Pamela was.

One night, I was at another bar in Huntington called New York Avenue, seeing a Grateful Dead cover band that I liked at the time when I met a friendly guy named Rob, who was a drummer looking for a band. For a while that night we talked and got to know one another a bit and decided that maybe we could find a guitarist and bass player and form band together. I was something of a singer and wrote bad poetry that might be adaptable to music. It was an exciting fantasy. Rob and I hung out a few days in a row, and it was obvious that he was more interested in me than I was in him, and it was not too difficult to figure out that he wasn't really a good drummer, either, but we were just hanging out. He invited me to a beach party in Locust Valley, where he used to live in northern Nassau County. I was in the mood to meet new people and try new things, so I happily accepted.

The party was in a private beach house, a gray, rustic two-story wind-worn house on a private beach that was open only to the residents of this highly secluded North Shore community. Rob introduced me to his friends, who were warm and welcoming. We all sat around a large, round table on the top outside deck of the house and talked. There was plenty of wine and beer and some *hors d'oeuvres* to snack on. I sat down after being introduced to everyone, and before long I was spontaneously singing and scatting with Rob's guitarist friend, who was playing random melodies for us all. This was something I would not naturally do—I would've been afraid of making a fool of myself, but that night I was feeling untethered and free. It was fun.

I was reinventing myself on the spot. I had a great time.

Soon, I noticed the guy who was sitting next to me at the table. He had been friends with Rob and all these lovely people his whole life and lived nearby. Everyone was talking and telling stories and as I was listening, I began to play with someone's keys on the table. They were his keys, and as he was reaching for them to get them out of my way and keep me from touching them, our hands touched, and I felt lightning.

OK. More subtle than lightning, but I felt something. He did, too. He introduced himself as Sam, and we spent the rest of the night talking to each other, and with each passing hour we were more oblivious of everyone else. He was very handsome, clean-cut, sandy brown hair, amazing blue eyes and was a tall 6-foot-4. At dusk, Sam and I shared a beach blanket, huddled very closely in the dark, illuminated by the bonfire and talked non-stop. We told our life stories, told jokes, nothing was off-limits. He told me some terrible jokes, which I thought were hysterical. I think I may have been the only person alive to have laughed at these awful jokes of his. He might have fallen for me right then. I know I was well on my way.

Sam confessed that he really liked me but felt guilty because he thought I was dating Rob. I wasn't dating him, I said; we were just friends. This gave him the green light. When the party was breaking up, we realized that Rob was gone. He had disappeared with another guy; they were smoking pot down on the beach and probably passed out. It was time to go home. Luckily, I drove myself to the beach party, so I was free and clear to go on my own without worrying about Rob's stoned ass. I wanted to give Sam my number, but there were no paper or pens. He told me his number, we kissed goodbye, and the whole way home as I drove, I kept reciting his number aloud over and over and over so I would not forget it. 626-8808. 626-8808. 626-8808. 628-8808. 626-8808. 628-8808. 626-8808 ... all the way home.

I wrote down Sam's number the second I got home and then, throwing all caution to the wind, I called him the next morning. We spoke and wanted to see each other again. Because he didn't want to wait another day to see me again, he invited me to go car shopping with him that afternoon. It was an unusual first date, but what the heck. We went shopping at a Dodge car dealership and decided to play good cop, bad cop with the salesman. I played an excellent good cop to Sam's bad cop, and we not only got him a good deal on a used Dodge Lancer, but we also realized we really were great together.

Two days after I met Sam, my mother married Alan in a lovely ceremony at a big, beautiful catering hall. I didn't bring a date to the wedding, as I was single. Knowing Sam for only two days, I thought that bringing him to my mother's wedding would be weird. I was maid of honor and walked my mom down the aisle to meet her groom. Alan was a very quiet man with a kind, warm heart. He treated me like his own daughter; I liked him. At the reception, I sang a song to them—Anne Murray's *Can I Have This Dance*—which is a lilting, romantic country song that appealed to Alan's musical taste. I remember having a great time and having a dance with my former high school band director, Peter Brasch, who had become friends of my mother's through their involvement with the PTA years before. Things felt complete and like they had gone full circle. Everyone was happy and the occasion was joyous. My mother was the happiest and her mood the lightest I'd ever seen. We were surrounded by the entire extended family on that side as well as Alan's family, naturally. It was a time of togetherness, peace, and love and I felt safe and connected.

Before the wedding, I sat with my mother and all the CDs we could find, and we struggled to pick a wedding song for her and Alan that expressed their deep love. The songs she was picking were beautiful and romantic, but the lyrics implied that this was their first and only love. Alan's first wife had died, and he loved her, so songs like this wouldn't fit. Eventually, she picked a Barbra Streisand song from the musical *Phantom of the Opera* called *All I Ask of You*. As the maid of honor, I threw her a wedding shower at a friend's house. I couldn't engineer a surprise, so she did know ahead of time, but we had a lovely time. Because she was happy and in a perpetually good mood, she was easy to be with, light-hearted and fun.

We went shopping for her wedding dress and picked out centerpieces for her reception tables. Planning this wedding with her was fun and she and I were unusually close in this period; I didn't know how long this Mary Poppins period would last, but for now things were great.

I wanted more time like this with my mother. I wished it could always be like this, but as her daughter I knew that this would eventually end, and Cruella Deville would return at some point. For now, I was going to ride this high and enjoy it for as long as it lasted.

Sam and I quickly folded our lives in together. My family liked him. His family liked me. His friends liked me and enveloped me into their group. I had no real friend group at the time, because I had distanced myself from the bar crowd, so I easily became part of Sam's. There were four main couples—the guys had all gone to high school together, and the girls all got along very well. Sam had graduated from college just the previous spring, was a year younger and also Jewish, which was more comforting to me than I had expected it to be. It was nice to share the same holidays and traditions, not having to explain everything. He was looking for a job in the environmental field and felt, as I did, that he wanted a career that helped make the world a better place. Meaning was just as important as money.

We dated and got to know each other very well. There was instant attraction between us, and what I loved the most about us was that there was so much more to us than sex. There were so many facets to who we were as a couple that I genuinely felt we were becoming best friends, which was wonderful but that was eclipsing the romantic and sexual side of our relationship. We had been quite hot and heavy at first—so much so that he was afraid that I would get the wrong idea about us or what he wanted from me. Soon after we started dating seriously, almost all physical contact between us, beyond a PG-13 rating, ceased to exist. After so many relationships that were really based on sex, this was refreshing to a point and felt mature and adult to me and although, in hindsight, I should have been alarmed by this, I wasn't. I let it go figuring that we'd eventually re-learn that part of our relationship. Looking back, this should have been the most sexually charged portion of our new relationship as sexual chemistry and attraction can't be learned. It's either there or it's not. And it was not.

As we got to know one another, we realized there was a pattern or synchrony in dates between our lives. Many iconic events in our lives happened on the same date, and we took this as a sign that we were meant to be—*bashert*. We spent more and more time together, and no matter which parent's house I was in at the time, he was welcomed as part of the family.

Before I left my job as a photographer, I brought Sam to my studio and took portraits of him. They were not my best work because I was a little nervous, but the experience of shooting headshots of him was flirtatious and fun.

Chapter 20

BE YOURSELF; FIND WHAT MAKES YOU HAPPY

"Be yourself; everyone else is already taken."

—Oscar Wilde

J ust after I turned twenty-four, in the autumn of 1992, I applied for a job and earned an interview for a position as a public relations assistant with a small public relations firm on East 41st, off Lexington Avenue in Manhattan. Job interviews are nerve-wracking, sometimes harrowing experiences, and I was very eager to make a great first impression and present myself well so they would offer me the job. I wanted to break into the PR game and knew that I was qualified for the position, but I had to convince them of that in my interview.

I had my new, tailored suit cleaned, the black one with the short jacket and pleated, knee-length skirt. I bought a new, pale-pink blouse for underneath and planned to keep my jewelry simple and understated, leaving the many rings and bracelets I usually wear tucked safely in the inside zipper pocket of my purse. I wore my long, brown hair up in a neat bun, which I felt looked more corporate and conservative than the wavy and wild style I normally wore; that morning, I put on subtler makeup as well. I kept my usual dark lipstick and the rest of my everyday jewelry in the zippered pocket of my messenger bag.

At the interview, I sat across from Holly, the office manager, at the end of the rectangular conference table in a small conference room. She had wild, curly auburn hair, wore glasses that fit her face well, and her outfit was stylish and bohemian. She was impressive. As she looked over my résumé and application, I silently speculated that she was only a few years older than I was, and in a few years, I could be in her position.

Holly asked the typical questions about my education and previous job experience, about my skills and what I saw as my flaws, which I answered carefully, by phrasing them as things I wanted to improve. I figured focusing on personal growth was better than just listing flaws.

We discovered some common threads: Her cousin went to the same summer camp as my younger sisters; we did our bachelor's degrees at the same college. About thirty minutes into the interview, she told me that I was certainly qualified for the job, but she thought that I was too conservative in manners, behavior, and dress to fit in with their creative, wild office culture.

I paused. Quickly, I thought that this could be the time to pull out the real me.

It was just as if it was a movie scene. I saw the camera pull out to a wide shot, turn and refocus on me. I slowly said that I disagreed with her assessment of me. I said that for this interview, I dressed very differently, much more conservatively, than I usually do because I was trying to appear more corporate, which is what I thought they would want.

While I was telling her this, I took my hair out of the bun and shook it into its long, wild waves. I opened the zippered compartment of my bag and put on all my rings and bracelets. I continued to tell her that I sang with a hard rock, garage band and we were practicing some Pat Benatar and Heart covers (which was only partially true—I met with a weird group of guys once to try to fit together a band), then I put on dark lipstick and her jaw dropped. She was speechless and sat mutely listening to me in awe of this sudden transformation. I asked her if she could guess what I did the night before. She silently shook her head no.

I told her that I went to a bar in Huntington to see a Grateful Dead cover band I loved and saw every chance I had. I bought myself a beer, said hello to the bartender, whom I knew on a first-name basis, and stood in the very dense crowd to watch the band. I noticed a really cute guy repeatedly glancing at me from across the smoky room (you could smoke in bars in those days), and I smiled at him. He approached me and we began talking. He had really beautiful eyes, so I was flirting with him, but once he really started to talk, or yell because the music was so loud, I realized he was dumb as a box of rocks.

When he asked me my name, I told him it was Pamela. Pamela Courson. I don't remember his name at this point, but I do remember that he didn't catch onto my game. I told Holly that Pamela Courson is the name of Jim Morrison's wife. The Doors are my favorite band, and this was my game to see if any guy caught on and knew who she was. He didn't catch on.

He joined me in listening to the band and I continued to talk to him for the rest of the night. I think he thought we were really hitting it off. At the end of the band's second set, he asked if he could call me and if he could have my number. I said yes, because saying no risked that the semi-drunk guy would get angry and ruin the relaxed vibe. I took a pen out of my purse and flirtatiously wrote a fake number on the palm of his hand. We parted company, and I never saw him again. Before cellphones it was easy to get away with this. Now there are very clever cell phone apps to help you by giving the guy a fake number and even rejecting him for you, if and when he calls.

Holly laughed along with me as I finished the story and then was quiet for a few very long seconds. I started to second-guess myself and panicked inside my head. Did I overdo it? Should I have not told the whole truth? Before I could beat myself up too much, Holly said I proved her wrong; I was hysterical and would definitely fit into their crazy, creative office culture. She hired me on the spot.

What's the lesson? You will get advice from well-meaning people. Some of it will be good, some of it less so. I've learned that I have to be my own barometer and stay true to who I am and how I am comfortable. It's one thing to blend in with an environmental expectation, like a company dress code, but it's another to ignore our own individuality. Try to make the best impression you can, but always be yourself.

It was now the summer of 1992, and I had switched jobs again. It was easier for work in New York City if I lived at my dad's, so I moved again. This time, it went better as there was a logical, logistical reason for the move, not just my whims or my parents' annoying expectations or habits. Sam had just finished a paralegal course and got a job with an environmental law firm a few blocks from my office on Park Avenue. We commuted together. He drove from his parents' house and picked me up, and we took one of our cars and drove to Queens, parked in a neighborhood off of Union Turnpike and took the Queens Surface bus to the city. It was fun. We had our little private jokes and peculiarities. We talked about the old man who always sat in the front of the bus whose few strands of white hair were very, very long and wrapped around his head like thread on a spool to cover his almost completely bald head. He had hair sprayed it in place so solidly, it resembled a white helmet. One morning while parking on the side of the road to meet the bus, Sam stood outside the car on the driver's side to guide me into a spot and I accidentally drove over both of his feet with the rear driver's side tires. He wasn't hurt, luckily, and we laughed about that for a long time. We had so many hysterical jokes and situations, we practically had a vaudeville act. Life was great.

I loved my new job for about a year, which was my longest stint at a job so far. I got to write copy for public relations promotions and put together press kits; I managed their computer network despite not knowing much about computer networks, but I was savvy and smart and whatever I didn't know I learned or called computer geek friends for help. I liked it a lot most days. The corporate heartlessness was too much for me. People in PR behave like what they do is as important as curing cancer. I get that a job should be done well—any job you undertake should be done well—but I couldn't take doing PR for a wallpaper company very seriously. Then, the last straw for me was when a co-worker got fired for being absent too often because her toddler son repeatedly was sick with strep throat. The irony was that the CFO, whom I reported to directly, had me babysit for his six-year-old daughter in my cubicle whenever his Upper East Side wife had a tennis lesson. I couldn't take it.

I found another job, this time doing PR and fundraising for the Boys' and Girls' Clubs of America, near Sam's parents' house. I quit my city job and Sam had to commute on his own. The Boys & Girls Clubs of America was a fun place to work. There was always something going on with a full program of activities for the kids who frequented the club every day. I organized charity events like art auctions and golf outings; I helped plan events for the kids and a host of other office duties. There wasn't much growth opportunity, but I made more money than I had in the city and was able to buy myself a brand-new car, which I desperately needed. I loved driving my new phantom gray (black) Honda Civic and was so proud of myself. It was my first new car, and its size and shape suited me perfectly. Zipping around in that car, I felt like a million bucks.

I thought things were going very well at this job, and throughout the summer and fall, they were. I have no idea what happened because it was never explained to me, but the day before Thanksgiving in 1993, I was fired. No notice. Just *sorry, you're out*. I kept running through all I had done recently. The fundraising art auction went well, as did the big golf outing. My interactions with the other staff were professional and pleasant, as were my dealings with the board of directors and the center's kids. I was shocked and devastated and had no idea what to do next. I kept replaying over and over all the conversations with co-workers and the center's kids, as well as my boss trying to make sense of it all. There were a couple of reports I typed up that had had a couple of careless typos that were caught before they were distributed; that certainly couldn't be reason to fire me without notice. The only thing that I could piece together was that maybe the director felt insecure in his own position with the board, and since they really liked me, maybe he fired me to eliminate his *competition*. I was young and naïve and had no idea that I could protest my firing and ask for reasons and documentation. I think that young people, maybe especially girls, weren't raised to question authoritative men in positions of power and I certainly did not know my rights as an employee. Sadly, I just left and had to come up with a new plan.

Obviously, going from job to job wasn't getting me anywhere. I needed to find a career I liked, one that would sustain my interest and give me enough money to finally be financially independent and out on my own.

For our second Thanksgiving, Sam and I decided to celebrate separately with our own families. I went with my mother and Alan to Aunt Maggie's and Uncle Isaac's house in New Jersey to spend the holiday warm in the embrace of my loving family and eat a delicious meal prepared by the three of the most important women in my life: my mother, my grandmother, and my aunt.

This would prove to be a pivotal day for me because of a late-night, after-dinner conversation with Aunt Maggie that was to be life-changing. After-dinner conversations like after-party conversations are always the best. The tension and expectation of the main event are gone, and people are more relaxed and open.

After dinner, once all the dishes were done and the kitchen was cleaned, Aunt Maggie and I sat at her beige Formica kitchen table and talked. We talked about my losing my job, and she tried to help me figure out my next move.

She asked me, "How do you picture your life in the future? What do you envision for your life? Do you know what you want?" Boy, that was a heavy question to drop on me with my belly still full of turkey and apple pie. I looked out of the kitchen window into the blackness beyond while nervously playing with my fingers. I wasn't sure how to respond. What did I want to do?

"The most important thing is to eventually have children and to be able to be a great mom," I said and then paused.

I had known, since I was a little girl playing with my baby dolls and arranging for my mother (their grandmother) to babysit for them while I was away all day in elementary school, that being a mom was the most important thing to me. More than anything else. "But I need a career, not just random jobs, that will bring some meaning to my life – I want to do something worthwhile – and, of course, I have to make enough money to support myself so I'm not living with my parents forever."

She nodded and looked at me with her warm, brown eyes and said, "I know you will be a great mommy. Just seeing you with Steven and Sarah shows me that."

Aunt Maggie had been a nurse but then became a real estate agent after her kids were born because real estate gave her more flexibility to be home when her kids needed her. "If I could do it all over again, I would be a teacher," she said somewhat wistfully. I had not heard her ever say this before and I must have made a scrunched-up face, because she repeated herself. Then she said, "You, Marci, would make a wonderful teacher." She paused looking at me sensing for my reaction. "I think," she continued cautiously, "that for many years, we have all thought you would make a wonderful teacher, but when your mom suggested it you shot down the idea so vehemently, we didn't bring it up again."

This was news to me. I didn't remember anyone ever mentioning teaching to me as a possible career, but I sometimes tend to dismiss things my mother says. Why had no one said anything again or more persuasively? It was something I had never considered before, but she was right? "That's an interesting thought,' I said. "I'd have a good salary and my workdays and vacation days would be very close to my future children's' schedules." Aunt Maggie nodded in agreement and said, "Those are the reasons I wish I had been a teacher. You have no idea how hard it is to be a working mom and have a completely different schedule as your kids. To be on the same schedule with them for each day and for weeks off and summers, would have made my life so much easier," she said. I had to admit it sounded pretty good. I told her that I'd investigate that after Thanksgiving.

I went to bed that night thinking about what it would be like standing up in front of a class of teenagers teaching them something. I was intrigued.

The next week, I had an appointment with an admissions counselor at Long Island University/ CW Post to discuss my options. I met with a lovely, easy-to-talk-to man with a kind face and a patient manner. We talked through my education and job history. He reviewed my college transcript and somehow within our three-jour meeting I had decided to go to graduate school to get my master's degree in secondary English education; I had applied, been accepted, registered for classes for the spring semester and was fully matriculated by the time I left. This was a big day. I was overjoyed and very excited to begin my next new chapter.

I love going to school, and I was eager to learn new things and start something that would lead to a solid career I could be proud of and hopefully would find meaningful as well.

I found a part-time job working as a nanny for a wealthy family who lived between my dad's house and CW Post's campus, so I had some cash and a job that would allow me to do my homework. I registered for twenty-one credits' worth of graduate credits, which was seven classes in one semester. I had to get the dean of the school of education to sign off on a course load like that, and he didn't think it was a good idea. It was one of those moments in life when I was being underestimated, and I had something to prove.

I was confident that I could handle the workload. I was highly motivated. I told him that he didn't know me and how capable I was. I only worked part time and had enough time to do all my coursework and do it well. He agreed but was skeptical.

I loved being back at school, and I loved being a graduate student. I excelled in these classes because all the course material was interesting, relevant and immediately applicable to my goal of being an English teacher. (Whereas, as an undergraduate, I just got by.) Educational psychology and pedagogical studies were so interesting and relatable to me. I sailed through my coursework with straight A's and ended the semester with a 4.0, despite a messy April and May, much to the surprise of the skeptical department chairperson.

Sam and I were very serious about each other, and in April of 1994, we decided to move in together. He had changed jobs and was now working for an environmental consulting firm on Long island and we could afford our own place. I hoped that living together would help us feel more like adults and less like old, celibate kids living in our parents' houses. For too long, I felt displaced living in my step-parents' homes and longed for a home of my own. I needed my own home. And I hoped that by living together, on our own, Sam and I would start to behave more like a cohesive couple—like two people in love with one another—and less like roommates. We found a newly renovated garden apartment that was in the same complex across the street from where my parents lived as newlyweds from 1964 to 1969. The synchronicity of this seemed somehow meaningful to me.

It was so much fun decorating and setting up our own place. Everyone we knew helped us furnish our place with extra things from their homes, and lots of gifts. We actually purchased very little for our place at first because money was tight, and we were just starting out. My mother and Aunt Marie, my mom's best friend, helped us decorate, unpack, hang curtains, and fix the apartment up. We got a little gray cat, named Phoebe, and were in love with our new place.

Everything was right in my world. We had three great couples to hang with who were all in the same stage that we were—living together, getting engaged, and getting married— and all starting out in life with more hope than money.

CHAPTER 21
FACING DEATH

In mid-May, I got a call from my mother, who was in Florida visiting her parents in North Miami Beach, that my grandfather was ill and near death. I needed to drop everything and fly to Florida to say goodbye. I was very upset, as my grandfather and I had always been close. My mother said that she had arranged for my stepfather and I to fly down to Florida the next morning, so I should expect my stepdad to pick me up in time to get to the airport. Before I went, that night I put the finishing touches of my final project for my educational methods class, called my professor to explain my situation and arrange to drop off my work early the next morning so I could fly to Florida to focus on my family without worrying about school stuff. My professor was very understanding, and after I got that squared away, off to Florida I flew.

Grandpa Max had had thyroid cancer some years before and despite surgery and cancer treatment it had come back and spread. What he had misinterpreted as repeated upper respiratory infections was the cancer spreading throughout his chest. The doctors had to do a tracheotomy because my grandfather had been fighting to breathe, which meant that he couldn't speak to us or anyone. I can't imagine how frightened and frustrated he was. He was quite medicated but was able to see us one or two at a time. I'm sure that he knew that his condition was serious because we were all there at the hospital: my grandmother, mother, me, my stepdad, my aunt and uncle and two cousins.

I was anxious and upset because I loved him so much, I couldn't imagine life without him. I was trying to be as calm as possible because I felt that my mother and my grandmother were barely holding it together. I think, deep inside, I was very hopeful that he would pull through this like he had pulled through so many other illnesses.

In a cream-colored damask quilted box, I still have the notes he wrote to me when we had what was to be our last conversation. I spoke and he wrote his half of the conversation on hospital stationery. His handwriting was shaky and wobbly, but what I notice the most about those notes was his ever-present hopefulness and positivity. I don't know if he knew how gravely ill he was and he was trying to be strong for me and the rest of us. I'll never know for sure, but the love he felt for me was evident on every page of paper. For two or three days, we all sat vigil at the hospital. Trying to busy ourselves in the various waiting rooms, I taught my younger cousins to do word search puzzles and together we completed at least two books of them while we waited.

Either my grandfather thought that he might get better and wanted to be in New York to be treated by his regular doctors, or he was trying to get himself moved to NY to take care of all of us. By the third week in May, they transported him back to New York via an air ambulance. My aunt, who was a nurse as well as his daughter, traveled with him. She said that it was one of the scariest times in her life. Despite my grandmother's and mother's fantasies that grandpa would play golf that summer, his situation deteriorated. Within a short time of getting situated in his hospital room in the New York hospital, on May 26th, my grandfather peacefully passed away.

According to Jewish law, a funeral must take place no more than forty-eight hours after a death. The grief process should not be prolonged. Life needed to resume sooner rather than later. Because grandpa had endured some other health emergencies over the previous few years, funeral arrangements had been prearranged a bit, so it was relatively easy to set up the funeral for the next day. My grandfather's funeral was on my twenty-sixth birthday—May 27, 1994. Somehow, I liked this. I know it sounds morbid, but I loved my grandfather a great deal and I felt that this linked us together more closely because his funeral was on my birthday. It was a terribly sad day and we were surrounded by more than a hundred people—family, extended family, friends, work associates—everyone who knew him, loved him, and came to pay their respects. We sat shiva for several days at my grandmother's apartment, then at my aunt's in New Jersey and then my mother's on Long Island. Each of my grandfather's ladies had the chance to grieve in her own home and have their own local friends pay respects, offering love and sympathy. Sam didn't leave my side.

About ten years later, my grandmother passed away surrounded by her daughters and me. She had been living with heart disease and high blood pressure for a very long time and was growing very frail and weak. It was clear, as she deteriorated, that the end was near. She was eighty-nine, a few months shy of ninety when she was brought into the hospital by her live-in caretaker, Lana. The doctors confirmed that she would likely pass away that day. My mother, Aunt Maggie and I sat around her bed as she lay drifting between this world and whatever is beyond. For hours we were talking, reminiscing, laughing and crying. We listened to her irregular heartbeat as we talked and then suddenly her heartbeat shifted to a perfect, regular sinus rhythm. We fell silent, clasped hands forming a semi-circle of love around her and watched her very closely. The air was still. The world fell away. We held our breath and waited. Then quietly and peacefully she exhaled her last breath and slipped away. No one moved. The machines started screaming their alarms and a nurse shut them off and left us to say goodbye. We sat there with her. The three of us, the women in her life, women of her blood, and bid her a peaceful and loving goodbye from this world.

It was sad to see her go, but it was one of the most profound moments of my life – to witness her last breath as we surrounded her with love.

CHAPTER 22
LAKEHOUSE PROPOSAL

"No one was more surprised than we were."

—Me

Before we knew it, it was summer and with it came more graduate classes to get myself ready to student teach in the fall semester at the high school and middle school in the public-school district from which I graduated. Sam was working hard at his new job and demonstrating to his superiors how on the ball and indispensable he was. He was doing very well and despite traveling a lot between various drilling sites and the offices on Long Island and New Jersey; he was thriving and loving it. I think this job was fulfilling all his requirements of job success—challenging work he was good at, growing financial independence, and a sense that his work cleaning up the environment was meaningful.

And I was feeling a similar growing confidence in my career trajectory as well. All in all, things were looking up and as long as I didn't think too hard about our relationship, I was happy. I already found Sam a little controlling—only in that he lost his temper when he was confronted. To avoid loud, scary blowups, I walked on eggshells around him on certain subjects like intimacy and the lack of it in our relationship. We were roommates who shared the same bed, not lovers, and this was not getting better even in our own place. We should have been all over each other, but we weren't.

During the winter of 1993, my father, stepmother and her sister and brother-in-law (my aunt and uncle) had purchased a huge, sprawling lake house in northwestern Connecticut that served as our summer compound with the extended family every summer. The house had room enough for all of us to sleep, eat, play games, have intense conversations, and frolic in the sun. It is a peaceful, serene and a remote hideaway, and since the summer of 1994, it has become one of my most beloved places.

On the weekends, we traveled to Connecticut to the family lake house. My dad and stepmother's side of the family had bought this gorgeous, lakeside house for us all to summer in. We quickly learned that having such a great place to relax, swim, talk, eat and sleep together was a rare and amazing privilege. From the first, this house has been a true oasis in my life. It has a weird sprawling ranch-style floorplan but from the street view outside, it looks like four, old-style Pizza Hut restaurants built ridiculously close together. It is quirky just like we are. The view from the backyard overlooking lake is tranquil and picturesque.

We still enjoy the familial togetherness every summer. The cast of characters has evolved as there have been marriages, births, divorces, and deaths, but the love and togetherness are ever-present. So many memories of elaborate meals, Jill's wedding, cute sayings and small silly jokes are buoyed around the house by loving breezes and laughter.

That same summer, two couples in our small group were married; we were in two wedding parties and got the marriage bug.

Little did we know all we needed was a nudge.

On a mid-August weekend at the lake house, my paternal grandmother Claire was visiting, and met Sam for the first time. She remarked that he looked like the spitting image of her late husband, my grandfather, Dean, who died when I was small. Somehow, this resemblance meant to her that we should definitely get married, especially since we were already living together. We hadn't even discussed getting married at all and were struck a little awkwardly by this suggestion. I think that everyone who was there felt the way we did, but it did get us thinking.

I knew we had issues, but it's easy to get swept up in the wedding excitement and sweep our fundamental issues under the rug.

We had been dating two years and were living together. I thought, what would be the harm in getting engaged? Sam was thinking the same thing, but we didn't want to discuss it in front of the whole family. That night, on our two-and-a-half-hour drive back home, we talked about it. I don't know which of us brought it up, but for hours this is all we talked about. We examined our relationship, what our plans and goals were, how we envisioned our own futures and how they could mesh. Somehow what should have been a direct two and a half hour southerly drive took us over five hours because we were so focused on our conversation that we didn't realize we had taken several wrong turns and were on the other side of the Hudson River in Orange County, and then had to make our way home. By the time we arrived home at our own apartment, we had decided to get married.

We were ecstatic.

The next night, we had dinner plans with Sam's parents, and while we were still at their house, before we left for the restaurant, we told them our big news. Instantly, his mother squealed with delight and asked to see the engagement ring. We had just decided to get engaged the night before in quite an unorthodox manner and forgot about an engagement ring. We didn't have any money to spend on one—I was in graduate school full time and Sam had just started working a few months back. His mother would not hear of this and insisted that I have a ring. She had just the thing for me. She ran upstairs and left us in the kitchen, staring at ourselves, wondering what she was up to.

A few minutes later, with an excited look on her face, she returned to the kitchen from her bedroom. She had two velvet ring boxes in her hands, and she presented them to me. She told me that one ring belonged to Sam's great aunt and the other belonged to her mother. They were both beautiful diamond and platinum rings and I could have whichever one I wanted as my engagement ring.

Let me tell you, they were both gorgeous!

After looking at them both, I chose Sam's maternal grand-mother's platinum, art deco ring from 1922. It was a round, very sparkly diamond in a low, square setting with tiny diamonds all around the perimeter. Inside it was inscribed with his maternal grandparents' names and their engagement date. And it fit me perfectly! I think we all thought it was a sign that this was meant to be. *Bashert.* She handed Sam the ring and made him kneel in front of me, as I sat at her kitchen table, to formally propose to me in front of them, and that is exactly what he awkwardly did. Sam did not like expressing his emotions like that with an audience, and we had a rapt audience for this. His mother and father were extremely excited, and so were we.

Over the next few days, we had a great time making trips to see family and friends in the area to share our news. Everyone was so excited and all our friends, who had us in their wedding parties, agreed to be in ours and plans were underway and quickly took on a life of their own, especially once my mother got involved.

Sam's parents insisted on throwing us an engagement party in November 1994 at The Milleridge Inn; it was like a miniature wedding with fancy invitations, seating arrangements, formal meal service and a big, fancy cake. I bought a beautiful cobalt blue dress that I felt like a million bucks in, and with all our family and friends around, we celebrated our engagement and were showered with gifts. I was so entranced by all the excitement and everyone's outpouring love and affection. All I heard from my family was how wonderful Sam was, how handsome and kind. Everyone I spoke to reconfirmed for me that we were a perfect match and they loved us together, so all my doubts, held in the dark recesses of my heart, were hidden away deeply in places I couldn't find. I only felt happy, hopeful, and in love.

As soon as my mother got involved, as predicted, wedding plans took on a life of their own. Her own wedding to my stepfather was only two years prior and they still had all their contacts for the catering hall, the florist and invitation printer. We went along with it and booked the same catering hall, that had just refurbished one of their rooms to resemble an indoor garden with three completely glass walls, for August 13, 1995. We used my mother's photographer and videographer, and really, very quickly all the plans were set, and we all rode a wave of matrimonial excitement. Everyone was so excited, including my mother, and this marked one of the longest periods of happiness in my mother's life. For the whole year of wedding planning, there was hardly a dark moment or even a shadow of one. She was Snow White all the time and I loved it. I tried not to think about Cruella De Vil's eventual reappearance.

I had a clear idea of the kind of dress I wanted and found it in a bridal magazine. Believe it or not, a bridal shop in the next county carried that exact dress. My mother, mother-in-law-to-be, and I went there for me to try it on and make sure that it was the one that I wanted. I loved that these two women, who I adored, were shopping with me for this magical moment. I put on the dress I had my eye on. It was huge and had to be clipped here and there to get it to fit well enough for me to walk around in it. It was a full skirt consisting of many layers of pure white organza, a fitted bodice with a sweetheart neckline made exclusively of delicate, floral lace with little cap sleeves of the same lace and delicate cascades of white silk flowers over the shoulders. I loved it. It was the dress. The very first one. Just to appease my mother, I tried on a bunch of other forgettable dresses and before lunch, we all knew we had found THE dress.

CHAPTER 23
FINDING MYSELF IN
MY CLASSROOM

"In learning you will teach, and in teaching you will learn."

—Phil Collins

I started student teaching high school English in September 1994, and it didn't take me long to gain the confidence I needed to realize that I loved this job. I was teaching five sections of eleventh-grade English alongside a veteran teacher whom I quickly grew to greatly respect. She taught me how to trust myself as an educator and how to put into practice my great instincts as well as what I leaned from graduate school.

Before I knew it, I was running the show each class and loving every single second of it. After the high school portion of the internship, I had to have a middle school (junior high school) experience to satisfy the requirements of my certification. For this portion of my internship, my cooperating teacher was my former seventh grade English teacher who was a very scary and intimidating dean when I was in junior high school. But when I met him now, he was just Joe. We chatted before school started my first day and he told me that he was going to sit in the back of the room, and it was all up to me from now on. I panicked momentarily but soon realized that I had this. I was totally able to do this – I taught three sections of seventh-grade English and two sections of eighth-grade English classes.

It was great. I was prepared, knew exactly what to do, or at least how to find out what I should do, and from early November until mid-December I was one hundred percent their teacher. Joe stayed in the back of the room with coffee and the New York Times, as he promised, and stayed invisible. Even when I had a difficult eighth-grade class, handling it was up to me. Despite the fact that it was a big challenge for me, I found that authoritative voice I needed to turn their behavior around. I did it, and those kids learned despite themselves. It was great.

Before the end of my time there, Joe told me that he was leaving for most of the spring term on a medical leave of absence and he wanted me to take over for him since I was clearly good at this and knew the classes already. There wasn't much of an interview process at all. The school sort of rubber-stamped the whole thing, and in January, after holiday break, I was the only teacher in the room. I loved it!

I took my last certification exam in January, and by February 1995, I was provisionally certified to teach secondary English classes. I had the leave replacement job for the spring semester of 1995, and during that time I interviewed for a job teaching seventh-grade English at another district about fifteen miles away, a position for which the principal at the high school recommended me.

In one year, I had gone from being a directionless, unemployed twenty-five-year-old to a twenty-six-year-old, New York State provisionally certified secondary English teacher with a leave replacement job that would last almost six months.

In July, I was hired to write the curriculum and teach a new seventh-grade English course starting in September in that district fifteen miles east. I was so excited. My life was finally coming together. I felt wonderful, and my cup was overflowing with joy and hope.

CHAPTER 24
DOUBTS AND SILENCE

"Lying is done with words, and also with silence."

—Adrienne Rich,
<u>Women and Honor: Some Notes on Lying</u>

I f Sam and I had any doubts about getting married, we
didn't talk about them with each other before our wedding. Sam and I talked regularly about our lives, or at
least I talked a lot and he agreed with me. These one-sided
conversations, that I didn't realize were one-sided until much
later, confirmed for me that we were on the same page with
virtually every major life decision I could think to bring up.
Of course, I was agreeing with myself since I was the only
one talking.

I was seeing a therapist on my own at this point, to help
me ensure that I was moving my life in the right direction. I
had spent so many years unsure of who I was or where I fit in,
therapy helped reassure me that I was in a healthy space and,
if I wasn't, it helped guide me back to a better path.

Despite the fact that I was the happiest I had ever been in an exterior sense—we had our own place, I had a career I loved, I loved my fiancé, and we seemingly got along with both sides of my family and Sam's—I wanted to make sure I was moving in the right direction.

I knew secretly that something was not right. It was gnawing at me but always stayed out of my line of sight.

The therapist was concerned about my future marriage's success because of our lack of emotional (and physical) intimacy and was curious about why Sam wasn't attending therapy sessions with me. He had some valid points, but I didn't want to hear them. He told me, against all therapeutic guidelines, to pack up, move out, call off the engagement, and move back in with my parents.

I refused to hear him. I had a home of my own for the first time and didn't want to move backward. I couldn't give that up.

I knew that we still had trouble maintaining a close, intimate communication, but I kept thinking we loved each other enough to figure it out together; we would learn this part of our relationship in tandem. For the first time in my life, I felt secure enough in a relationship to not be looking over my shoulder at other prospects. All we needed was love and time, I told myself. And we had both of those in abundance.

I remember feeling very comfortable with Sam in our home, just doing whatever we were each separately doing. One night, I was engaged in some art project in the living room and he was reading in the dining room, and out of nowhere Sam said, "I love that being with you feels the same as it feels to be alone." At the time, I took it as a compliment and a testament to how comfortable he felt with me that all self-consciousness or awkwardness was gone, and he felt one hundred percent comfortable being himself. This may have been exactly what he meant, but years later I began to wonder if what he really meant was that I mattered so little to him that he hardly noticed me and therefore I didn't cramp his style. I guess I will never know.

In hindsight, a little later, I felt that I did not matter to him at all. I was there just like a piece of furniture that was there for his convenience. He certainly didn't pay attention to any of my needs and even when we did talk, when I got up the courage to talk about sensitive, deep things that were important to me and the health of our relationship and future marriage, I was placated and dismissed. Or he'd promise to be on the same page, but then go back to his old ways soon enough. Nothing changed. I would get frustrated and then life would distract me and time marched on.

I had flirtations with a new friend of one of his old friends. This guy was a social studies teacher and very interested in civil war reenactments and it was obvious that he liked me. He flirted. I tried not to flirt because I was engaged, but it was so tempting to flirt with him and, in my mind, I imagined having wild sex with him in our bed. He was a dark, handsome man with a quick intelligent wit, and he could not for the life of him figure out why I was with Sam and why I wasn't demanding to have my needs met. Deep inside I truly wondered the same things, but my blinding fear held me back. Deep, all encompassing fear. I had my own home. I was engaged to a man my family liked. I loved his family. We shared a fabulous group of friends whom we socialized with all the time. I worked very hard to convince myself that sexual chemistry, mutual affection and kindness could be learned. But that is absurd. Those things are either there as essential parts of people in a relationship or they are not.

August 12ᵗʰ, 1995, the day before my wedding, after I got my special bridal mani-pedi and facial, I traipsed all over Long Island looking for a pair of black flat shoes or dressy black slippers for my mother to wear with her mother-of-the-bride gown the next day because she broke her right pinky toe - again. The toe was about five times its normal size, and she couldn't wear a shoe. She was making a huge deal over this—after all, she was walking down the aisle with my father to give me away, so people would see her, and she needed decent shoes to wear.

Even my wedding day eve was all about my mother. Part of me wonders if she didn't subconsciously break her toe on purpose to ensure that more attention was paid to her and she wouldn't be sidelined. Afterall, my wedding day was about me and not her. She had done things like this before when her husband had a social engagement that he was excited about but held no interest to her, she coincidentally had broken the same toe.

Using her credit card, I bought every single potential option in a size ten that I could find. Without any hyperbole, I brought her at least fifteen shoe boxes of options by the time the stores closed. Something would work, but by this time I was exhausted and no longer cared what shoe she wore or didn't wear to my wedding.

Geena, my hairstylist and make-up artist, came to my mother's house, where I had slept the night before, on the morning of my wedding to help me get ready. I planned to get dressed in my gown at the Huntington Townhouse before we were to meet the photographer for pre-wedding pictures. When it was time for my mother, stepfather and me to leave my mother's house, my mother was not ready. She had taken pain pills for her *horrible* broken toe—over-medicated with her friend Vicodin—and was moving slowly and running late. (She's the only one who would medicate a broken pinky toe with Vicodin.) I was furious with her. I did not want to be late for my own wedding because of my mother, so Geena drove me. We bundled my dress, shoes, and all my stuff into her Jeep and drove off. I arrived barely in time to get dressed in the bridal suite before the whirlwind of the day took over: pictures, guests arriving, ceremony, video, more pictures during the cocktail hour we didn't get to go to, and the rest of the reception. It was great!

I had an assistant for the day who kept asking me what she could get for me. She kept asking me if I wanted drinks, but since I usually get overheated from alcohol, I asked for a chocolate milkshake. Having as assistant like that was great. I want one every day. And milkshakes, too.

Sam and I made our rounds to all the tables, mingling with our guests and dancing. It was overwhelming. My stepsister, Beth, noticed that I was getting a little swoony and sat me down. She made me take a long drink of water, breathe and take a minute to be quiet. Then she whispered into my ear, "Take a look around you. This whole room is filled with people who love you and came here to enjoy the day with you. They are all here for you." This was exactly what I needed at exactly the moment I needed it. She helped me get back in the present moment, and I was able to enjoy the rest of the party in a much more calm, peaceful way. Because of how much I appreciate what Beth had done for me, I make it a point to do that exact thing for every bride at every wedding I attend. I think it makes all the difference and brings a bride back into that moment of her life and probably helps her remember the day after it's over.

The wedding was great, but it was not perfect; nothing is. During the hora, the quintessentially traditional Jewish circle dance (like a polka), my cousins and our friends lifted Sam and I on chairs in the center of the concentrically spinning and dancing circles, as custom dictated, and for some reason my cousin, Drew, lifted my chair too high, thrusting my head into the crystal chandelier, and then dropped the front left side of my chair, plummeting me into the crowd and onto the floor. I was shocked but unhurt.

Later, I found out that the videographer got drunk and passed out on the men's room floor and didn't videotape any of the reception at all, which was the reason we hired him the first place. I wanted video record of my grandparents and their whole generation. Regardless, by the end of that day, we had gotten married and enjoyed the company of 177 of our closest friends, family members, and quite a few of our parents' guests whom we didn't know.

It had been an afternoon wedding, and it was over by six o'clock that evening. After the reception, many of us—mostly Sam, our friends and I—headed back to my mother's house to change. I thought Sam and I would go home at some point early in the night to spend the night in our home as husband and wife, but he didn't want the festivities to end since all our friends were still with us. We wound up at a Tex-Mex restaurant for a late supper. It was a fine way to spend time with friends, but I remember very specifically feeling disappointed that Sam would rather be with our friends until all hours than be alone with his new wife.

I sat there in a simple cotton, black floral dress that was so different than the white lace and organza wedding gown I had worn earlier, eating quesadillas and feeling letdown and sad inside. I kept my mouth shut and didn't tell him how I felt, always wanting to keep everything happy and light. Sam didn't know I was upset, and I suffered in silence and resentment.

This was wrong. I should have spoken up. My magical, romantic wedding night, that I had been idealizing and fantasizing about forever was being ruined by a mundane and trivial dinner. We had this gloriously fun and important day, dressed up, reciting vows in front of everyone we knew, and now we were eating tacos? It was absurd. I didn't say anything because I was chicken shit. Sam really wanted to go. All our friends were there, and I repressed my own feelings to avoid upsetting him, to avoid starting an argument and to avoid hurting our friends' feelings. And later that night back in our own bed in our own apartment for the first time as husband and wife we went directly to sleep after separately showering off the day. We did not consummate the marriage. He turned his back to me in bed and was asleep in two minutes.

I went to sleep fighting back tears.

Two weeks before our wedding, Sam and I bought a brand-new forest green Ford Explorer with a beige leather interior (it was gorgeous), and the Tuesday morning after our wedding we packed it up and drove north to Canada for our honeymoon. We decided on Canada because August is hot and since I don't fare well in the heat and I wanted to feel cool and sexy on my honeymoon, we went north instead of south. The average temperature, so we thought, was going to be around seventy degrees Fahrenheit during the day, and we packed accordingly. Unfortunately, the week we were in Quebec, they were having a heat wave and temperatures were in the 90s every day. We had to go shopping for summer clothes since next to nothing we brought was wearable. Luckily, Montreal has one of the greatest multi-floor shopping malls I had ever seen. Plenty to choose from, and we browsed and shopped and found everything we needed in one place.

Sam and I had never traveled by ourselves before, and it didn't dawn on me that we should talk beforehand about our expectations for this honeymoon trip, just like we should have talked about our wedding night in advance. I just took for granted that we both wanted the typical honeymoon—some sightseeing, some activity outside the room, but that we would take full advantage of our honeymoon suite in the Ritz-Carlton, with baths for two, room service, and the big, comfy king-sized bed. Turns out, we didn't want the same thing at all. Sam wasn't interested in any of the in-room activities since we could do them all at home even though we never did. Instead, he insisted that we get up at seven o'clock in the morning every day, eat a quick breakfast, and go out sightseeing from 8:30 a.m. until after midnight every night. He wanted to do everything.

Granted, we did see some very interesting and historical things, we learned a great deal about Montreal and Quebec City, but by the fourth day of the seven-day trip, I had blisters all over my feet from my new Birkenstock sandals, I was sweaty and exhausted, and we were married for almost a week and still hadn't consummated our marriage. I was done. I was limping down the busy street in the middle of the city right behind him when I stopped walking and sat down on the curb right where I was and burst into tears. I refused to take one more step unless it was to go back to our hotel. I was inconsolably crying. Sam's expression was one of disgust, and he looked at me like I just shot his dog. I told him that I was going back to the hotel and he could either join me or go ahead alone. It seemed that he could not understand why I was upset, or he refused to care.

Now, every woman knows that giving a man the choice to follow you is meant to tell the man that he has no choice— he *has to* follow you. But Sam did not know this fact about women, and he let his new wife limp back to their honeymoon suite alone while he set off in the opposite direction to do whatever. Later, back at the hotel alone in the honeymoon suite, as I slipped myself into a solitary bubble bath, I had my first thoughts of annulment.

He arrived back at our hotel several hours later, after I had already ordered room service and had my second and third thoughts about annulment. It's not like we had even consummated the marriage yet. We could have just ended it then. "Oops. Sorry. Our bad." Funny, not funny.

We didn't get an annulment. In fact, I never mentioned it to him at all.

When Sam returned to our hotel room without an apology or explanation, I was angry. He dealt with my anger by freezing me out and giving me the silent treatment. This was going to set the tone for the rest of our marriage. He hurt my feelings by making me feel invisible and forgotten, and instead of apologizing to me, he froze me out as he was angry at me for having been hurt. He couldn't dream that he had done anything wrong, so if I was accusing him of something and was angry, it had to be my fault. My feelings were hurt, and yet I was continually forced to be the bigger person and force my way through his silent treatment, push the transgression away and forgive him without his ever having to acknowledge that he hurt my feelings or ever apologize. Of course, I say force, but I did this willingly because this felt normal to me, as this was the blueprint for my relationship with my mother. Only this time, I got to have this dysfunction, my own home, a second family, and a group of friends I loved.

Marriage is compromise and trade-offs. I think I felt that I was making mine.

Over the next three years, we continued to work hard at our jobs. Sam got promoted twice, and his salary increased along with his job responsibilities and hours. I continued to love teaching, won the Best First Year Middle School Teacher Award in 1996 and felt confident in my new career. I still was unsure if I'd last more than ten years as a teacher, since my track record for staying interested in jobs was abysmal. Only time would tell. We moved from our one-bedroom apartment to a two-bedroom townhouse closer to my school and, since Sam was working a long-term job for his company at Brookhaven National Lab, it was closer to his job as well. From the outside, our lives looked perfect. From the inside, nothing had changed.

CHAPTER 25
LIFELONG FRIENDS

"A true friend is someone who thinks that you are a good egg even though he knows that you are slightly cracked."

—Bernard Meltzer

Time flies relentlessly. Days seem to take on a rhythm of their own and life beats on, but before you know it, months and years have gone by. As I was completing my first year of teaching, I reached another milestone—my ten-year high school reunion. I had lost touch with most of my high school friends. Melanie and I had stopped talking years earlier for some unknown reason, and everyone else scattered to the four winds, so I was looking forward to seeing who showed up and hear about the lives my classmates made for themselves. It seemed weird to me that even after ten years people gravitated to the same cliques from high school. This does make sense though because we all just wanted to catch up with our friends. The big surprise for me, as Sam and I walked into the Smithtown Sheraton hotel, was the smiling faces who were happy to see me. There were so many people with whom we sat and spent the evening catching up and rekindling friendships and even starting some new ones.

The ten-year reunion was responsible for bringing me some very valuable friendships that have stood the test of time. Sure, we knew each other in high school, but we weren't close then. Now, as adults, we are in more regular contact and see each other several times a year as we take turns hosting parties. Facebook has been instrumental in fostering continued communication and kept us in each other's lives more than would have been possible without it. Sharon and her husband, Sebastian, have parties at least twice a year, invite everyone, and are the most gracious hosts. Rose was in my primary friend group in high school with Melanie, and about a year into my new career as a painter, she bought my gigantic butterfly painting. She is a Jane of all trades and can do anything she attempts. Rose has remade her life at least twice and has more energy than five women.

Gloria and I weren't really friends in high school for some reason but had a lot of friends in common. We had a lot to talk about at the reunion, and over time at the various parties, we have become very close. Of all the ladies from this era of my life, she is the one with whom I am the closest. Gloria is independent and strong, she's fierce and funny, and in the middle of getting a divorce, selling a house and buying another, she discovered that she has a knack for stand-up comedy. We all go through rivers of shit at times, but Gloria can take any situation, and, in the retelling, make it hysterical. Over the past couple of years, she has taken it to the stage at comedy clubs in the area. I applaud her and am in awe. When Michael and I were about to get married in 2017, she orchestrated an almost surprise wedding shower for me with all our local high school girlfriends. I was speechless.

It was so touching that they would all get together for me to help me celebrate this milestone event in my life.

The qualities I love the most about them are their resilience in remaking their lives when life is all lemons, thrown off-course by unforeseen setbacks and, of course, their openhearted generosity. When Gloria bought her own house, I gave her a painting of mine that she has loved since she saw it in my studio the year before. It was the perfect complement to her new living room furniture in her own new home. Last year, when I needed to drive my daughter, Simone, back to college in Massachusetts and Michael couldn't get out of work, Gloria was the first companion I thought of to take on this journey. She's so much fun to be around and I knew that driving with her, I'd never fall asleep at the wheel. Plus, Simone loves her and the three of us had a blast on our mid-winter road trip.

CHAPTER 26
MOMMYHOOD —
ETHAN ARRIVES

"Birth is not only about making babies. Birth is about making mothers — strong, competent, capable mothers who trust themselves and know their inner strength."

—Barbara Katz Rothman

S am and I both very much wanted children and it was one the things we could solidly agree on. I wanted to be a mommy more than anything in the world and it was the one goal I had had for my life since I, myself, was a young child playing with my baby dolls. In the spring of 1997, we agreed it was time to start trying to conceive. I wanted to become pregnant so badly. I did my best to reduce my stress and eat more healthily. I obviously stopped drinking alcohol entirely, avoided soft cheeses that could have the listeria bacteria, and sushi, as well. I got plenty of sleep and focused on making my womb a hospitable environment for a growing fetus. Luckily, we were young and fertile, and we got pregnant the second month we tried. We, and both our families, were so very excited.

Two months before I turned twenty-nine, in March 1998, our son, Ethan, was born. We named him after Sam's grandfather, Emanuel. My pregnancy went well, and I loved every second of it. I felt like an Amazon queen creating life. I remember very clearly imagining that at any specific moment I was creating neurons or a pancreas. Pregnancy is amazing. Ethan was supposed to be about nine pounds at thirty-six weeks and was very breech. His head was under my left rib cage, his butt in my pelvis, and his feet up near the right ribs. My obstetrician tried to turn him by performing an external cephalic version, or ECV, but Ethan was comfy and refused to turn; we scheduled a C-section delivery for the thirty-seventh week, and I got to pick the date. My choices were March 17th or 19th. I decided the holiday was better—this way, every year there would be a parade, and when he was old enough, his friends would celebrate with him and buy him green beer. (Twenty-one years later, on his birthday, Ethan's college girlfriend, Annie, would do just this and text me the picture commemorating the celebratory green beer that I had predicted even before his birth.)

The night before my planned Cesarean section delivery, I sat alone in my darkened dining room and I wrote in my journal.

Here I am on the eve of my son's birth mentally preparing for our big day. I am filled with awe, anxiety, a bit of trepidation and excitement. It will be a day I remember for the rest of my life, and one that Sam and I will recount to our son many times as he asks about the day of his birth. I feel him restlessly moving around within my womb as he has for so many nights before, and I realize that he has no idea what an adventure he embarks on tomorrow morning. The trauma of a regular birth will be avoided, so he will come into this world peace-fully and quietly.

All of our family will be there to greet him hours, or minutes if they can help it, after this birth to welcome him into the world and their lives and hearts. Everyone called today to tell us we are all in their thoughts and prayers and to offer emotional support.

Sam and I made a quiet dinner and watched the TV film version of Moby Dick with Patrick Stewart as Ahab, and then Ally McBeal which I taped earlier in the evening.

The next time I write, my son will be born, and I will officially be a mommy.

Ethan's birth was delayed several hours because the full moon the night before caused dozens of women to give birth in the rooms and even the hallways at the hospital. This was a nurse's explanation. A desperate woman said her baby was crowning in the waiting room. This made the morning hellish for the nursing staff and, somehow, between the operating room remaining empty for hours and the dozens of people in attendance during my Cesarean section all talking about their St. Patrick's Day drinking plans, I wound up with a nasty infection in my incision. I remember, I was strapped down on the operating table, arms tied to supports out to my sides hooked up to IVs and monitors, literally being cut open to birth my son – quite probably the single most profound moment of my life at that point – and I remember thinking to myself, *how dare these strangers hang out discussing their drinking plans for St. Patrick's day while I am having this life changing moment!* I didn't know that I had the right to kick them out if I wanted to so I said nothing and did my best to ignore them. Truthfully, once Ethan was born and I heard him cry, everything else melted away anyway.

By day two in the hospital, I noticed my incision was oozing a clear, reddish fluid. As it turns out, I had an infection in my incision and all the staples had to be removed and the wound debrided, removing the necrotic tissue from all the raw surfaces. It was excruciating, even with Vicodin and because of this we stayed at the hospital a full week. Our extra hospital time was because of my complications, and because I was breastfeeding Ethan, he stayed with me. I required massive antibiotics to eradicate the infection and wound care for my gaping incision.

The next several months were a blur of sleepless nights, breastfeeding around the clock and getting used to the demands of a newborn. My incision took a full six months of healing incrementally from the inside out. It was a disgusting and horribly painful process and required twice-a-day nursing care for months to ensure that it healed properly.

Despite this, I was in love with my son and with being his mommy! We slept next to each other every day, did baby yoga and baby massages. We played, and I reveled in mommyhood.

I took the rest of the school year off from work, from March to June, and then had the summer to stay home with him. I wouldn't have to go back to work until Ethan was almost six months old. Everything was fun with him even when I was exhausted. We took mommy-and-me classes at the local library and made new friends, we went to parks, and visited friends and family. Luckily, our group of close friends was also having babies at the same time, so there was always something to do and someone to play with.

In May, I was so engrossed in being a mommy that I completely forgot that my thirtieth birthday was coming. Sam did not, and he planned for weeks to throw me a surprise party. Our next-door neighbor was away, and we were cat-sitting for her, so Sam used her apartment to store all the party supplies and food. While Ethan and I were taking our late-morning nap, he silently set up the whole downstairs of our townhouse for the party. By the time Ethan and I woke up, everything was set. When I came downstairs, our apartment was filled with people all shouting "Surprise!" It was a lovely party and a great day. I loved that Sam went to all that trouble to celebrate my thirtieth birthday. I was utterly shocked that he had planned and secretly executed the entire party without my even suspecting any of it.

That summer, I took the last class of my master's degree at CW Post, graduating summa cum laude with my dual master's in secondary English education and curriculum and development. (Take that, skeptical chairperson!) Sam, baby Ethan in a stroller, and I unsuccessfully tromped across campus in the rain, looking for the small departmental graduation ceremony and eventually gave up. I had certain physical limitations still because my incision still hadn't healed completely, and I tired easily. I made my apologies via a phone call the following Monday, and the school sent me my diploma in the mail. When it arrived, my first name was spelled wrong—MARCIA—so it had to be sent back. This same mistake happened again until they finally got it right. So, it's like I have three suspiciously similar master's degrees from CW Post.

Initially, Sam and I were great parents together. We wordlessly divided up parenting tasks, and Ethan blossomed into a toddler with loving parents catering to his every need and doing everything in their power to stimulate his curiosity and learning. We established routines for every facet of his day, and even from newborn-hood, I was reading to him every night before bed. Books and reading together while snuggling in the glider rocker in the nursery became my favorite part of the day and Ethan's (I'd like to think).

By the time he was a year old, Ethan weighed thirty-six pounds, and carrying him around was a loving chore causing my first carpal tunnel symptoms that would worsen over the next twenty years. Ethan could say a few words, like mama and dada, make his desires known through gestures and sounds, his favorite dinner was my homemade chicken *francese*, and he loved *Clifford the Big Red Dog*, but he couldn't walk yet. It wouldn't be until after we had purchased our own single-family house in Kings Park, when he was just shy of fourteen months old, that Ethan would take his first steps. Once he did, he would scarcely sit still again.

Our family doted on Ethan. He was the first grandchild on all sides of the family and had three sets of grandparents to spoil him. He shared a love of model trains with Sam's dad, and the two of them would play with his train setup in their basement. Sam's mom painted Ethan an elaborate train table for his *Thomas the Tank* magnetic and wooden trains; it was gorgeous, and Ethan played with it for hours at a time. My mom adored Ethan and loved to do crafts with him, read stories, and go to the movies. She started her tradition of having a strip of pictures taken in a photo booth after the movie. She would continue this for many years, and I have taken it as my tradition as well, taking pictures strips in a photobooth whenever I have the opportunity. With my father, Ethan played catch and softball-light—after all, Ethan was a little boy. He was the first-born grandchild to all our parents and was therefore the object of much love and devotion.

Despite being great co-parents and loving our son more than either of us ever thought possible, Sam and I were still dealing with the same problems with our marriage that we had been for three years. Nothing had changed except that we now owned a home and had a son and were busier than ever. I loved being a mommy more than anything, and co-parenting with Sam in the early years was great. I loved my teaching job and all my students, but I felt, in all of that that I was losing me. I was Mommy.

I was Mrs. Goldstein at school. I was Sam's wife. But I was losing track of what made me Marci.

I talked to Sam about it and he said he understood what I was feeling and seemed compassionate. When I directed the conversations back to our ever-present, *hiding in the shadows* problems with emotional and physical intimacy, Sam got defensive. We fought. Eventually, Sam would tell me that he agreed with me and wanted the same exact things I wanted, and I bought it every time. I guess I wanted to believe that he did want what I wanted and that he did love me the way I needed to be loved. Each time, things would improve for a while and then revert back to the way they had always been. Sam admitted to me while we were in the process of getting our divorce years later, that each time he told me he understood and agreed with me was a lie. He lied to me every time because he didn't understand what I wanted at all, wasn't interested in figuring it out, and was tired of talking about it. He lied to shut me up. That hurt a great deal to say the least.

I had been married to a man who did not care about me and was uninterested in learning what I wanted or was feeling. (To use Brené Brown's metaphor, he was not a marble jar friend.)

So obviously, nothing ever changed. I wasn't happy. I mean, I loved our child, our house, and our lives, in general. I loved our combined families and our group of friends. I loved our son with every breath in my lungs. I was not very happy with my marriage. I had flashes of ideas of divorce, but there was too much to lose, too much connectedness and connection that I not only loved but also needed to hold. Marriage is compromise and trade-offs. I felt that I was making mine.

New Year's Eve 1999-2000 was approaching—the big millennium New Year's Eve—and we had offers of babysitting from all three sets of grandparents. I thought it would be fun to go out for a change, see our friends and enjoy a baby free night. Sam was adamant that he did not want to go out. He wanted to stay home with his wife and infant son, so we stayed home. I made a nice dinner, and we were going to watch the ball drop on television. While I was putting Ethan down for the night in his crib, Sam had been on the phone with his friend Tom, who was having a party and called to wish us a happy new year.

Sam panicked and suddenly freaked out about his life and said to me that he was sorry he said we should stay home. He wanted to go to Tom's party. He regretted his previous decision—in fact, he said that he regretted getting married and having a child because now, not only didn't he recognize his life, but he was also missing out on partying with his friends.

I was stunned. Without waiting for me to respond, he said he was going to Tom's party without me. He defrosted food I cooked from our freezer to bring with him. I stood in the kitchen, silently watching him.

"Are you going to stop me?" he asked me.

"No," I said. "If you don't want to stay, then go. I want you to want to be here with us."

He didn't say anything in return. He shrugged, put on his coat and left. I cried for a while, but then my son woke up and wanted a bottle. After feeding him and changing his diaper, I went to sleep. I slept through the ball dropping. I slept through Sam's call after midnight as everyone around him was kissing and he stood there alone like a fool. I didn't hear him come in sometime in the middle of the night. I didn't feel him slip into bed beside me.

The next day, when he woke up around noon, I had already been up with the baby for hours. He came downstairs and could tell I was angry. He tried to get me to feel sorry for him because he'd had a bad time at the party. He said he felt like an awkward third wheel all night and had no one to kiss at midnight. But going was his choice. He could have stayed with his wife and son. Instead of being sorry for going or even just telling me he was sorry or wrong, Sam spent the rest of the day giving me the silent treatment for my feelings being hurt. He was unable to take responsibility for his own actions and feelings, but he could be angry at me for being hurt by him. This was a pattern with which I was intimately familiar. Sam and my mom had a lot in common.

I kept repeating to myself "marriage is about compromise," over and over and over, but I also heard my mother's voice in my head saying, "We teach people how to treat us through what we accept." I heard her and didn't hear her. I certainly didn't absorb this information until many years later.

It was ironic to be told to set boundaries and limits on behavior and how I expected to be treated by the woman who taught me to accept less than I deserve and to expect to be treated badly. Because of this, I really didn't hear what she was saying, despite it being one hundred percent true.

By April 2000, I felt it was time to give Ethan a sibling. I was an only child biologically, and I wanted Ethan to not have to grow up alone. Sam wanted another child, too, but this time it seemed to me that he had to force himself to engage in activities with me to make that happen. I don't know what was going on in his head. Since he would never open up to me about it and it was an impossible subject to broach, what I told myself was that he was not attracted to me.

I had internalized his rejection of my femininity and sexuality as my own fault. I wasn't pretty enough. I hadn't lost enough of the baby weight from my first pregnancy, despite dieting and exercising. He was grossed out by my ugly abdominal scar from Ethan's birth. I wasn't enough of what he wanted. I took my hurt feelings and anger at him and turned in inward onto myself. This was psychologically a very unhealthy thing to do and would take me a very long time to undo.

Luckily, our mutual desire to have another baby motivated us and by the second month of trying, I was pregnant again. I was relieved and surprised how easy it was to conceive again. After a long time on birth control pills in my twenties, I was thrilled.

In order to share the news with Sam, I made a home-made greeting card, with Ethan's help, that said, "Dad, guess what!" on the outside, and inside it said, "I'm going to be a big brother." I thought that was a cute way to tell Sam. In the morning, Ethan woke Sam and gave him the card. Sam, and everyone else, too, was surprised and overjoyed. Another baby to bring our family another heart to love. I was ecstatic to be pregnant again and overjoyed that this would get me out of a family camping trip we had planned with Sam's friends. I hate camping and was going along with it just to be a good sport. Now, I didn't have to.

My pregnancy was going perfectly, and my baby was growing well. At my four-month sonogram, the sonogram tech told me that my baby was a girl. I was thrilled! I so very badly wanted a girl. Of course, either sex would have been fine, but I really wanted a daughter. On my way home, I stopped at Baby's R Us and allowed myself to buy one pink, girly thing for my daughter. According to my grandmother's and my great-grandmother's old-country, superstitious folklore, expectant mothers were not supposed to buy new things for their baby before the baby is born. It supposedly was bad luck. When Ethan was born, although we bought everything before he was born, my mother insisted we leave all his stuff at her house until after he was born. For good luck. But this time, I needed to buy something pink.

What I bought was one crib-sized, fleece blanket. It had a white background with pastel hearts in pink, lilac, yellow, and light blue. It was adorable, soft and decidedly feminine. This blanket would come to be known as my daughter's beloved Blankie and not only would be her everything companion for many years but also would accompany her to college. She sleeps with it every single night. I love that.

That winter was a snowy one, and I left for work earlier than Sam did at this point. He stayed home in the morning to get Ethan to day care, so he slept in. In the mornings, after it snowed, I had to shovel the snow to get out of the house and to my car, cleaning that off, too, despite being very pregnant. Sam refused to wake up any earlier to help me. There was a blizzard one day on a weekend and we needed milk and supplies for Ethan, but Sam refused to go to the store because he was watching a football game. I think he knew I'd go if he refused, so I went. I had to shovel my way out to the car and drive in a blizzard with a huge, eight-months-pregnant belly. He didn't give a shit. I guess he knew I was competent and stubborn and wouldn't not provide for my son. I got to prove that I am a reliable mother, maybe martyring myself in the process, and he proved he was a selfish asshole. But, again, I didn't call him on his behavior at the time.

I sublimated my feelings and said nothing. I taught him to treat me like crap and take me for granted.

Still I stayed and let him treat me like an afterthought, never acknowledging when he hurt my feelings or failed to apologize for anything he did. I had gotten used to being ignored. It's awful and painful, but it felt familiar to me and I knew how to deal with it. I hunkered down and devoted myself to what was important to me: my son, my new baby on the way, and my career. A lot of time passed like this. I was making my compromises. I was protecting what was important—home, belonging, children, love—and ignoring that ever-present hole in my heart.

The months before my daughter's birth were not calm and peaceful for our extended family. Sam's mother was diagnosed with hepatitis, had a yellow skin tone, and was quarantined in her own house for more than a month, maybe two. My own mother, who had Crohn's disease, had an emergency abscess and required an intestinal resection surgery to remove several feet of her intestines. She was terrified that she was going to die and never see her granddaughter born. My mother's surgery went well, as we predicted, but while she was recovering at home, her husband, my stepfather, had a heart attack and needed a triple-bypass operation. Things were falling apart.

I remember waddling around the hospital with a huge belly (Ethan was in day care), trying to hold up my mother as she hobbled around, hunched over, talking to nurses and doctors to ensure her husband had the best care possible. My mother was usually good in a medical crisis, but this was just too much for her, and she was a total mess. His bypass surgery went perfectly, and after a time he was released to go home. Because they were both recovering and could not take care of themselves, they had daily in-home nursing care. The combination of pain, confinement, and anxiety threw my mother's fragile disposition over the deep end; she became depressed and refused to see anyone.

I tried to talk to her. She dismissed me. She rarely got dressed, rarely left her bed. We tried an intervention, and she stormed off, slamming doors and ignoring us. I wrote her a long letter expressing love and concern over her depression, her worsening psychological state, and what I noticed was an increased dependence on opioids and other medications. She ignored all of it, refusing to listen or acknowledge what was happening. I was powerless to do anything about it, and I had my own responsibilities to take care of as well as my own maternal health, a toddler son, and a full-time job.

CHAPTER 27
MOMMYHOOD — SIMONE'S FIRST APPEARANCE

"In giving birth to our babies, we may find that we give birth to new possibilities within ourselves."

—Myla and Jon Kabat-Zinn

M y daughter, Simone, was born on March 12, 2001. Her delivery was also a Cesarean section, but this time the hospital was calm, and her delivery went without a hitch. The doctor was even able to remove some of the internal and external scar tissue from the previous delivery, which I was very happy about because I had a nasty scar and bulge from my C-section from Ethan's birth. It would look so much smoother and more attractive after it healed. In attendance at the hospital was everyone in our immediate family circle except my mother and stepfather. Sam's mother and father were at our house, hanging out with Ethan, since my mother-in-law had recovered from her bout with hepatitis. Ethan seemed excited about the arrival of his new baby sister, although I am not really sure he understood what was going on at the tender age of three.

We were all overjoyed with Simone's arrival, and I felt that our family was complete. I had a handsome boy and an adorable baby girl. One for each hand. Luckily, I decided that I didn't want any more children, because I was advised by my doctor, immediately after the delivery, that there was a great deal of scar tissue on my uterus from the previous delivery with Ethan, and that my uterine wall could not handle another pregnancy. If fact, had I not opted for the early planned Cesarean section and had a contraction, even one contraction, my uterus would likely have ruptured, possibly causing mine and Simone's deaths. That's some scary shit! The doctor said my uterus was stretched so thin that it appeared translucent, like a window, and he was able to see my baby still inside.

Beth's best friend, Jana, was in medical school doing her ob-gyn rotation at the same hospital where I delivered my baby. Jana asked me if I would mind if she scrubbed into my surgery. I was overjoyed to have someone I knew well and loved in there with me, besides Sam. Jana held me while the nurse gave me my spinal injection, and during my actual Cesarean, she assisted my obstetrician. We joked for years that she had her hand in my uterus and saw parts of me that I had never seen.

As an only child until I was seventeen, I had always wanted at least three children, but when I was talking care of Ethan while pregnant, I realized I had just two hands—one for each child. What would I do with a third? I joked that to have more would be inviting mutiny. Many people have large families and lots of children and it works out fabulously. For me, I knew that two was going to be enough.

The day after Simone's birth, as I cracked "what, were you born yesterday?" jokes, I wrote in my journal while she slept soundly on my lap.

Simone was born yesterday weighing 7lbs, 2oz and measuring 19 ½ inches long. She is pink and sweet with a full head of light brown/ dark blonde fuzzy hair that stands up in sweeps on her head. Her eyes are deep blue, she has dainty fingers and is the spitting image of me as a newborn. She is quiet and easy going with a sweet, high pitched cry. She is nursing well and makes the cutest gurgly, squeaky sounds. She is perfect and nothing but wonderful.

Ethan is quite interested in his baby sister and asks all about her. When she was crying while I was changing her diaper, Ethan tried to comfort her. He leaned close to her head and whispered, "It's ok, Simone. Ethan is here." I love being a mother and am so excited for the adventures I will share with my perfect children.

We brought Simone home from the hospital on Ethan's third birthday. He was wearing his Buzz Lightyear wings and green, plastic wrist cuffs and running through the house shouting, "Infinity and beyond!" As I carried Simone into the house, Ethan ran over to me and hugged my leg, exclaiming that his "baby sister is the best birthday present ever." A little later, I gave Ethan a small birthday gift from his baby sister. It was a Matchbox car Corvette. He was thrilled and innocently asked me how Simone knew he loved Matchbox cars.

Simone took to nursing easily, and since I had done it before with Ethan for eight months, I was more comfortable, which I am sure helped. Sam stayed home with us for two weeks, and since I delivered in March again, like last time, I planned to take the rest of the year off and go back to work in the fall. Meanwhile, we were all home for a bit.

Another adorable and memorable Ethan story happened during Simone's newborn period. Each time I changed her diaper, I was still swabbing her umbilicus with rubbing alcohol to keep it clean and help it dry and fall off. Ethan loved to help me change her and stood on the stool at the foot of her changing table, watching with rapt attention. His eyes fixated on her umbilicus. He thought it was her penis, but I didn't know this is what he thought. He pointed and asked me why it was dark blue and black, and I explained that it was drying out and would fall off soon. He freaked out and screamed, "I don't want her penis to fall off!" I had a hard time not laughing at this innocent mistake and confusion. I had explained through books for very young children that girls have vaginas and boys have penises, but without a frame of reference, he had no idea what we meant. Everything was quickly resolved, but I love this story, for his innocence and his sincerity.

Simone was two months old before she met my mother. This whole time, my mom and stepdad were still recuperating and were so depressed that they refused to let anyone into the house to see them. Only my Aunt Marie, my mother's best friend, was allowed to visit. One afternoon, while Aunt Marie was there, I came over with Simone all wrapped up in a red-and-pink striped onesie and a matching blanket. These women, who had loved me my whole life, finally got to meet my sweet, pink Simone. For both, it was love at first sight. I was hurt that my mother didn't want to see her only grand-daughter (or anyone else) and hadn't wanted to meet her until she was over two months old, but mom was depressed after the surgical and emotional hell they had been through since February. I had to let that go and just be there for her as best as I could with a newborn and a three-year-old to take care of and a husband who, by this point, was working very long hours in New Jersey and was often gone. Sam was working hard for his family.

Who could fault him for that?

Since Sam worked such long hours and needed his sleep and Simone was up many times a night to nurse, he moved downstairs to the den. For the first six months of her life, Sam slept apart from us on an aero bed. This put a huge physical distance between us, and the resulting further emotional disconnect was never fixed. Although we were great parents together and were living what looked like from the outside as a charmed life, I was deeply lonely and was starved for genuine love and affection. My children filled some of this void with their endless hugs, kisses, and cuddling. Only time would tell what would happen with our marriage. We were strangers, cohabitating and co-parenting together.

We were living inside a fragile house of cards.

I stayed home with both kids for that summer and applied for a leave of absence for a year to stay home longer. Sam and I felt that having me home for longer was important for their development. Plus, my father and Kay generously offered to give us some extra money each month to offset some of the loss of my salary, since they, too, believed it was important for me to stay home. When each child was born, they offered to hire a baby nurse to help me, but since I was exclusively nursing, there wasn't much a baby nurse could do. They now used that money to help us, which was a great idea. It was the best gift ever because it gave me more time at home with my babies and I was able to take a second whole year off, making my leave after Simone's birth two and half years. I loved being a stay-at-home mom and being fully present for my children, but it got lonely at times, as I felt starved for adult conversation and companionship.

My most serene memories that summer were the weekends at the lake house in Connecticut. Sitting lakeside in an Adirondack chair in the early morning before anyone else in the house was awake with my newborn baby at my breast is, to this day, my happy place. I got to do this with Ethan and Simone when they were infants, so I got to enjoy this many times, twice. The lake was quiet and still as the early-morning sun reflected off the water's smooth-as-glass surface. The birds were cooing, waking for the day and all the natural world was slowly coming to life. I would sit in the slightly recumbent position that an Adirondack chair permits, a sweater or blanket wrapped loosely around my shoulders as I cradled my baby in my arms. It's the most at peace with the world I have ever experienced. Quiet and transformative. When I try to meditate, it is these moments that I picture in my mind.

When Simone was about nine months old, she developed a high fever with no other symptoms, which lasted for days and days. I kept going back to the pediatrician for more tests to figure out the cause of the fever that would not abate even with regular doses of infant Tylenol. I was at the doctor's office so often, I suddenly found myself on first-name basis with the doctor and his fabulous staff. Repeated urinalysis tests came back positive for infection, and it was determined that she had a horrible UTI. After a full, strong course of antibiotics, Simone had to endure a string of tests to determine the cause of the UTI as per American Academy of Pediatrics guidelines. She had a congenitally malformed valve in her left ureter that didn't prevent the backflow of urine into the kidney. The fear was that with repeated UTIs, if she were to get them, the back-flowed urine could damage her kidney, hampering its development and causing larger, more serious issues down the road. I conducted my own research online and scared myself to death with all the complications that could arise if this were left untreated. Simone's pediatrician told me in very clear and forceful language that I was not allowed on WebMD ever again. He said that his treatment would prevent all that other stuff from happening and if he could choose a congenital defect for a baby, this one would be it because of how often they fix themselves.

Simone was put on a low-dose, prophylactic course of antibiotics for a solid year to prevent UTIs and to allow extra time for her body to potentially grow this missing valve. Studies showed that in cases like these, babies' bodies tended to fix themselves given enough time. It was like her body needed an extra several months to finish developing. It's the miracle of human biology. After the year, all the tests were repeated, and she had indeed grown the previously missing valve. Hooray!

Maybe human babies are born at forty weeks' gestation, so they fit through the birth canal, but often need longer than that to fully develop.

When Simone was eight months old, I started what would be one of our favorite annual traditions. Following a recipe that I found in *Parents' Magazine,* we made our first ever three-dimensional turkey cake. It is made with two nine-inch round cakes, lots of orange and brown frosting, candy corn, Vienna Finger cookies, sprinkles, and red fruit roll-ups. The first time we made it, Ethan was about three and a half and Simone young enough to cluelessly gnaw on a cookie in her highchair. We got to share this experience—this whole messy kitchen escapade—with my mother. The first time we followed the recipe exactly, and in each of the subsequent years, we altered it here and there to suit our own fancy, but they all do look very similar. In 2019, we marked the eighteenth consecutive Thanksgiving turkey cake. Each year, we bring the cake to the family gathering, and while other desserts are enjoyed as well, our turkey cakes are a hit.

During these brief years of being home full time with my babies, we filled our days with books, crafts, games, naps, playdates, picnics in the park playing on the swings, and visits with friends and family. We had a great time together just the three of us, dancing around the house while strains of Raffi and classic rock music filled the air. I loved being home with them, but after a while, I missed working.

When my kids were little, I used to imagine writing a book or a narrative of my day taking care of the millions of little tasks that encompasses the life of a stay-at-home mother with two small children. At that point in her children's lives, every mother is sort of an isolated little island. Until she reaches out to a friend to bridge the gap between the two isolated islands, she doesn't know that she is just like every other mother out there—overwhelmed, overtired, overburdened, and more importantly, I suppose, more overwhelmed with the love that she has for her children and the miracle of their existence.

We had Ethan in part-time preschool at Tutor Time. I became friendly with the staff, they knew I was a teacher, and I was offered a job teaching three-year-olds, since they were over their ratio with their three-year-olds and needed another teacher. I took it. The salary was small, but both of my kids got to go for free, and we were all in the same building.

Simone was born stubborn and sassy. She refused to speak more than two words for a long time: *Mama* and *No!* Ethan and I anticipated her every need and desire, so she had no need to talk. We made it very easy for her to get by on two words and a few ad-hoc sign-language moves I taught her to ask for milk, bed, and to get down from her highchair.

Eventually, Simone was speaking only four words for no other reason than her stubbornness. After the audiologist told me her hearing was fine, she suggested pre-school so Simone would be with people who didn't know her sign language and it would force her to learn to talk to make herself known. The timing was perfect. Putting Simone in the Tutor Time twaddler class worked like a charm, and within a few months she was speaking hundreds of words, and we haven't been able to shut her up since.

I had a class of six three-year-olds, which I liked for a few weeks. The school gave me a budget to order whatever I would need to set up a brand-new classroom, which in itself was new and fun. Circle time was so much fun, with songs to teach them colors, numbers, dates, holidays, and manners. I rubbed all their backs as they settled down for naps after lunch. We did arts and crafts every afternoon, played games, and learned songs. It was rewarding for me, but not as much as raising my own children and not as much as teaching middle school and high school kids. Teaching pre-school was a little too far out of my wheelhouse, plus I had a two-year-old and a five-year-old at home, and soon I burned out.

I wanted to go back to teaching older kids a year earlier than I planned, but my union wouldn't allow me to return to work a part-time position, and we had a scheduling nightmare. Ethan was going to start kindergarten in the fall, and our town had only a half-day kindergarten program at the time; he would be home by noon each day. I had to be home before then.

Part-time public high school teaching jobs are very hard to come by. There aren't many of them, and usually a thousand potential employees seek them out. Surprisingly, I found a part-time teaching job at another high school not far from home, and I joined their staff temporarily. This was a one-year position, and we all knew that. It was perfect for me; it would allow me to teach three classes in the morning and be done by 11 a.m. so I could get Ethan off the school bus at noon. Simone would stay in her class at Tutor Time and either I would get her before I met Ethan's bus, or we would both go to get her afterward. This was the best of both worlds. I got to go back to teaching, which I loved, got to earn a respectable salary again and got to be home a great deal with my adorable munchkins.

Balancing schoolwork—planning and grading—while being a mommy was a delicate juggling game but would be good practice for when I would go back full time the following year.

My classes were great, and it was so nice to talk with older teens about literature again. My transition into this new school environment was very smooth. The staff was welcoming as were my students. Everyone in this school, faculty and students, had a lot of school spirit and treated everything from football games to PTA fundraisers to holidays as celebrations. For almost the whole month of October the school was bustling with Halloween spirit – everything was decorated, and students excitedly compared costume ideas. The school was buzzing.

I've always loved Halloween. Ever since I was a kid, I've loved dressing up in costume and being silly. Every year when I was in elementary school, my mother made my costumes, mostly with random things cobbled together from around the house, some makeup, some minimal sewing. For the most part, I was doing the same with my kids. So, I got swept up in the Halloween spirit of this school and put together one of my most outrageous costumes ever. I was inspired to tell them that this Halloween I was going to convert my wedding gown into a costume, but I wouldn't tell them what it would be. On Halloween morning, I walked into school dressed as Glenda, Good Witch of the North (from *The Wizard of Oz*), having added sparkles to my old, white wedding gown, pairing it with a sparkly tiara and magic wand. As I walked in, I saw the principal of the school, a man I had only known a short time but who obviously had already sensed my quirkiness and bubbly enthusiasm, doubled over in laughter. He said to me, "Of course, you come in costume, Marci! You, of all people!"

I froze on the spot and looked around. In a split second I saw that none of the faculty members were in costume. All the kids were, but the adults were in regular clothing. I was crestfallen. Quickly, I learned that none of the faculty members at this school ever dressed up for Halloween, although they allowed and encouraged the students to do just that. Weird. After a lightning fast assessment, I realized I had no choice but to go inside to do my job. I really had no choice but to own it—leaving was not an option, as I did not have a change of clothes in my car.

I made best of it. I stood straight and tall and walked right over to the principal with a full smile on my face and said, "Of course I dressed up. It's the best day of the year!" Then I waltzed up the stairs to my classroom without looking back. I spent the entire day teaching in my revamped wedding gown and spontaneously singing songs from the *Wizard of Oz* as Glenda, Good Witch of the North. I welcomed the kids into my classroom with a dramatic flourish, and we all enjoyed the fun day.

This episode reminds me of the movie *Legally Blonde*. Reese Witherspoon's character, Elle Woods, was invited to a costume party by some of the Harvard Law School students with whom she wanted to become friends. She arrived at the party wearing a Playboy bunny costume before quickly realizing she was the only one in costume. They had played a trick on her, and it wasn't actually a costume party at all. But instead of turning on her high heels and running with her a little bunny cottontail bouncing in the wind, she went inside, faced the awkwardness head-on with self-deprecating jokes, and owned that she was the only one in costume. Turns out, she was the most beautiful, sexiest, outrageous girl at the party, and everybody wanted to be her or be with her.

I always want to be that woman—the one who fully embodied her life and was fully engaged in each experience.

Simone was having a little stint with night terrors, and for a few weeks that spring she regularly woke up in the middle of the night, screaming her lungs out. She needed to be rocked back to sleep and eased into peaceful slumber. In the middle of one night in early April 2004, I got up to comfort her as I had for so many nights, and while rubbing my eyes, I bolted down the carpeted stairs in my socks, slipping forward and twisting my right leg and dragging it behind me. As I continued to slide down the stairs, unable to stop myself with the handrail, I heard a loud pop from inside my body and then felt excruciating pain from my right knee.

Sam thought I was being hyperbolic, and he dismissed my pain and discomfort. He refused to take me to the emergency room or to the doctor. The next day, his mother took me to the doctor to have it examined. Turns out, I had ruptured my already torn ACL, which required ACL replacement surgery. I had a great orthopedist, who was also the official ortho for one of the local professional sports teams. I forget which one, but it evidently was a big deal considering the number of press clippings and signed photographs he had hanging on the walls of his office. He fixed up my knee with arthroscopic surgery that basically screwed the ACL from a cadaver into my right knee. I eagerly stayed awake to watch the whole thing. First of all, I hate the general anesthesia feeling and the loss of time, and I thought it would be cool to watch, like they used to have surgeries on television sometimes. And I was right. A little valium and a strong spinal, and I was happily watching my knee surgery live on a huge television screen in the operating room, chatting with the anesthesiologist and listening to The Doors.

We hired a former co-worker of mine, Veronica from Tutor Time, to come help take care of the kids while I recovered for the few weeks I took off from work after the surgery. She was a big help at home and drove us around to their schools and to my physical therapy sessions. This was a lifesaver since Sam was working in New Jersey still and was gone a great deal of the time. Both of our mothers helped out a lot because they were home—Sam's mom had retired from being a nurse, and my mom had never worked more than one day a week for her whole adult life and had not done that since my grandfather died in 1994. They were available, loving, generous with their time, and very helpful. I could not have managed without them.

One day, Veronica didn't show up for work at my house and didn't answer any calls. It was very weird. We cobbled together childcare, and I was able to do more by then, so we managed without her. A few weeks later, there as a knock at my door and one of Veronica's friends came by to return my house key to me. Evidently, Veronica had stolen a whole bottle of Vicodin from me and a whole lot of pills from the nursing home where she worked at night and was in jail or court-ordered rehab. That's why she disappeared so suddenly. And we solved the mystery of the missing prescription, which I'd had refilled.

Addiction of all kinds is an awful disease that affects everyone who knows the addict.

Opiate addiction is particularly awful. Opiate addiction is way too prevalent in our society. Big Pharma reaped in profits as doctors were prescribing tons of pills to patients who then became dependent upon them. This tears families apart and drives seemingly normal people to commit crimes to get more pills. I'm grateful for the nationwide medical database that records medication intake and prescriptions like these, but we need to do more to stop these drugs from being so abundantly prescribed and available. It started too late to help my mother but is helping keep the whole system in check now.

Needing a creative outlet and a creative community to be part of, I started to sing soprano with The Northport Chorale, a local community choir. I fell in love with singing again, and this community of musicians became devoted friends. I had sung in Geneseo, in New Paltz, and with the choir at CW Post in graduate school, but it had been a few years since I enjoyed the regular discipline and joy of creating music with people I liked. These men and women each touched my life with music and friendship, but also wisdom, creativity, and enthusiasm for life. For a long time, I was included in their weekly social gatherings after rehearsal at a local pub and earned myself a seat on the board of directors. I also volunteered to design the programs for the twice-a-year concerts; my co-designer was a new friend, Julia.

Julia became like a sister to me on the very first night we met. She joined choir a year or two after me and sat next to me during her very first rehearsal. We chatted and instantly clicked. We could just as easily have had a five-hour conversation as a five-minute one. We never ran out of things to talk about or different ways we could connect. She is an amazing woman, and I will always love her. I was a bridesmaid in her wedding and helped her and her husband move into their house. I corresponded with her regularly while she was deployed in Iraq with the U.S. Army during the second Gulf war, and when she came home to a husband who wanted a divorce, I helped her move out of the house and into a new apartment.

Friends are there for one another no matter the circumstance. And I was lucky enough to witness her fall in love again a few years later and again was honored to be part of her wedding ceremony, this time reading one of her favorite Emily Dickinson poems. She and her new wife moved to Australia and are much happier with their lives there than in the United States. Their daughter is beautiful and thriving. Friends like Julia are such a valuable part of life. I know that we don't speak as often as we would like, but I also know that we are both people who get swept up in the million activities life presents and time is always in short supply. Despite this, she is always someone I will treasure and be honored to know.

Two of my favorite moments with the chorale involved singing duets with my friends at concerts. The first was with Peggy, another soprano and a beautiful soul. She and I sang a very harmonious and cheerful rendition of *I'll Be Home for Christmas* to an audience of friends and family looking for holiday cheer at our early December concert one year. Several years later, another friend with a warm, soulful tenor and I sang *Mr. & Mrs. Smith* from the television series *Smash* for a Northport Summer in the Park concert to an audience sitting on lawn chairs and drinking wine from disposable cups. I love sharing music with another singers, friends, strangers, anyone. The act of sharing is communal, generous, and kind, and it creates a cohesive community even if for only the two to three minutes of the song. Plus, there is a part of me that likes the spotlight when I am creating something that I am passionate about and feel that I have a reasonable amount of skill or at least practice doing.

A few years passed as life carried us forward. Sam, the kids, and I were living life, swept up in the busy-ness of day-to-day living. We were both very driven in our careers. We took pride in our jobs because we excelled at them, but also because the work made the world a better place and brought meaning to our lives. We felt that our jobs gave back to the world in a positive way. We were alike in this.

We focused on raising our kids and supporting their growth in every way, shepherding them though valuable experiences and activities: baseball, basketball, karate, Cub Scouts/Boy Scouts, Brownies/Girl Scouts, dance classes, soccer, cross country and track, and many, many art classes. Experiential learning teaches kids invaluable lessons about themselves, and our consistency in creating a safe home for them that encouraged work ethic, growth, and challenges helped them grow up into kind and interesting people.

As a teacher, I nurtured in them a love of learning and a discipline for homework and studies. It was always *Have Tos* before *Want Tos* after school in our house. We collectively read every night, talked about books and characters and how they faced obstacles. My kids knew about Macbeth's treachery and Atticus's fairness long before most kids. We worked on science projects and staged elaborate experiments, staged and videotaped plays, skits, and dance routines.

Learning, discovery, creativity, and work ethic were big parts of our lives.

My grandparents
Max & Betty 1940s

My mom & me 1968

Me in 1972

My parents & me 1974

Me in 1984

Beth, Jill & me the
day we met 1985

My high school
graduation 1986

Michael &
me 1987

Me in 19990
College graduation

Ethan & me 1998

Simone & me 2001

CHAPTER 28
CAN YOU SAVE A MARRIAGE WITH REAL ESTATE?

S am and I were growing further apart. When I brought it up, we would talk and argue about the state of our marriage and lack of emotional connection. Nothing changed. We'd fight over chores and household tasks; we'd fight about money. We'd fight just to fight, but at the end of each argument, he would agree with me just to shut me up. He'd tell me he would try to be more understanding and do more around the house. For a few weeks, it would get better and we'd seem to be growing closer again. As I said before, he was lying to me, telling me he agreed with me just to appease me temporarily and get me to leave him alone. I wrote about each time in my journal, full of hope that this marriage would work, that maybe this time it would be different, and we would find each other again and remember the love that we once shared. After a time, every time, it would go back to the way it had been before. The kids and work were taking so much out of us both that we were able to keep ignoring all the problems.

It was easy to ignore it all and sweep everything under the rug when we had the kids to focus on.

Foolishly, I thought that maybe if we had a bigger house—our dream house—the marriage would miraculously improve. If we had a house we could be proud of, not that our original house wasn't nice, that we could host holidays and parties in, we would feel more grown up and solid, more trustworthy and safe. Since we didn't know that you can't save a marriage with real estate, we moved into an amazing house. A beautiful, modern colonial with a wraparound porch, four bedrooms, a huge living room, a full formal dining room, a spacious eat-in kitchen, three and a half baths, a cozy den with access to one of the two decks, a full finished basement with an apartment and a second kitchen and another outside entrance. The wooded yard surrounded a full-size in-ground pool. It was gorgeous. We all loved it!

As we unpacked our things, decorated the new house and settled in, it was obvious that we still had all the same problems that we had before. Now, we just had a bigger mortgage and more upkeep to do.

Duh. It seems obvious to me now that our problems wouldn't go away, but at the time, I thought it would help. Maybe we both did.

In the late fall of 2005, we had just moved into a new house and hadn't met any of our new neighbors yet because I always felt awkward introducing myself to new people. I put off doing it because I was unsure how to start the conversation. The only neighbors we knew were next door to the left, because they were friends of friends already. Our boys rode the bus to school together and had mutual friends.

This is how I met my new neighbors. My children were playing in the backyard and I was working on schoolwork for graduate school. Ethan was seven and Simone was four. From the kitchen window, I could see them playing with a soccer ball and hear their laughter as they innocently kicked it around the lawn.

After a while, I realized that I had been focusing on my graduate research and it was eerily quiet outside. I walked out onto the deck and looked over the yard and didn't see them. I called their names but got no response. I shouted their names. Louder still. No response. They sometimes liked to hide and scare me, and I initially thought that this was what was going on. I screamed, "I hope you're not hiding. Please come out now, it's going to get dark soon." There was no response but the late fall breeze rustling through the leaves. From the second-story deck I could see the entire backyard, and they were not there.

I ran inside and searched the basement, their bedrooms, under beds, the bathrooms, closets, toy boxes, shouting as I scavenged through the house. Still nothing. The house sat silent. I ran out front, searched the pool and shrubs. Nothing. I searched the side yard. Nothing. I ran to my next-door neighbor's house—their son was friendly with my son—but my kids were not there. Nick's mom, Elizabeth, immediately mobilized and volunteered to go look. She and her son hopped into their minivan and started to search.

Meanwhile, I called Sam and told him the kids disappeared.

He panicked, got in his car and drove home at speeds that would have broken the sound barrier. He reminded me of the little girl who was kidnapped out of her front yard recently, and this sent me into a more frantic tailspin, if that was at all possible. With the house phone in one hand and my cell in the other, I ran from house to house, knocking on doors, ringing doorbells, retelling the story:

Hello. My name is Marci. I just moved in next door or across the street or down the block. My kids ... ages four and seven,

both blonde, were playing in the yard and are now missing.
Have you seen them?

I went from house to house knocking on the doors of my new neighbors and retelling my story. House by house, they were all coming out to help me look. They all looked similar to each other; they were all gorgeous Bengalis. I found out later that they were all related. Most of the families on this block were a family of sisters and their families. They all wandered around the block, the yards, the woods behind the houses searching for my lost children. I remember looking at the massive number of neighbors swarming the neighborhood looking for my children, and although I was terrified that something had happened to my kids, deep down I was glad that this was my new neighborhood. These were wonderful, caring people. Sam arrived at the house and started to look with the neighbors. I paced the driveway and waited in case they should return or call.

After what seemed like forever, but was a little shy of an hour, Elizabeth and Nick drove up to my house, and in the back seat were my kids. I ran over to the house, and all I could think was "thankfully, they are fine and in one piece." Crying, I hugged them and kissed them and then yelled at them for disappearing. I demanded to know where they went. It turns out their soccer ball bounced over the fence that separated our yard from the woods and they went after the ball. They kept looking at cool things in the woods, not realizing how soon it would get dark, and they lost their way. Nick spotted Simone's pink coat from their car, and the kids were found as Elizabeth and Nick drove around the adjacent block and passed the sump, which was bordered by the opposite side of the woods.

That night I bathed them, fed them, and tucked them into their beds. They decided to sleep in the same room, on Ethan's bunk beds. They slept together for safety. For years, they, more often than not, slept together on the bunk beds. Simone liked to call the top bunk, where she slept, Paris, and loved to say that she was going to sleep in Paris that night. I sat in the room for hours, watching them sleep peacefully and being so very thankful they were safe and sound. We had only been in the new house a few days, and this was how I was met my new wonderful neighbors.

Before we moved, I started a Ph.D. program with an online university to earn a second master's and eventually my doctorate in education. Not only has school been very important to me as it fulfilled my quest for information and knowledge, but it would make me a better teacher and increase my salary. I also really wanted the credentials. I thought that one day, I could teach at a local university or publish research papers in professional academic journals. *Win, win, win!* Soon after completing my first semester at this school, whose mission statement included a strong sense of community service and improvement, I spent a week at a residency symposium in Seattle, which was interesting and fun. However, I realized that this school and I were not a good fit. I was uncomfortable with the way their program was run and billed and decided to look elsewhere for my next graduate degrees. I finished my current courses and withdrew. The only great part of this experience was spending a week in Seattle. All my new friends, whom I didn't ever see again, stayed in the same hotel as the symposium, which made it easy to get together. We all explored the famous Seattle Pike Place Public Market with the huge, red neon sign. We excitedly walked among the crowds browsing the wares of all the merchants and booths. Everywhere I looked, there was so much to see and taste.

One especially nice day, I went out on my own and found the street where Seattle keeps all its art galleries and spent a glorious afternoon looking at some beautiful pieces, after which

I went up to the top of the Space Needle. The view of Seattle and the surrounding beautiful landscape was gorgeous and breathtaking. It was refreshing and a little weird to be away from home without my kids for the better part of a week, and we did speak every night, but it was also refreshing to reconnect to myself again and so peaceful to have a hotel room to myself for a few nights. I liked being on my own. Being independent was certainly something I found very attractive.

My next move was starting a master's program at University of Phoenix to earn my second master's degree. Its program suited my academic and financial needs a bit better. I took one class at a time, and in two years I had a second MA. This one a dual major as well: curriculum and instruction and educational technology. Rules were changing in school districts with regard to salary scales, and I wanted to move myself to a place where I could maximize my salary as quickly as possible.

This was vitally important because I needed to be able to support myself and my children if my marriage should end. Unconsciously, I saw the writing on the wall.

I developed a friendship with my research partner in my program, a retired Army officer who was training for his second career, as a teacher this time. Jim was a gifted writer and a deep-thinking academic with strong opinions and convictions. We learned a great deal from one another as we worked our way through the program together from opposite sides of the country. Over time, he became an extraordinary friend, and we talked about everything in life. He was a wealth of knowledge and perspective having been married a few times, raising three children and enjoying a long career with the military. After a few months, I started confiding in him about my disappointment in my marriage and how unhappy I was settling for the status quo.

One night I said to him, "In my next life, I will choose a husband I am more compatible with."

Incredulously, he said, "What? You're only thirty-eight years old and you have your whole life ahead of you. Why not be happy now?"

"I'm stuck. What can I do? I made a vow. I have young kids," I said in a defeated tone.

He said, "You're not stuck. You just haven't figured your way out yet." Then he carefully asked, in a quiet voice as if testing the waters, "You do know that you can divorce him, ya know?"

Somehow, I was surprised by this, but he was right. I *could* get a divorce. I had thought about it before but had no real impetus behind me to follow through. Even though I had thought of annulling my marriage early on and several times thought about divorce, it really wasn't anything I seriously contemplated, until this very moment.

That August night, I stayed up all night, anxiety and indecision ripping through my gut, torturing myself with deep, complicated questions. *Could I do this? Could I rip my family apart, disassemble everything we had just built? We just bought this new house. Would my kids be OK? If I didn't, would I be OK?*

What kind of example was I setting if I stayed with this disappointing marriage? Would Simone ever know how she deserved to be treated? Would Ethan learn how to treat a woman? Would they ever learn that they are deserving of happiness and love? When I realized I'd be a better mom and role model for them if I got a divorce, I realized that I could do it. That's how I decided. Everything has been about them and giving them the best life and most meaningful life filled with healthy lessons and examples to follow. If you're unhappy with your life choices, change them and remake it all differently to try for happiness.

I was motivated by realizations that this divorce would *improve* our children's lives. And if I didn't act for myself, I would act for them.

By the time the early morning sun was rising, and the shadow of the French doors was long and sliding across the tan Berber carpet on the floor of the den, I had decided to tell Sam I wanted a divorce. I went upstairs while he was in the shower and sat on my side of the bed, with coffee for us both, waiting for him. He knew something was wrong the moment he saw me. I burst into tears and let the whole thing spill out of me. I told him how miserable I was, really how miserable we both were, but he didn't know it. I told him that I was lonely, isolated and had fallen out of love with him and we owed it ourselves and to our young children to find happiness in our lives. I needed a divorce. Sam was devastated. He felt blindsided and said that he didn't see this coming. When I would later tell this story to my family and close friends, they all confirmed that they saw this coming from a mile off. Only Sam was clueless.

Sam went to work after our very intense conversation that left me alone crying and drained in our bed. Before he left, he called his mother and asked her to come over and take the kids to camp so I could sleep. He told her I had a migraine. I spent the day alone in bed, crying and writing convoluted nonsense in my journal. It was a terrible day with a thousand unanswered questions swimming around in my head.

When Sam came home later that evening, he confessed that hadn't been at work at all. He ditched work and went to a Yankees game with his single friend Jake. He confided in Jake, who suggested that we seek a therapist as a couple. Sam agreed with him and told me that he already made us an appointment for that very night with the therapist he had been seeing off and on for a couple of years. We got a babysitter, and together we went to his therapist. I had never met him before, and I could tell right away that this guy was not going to help us. This therapist kept thinking that all our problems could be solved with date nights and an occasional sexy shower for two. If we made time for one another and remembered why we were attracted to each other way back when, then all our problems would vanish.

This was an oversimplification of astronomical proportions. Our problems were more serious than one night of sex could fix. Sam still thought there was hope. The more he had, the more mine drained out.

One morning several weeks later, while I stood in my bra and panties quietly putting on my makeup in our bathroom before my day started, Sam surprised me by creeping into our bathroom behind me. He started to rub my shoulders and kiss my neck, two things he hadn't done in years, or ever. Before I knew it, he had swept me up into his arms, carried me to our bed, and aggressively tried to have sex with me, things he had never done. He was not the sexual or romantic-overture type and always let me attempt do the seducing, which I did not do often at all because of how distant and unaffectionate he was and how many times I had been rejected. But this was not sexy or seductive. This was angry, caveman-like aggressive, like he had something to prove. I threw him off me and told him that this was not the way to fix our marriage. This was not the way to make me love him again. This was just hurtful and mean. I called him and his therapist fucking idiots to think fixing our marriage was as simple as this. I stormed angrily away back into the bathroom, physically shaken and took another shower so I could cry and not be heard.

The angry violence of this was overwhelming and terrifying but I couldn't reconcile this Sam with the Sam who laughed at me when I tried to seduce him two years before. To this day it is impossible to understand how these two Sams were the same person.

One time before we had moved to this new house, probably in 2004, I had planned a big seduction in an attempt to kick start our sex life and build a new bridge toward some kind of intimacy in our marriage. I put on a very sexy, push-up black negligee that made the most of my assets, lit tea light candles all over our bedroom, and waited for Sam to come upstairs with his glass of wine at the time I had pre-arranged with him a half-hour before. He opened our bedroom door to find me seductively lying across the bed, candles around the perimeter of the room, soft music playing in the background. The scene was set for seduction and romance.

Sam's reaction hurt me like a thousand knives through the heart.

He stood in the doorway and laughed at me. He was pointing and gesticulating while hysterically laughing at me. I burst into tears, mortified, embarrassed, viscerally cut down and ran into the bathroom. He didn't try to get me to come out. He didn't apologize. He left the bedroom and returned to what he was watching on television in the living room. We only spoke about this once afterward. I told him I was devastated by his hurtful rejection. He shrugged his shoulders and gave me the silent treatment for having the audacity to be hurt and angry with him.

Our failed couples' therapy sessions proved to me that there was really nothing left of this marriage. I couldn't pretend any longer. I could no longer sweep it all under the rug. No one owned a rug that big. Divorce was imminent. After about a month of weekly therapy visits with this yahoo of a therapist, I told Sam I wanted a divorce. For real this time.

Sam was shocked. He was hurt. In one mood, he tried to get me to change my mind and told me I was the best thing that had ever happened to him. In another mood entirely, he woke me in the middle of the night, standing his full height

- 6 feet 4 inches - over my bed in the guest room, where I was now sleeping, screaming and hurling insults at me and telling me I'd be alone forever and if I died no one would miss me. I remained outwardly calm in the face of these scary, abusive onslaughts because my Psych 101 class taught me that he was transferring his own pain onto me, but I was scared for my safety. Everything he was saying about me, he meant about himself. These wild shifts in demeaner and his emotional manipulation were classic characteristics of a narcissistic personality disorder. The more I realized this, the calmer I appeared, and the more enraged he became, but the kids never knew. We both hid it all from them. I hope.

We found a lawyer to serve as our divorce mediator in November 2006. I found my own therapist. She helped me keep perspective on my goal, which was to take apart our marriage with the least amount of pain for each of us as possible while trying to maintain as much normalcy as I could for my kids. I wanted to do a better job than my parents; I wanted it to take less time, cost less money (especially because we had no money—we had only debt) and I wanted to get it all done with a minimum of ugliness. If that was possible. Afterall, I was realizing that I was an emotionally battered wife who was physically afraid of her abusive husband, and no amount of intelligence and inner resolve was going to wash that way so easily.

We had been good friends, good co-parents, decently compatible homeowners. We respected each other's families and friends and careers, but something was missing. It was that extra connection, intimacy, intense compassion, heck, any compassion, and any shred of physical chemistry. I doubt it was ever there. We probably liked one another, somewhere deep down, because of our shared history and our children, but we hadn't been in love for years. I don't think we were ever *in love* but just loved each other, which is a huge difference.

And without that piece, the marriage was a sham. After all that had transpired between us, there was nothing left. Even I couldn't force myself into that daily acquiescence and compromise anymore. No matter how much we thought we loved each other at the beginning, this couldn't be fixed. There were many hurtful incidents, sinking suspicions, and aggressively disrespectful betrayals along with unrelenting silences, broken promises, and chronic disappointment—Suffice to say, we tried to fix it with new houses; we tried to fix it with new cars. Nothing worked.

At some point in this mess, when doing our family laundry, I found a pair of sexy women's thong underwear in my master bedroom laundry basket. It was hot pink with leopard patterned fabric and didn't belong to me. It was much too small. Instantly, I knew that Sam was having an affair and instead of being upset or jealous, I was actually happy that he was finally interested in someone. It was another confirmation for me that this marriage was seriously over. He never admitted it, but he had also never once admitted anything that could be considered hurtful or disrespectful to me.

Asking for a divorce, after couples' counseling that wasn't cutting it, was the most difficult thing I've ever had to do, but I knew that we would both be better off divorced. Our kids would be better off in the long run. They needed to know what it was like to live in a peaceful household. They needed to see what a healthy, loving relationship between two people would be like, if I would be lucky enough to find one for myself in the future. Making them grow up in this tense, angry house, with a mother who was afraid of their father who ran the house like a bully, would have been devastating for them. I've discovered throughout my adult life that I can withstand almost anything myself, but to protect my kids, I'd walk through fire. Every day of the week. The only way out is through.

One afternoon, while the kids were down in the basement playing, I was upstairs putting laundry away when Sam came upstairs full of anger. The whole energy of the upstairs hallway changed as he walked over to me and cornered me between the adjacent doors of the hallway bathroom and Simone's bedroom. He stood over me, one arm on each of the walls beside me, boxing me into the corner and drew in close, leaning down in my face and demanding that I give my engagement ring back to him immediately. His proximity and size were physically threatening and terrifying, but in the calmest voice I could muster I said that it was a gift from his mother directly to me before our marriage and I was saving it for Simone, just as I had long ago told his mother I would. He said that he didn't trust that I wouldn't sell it, and because it was a family heirloom, he wanted it back now. I felt I had no choice. I didn't know what he was capable of, especially when the children weren't around. I went into the guest room, where much of my stuff now was, found the ring and gave it back to him.

Instantly, I had the suspicion that he was going to take the ring, do something with it and then lie and say that I lost it or sold it, so as soon as he left my room, I called his mother and told her that Sam intimidated me into giving him back the ring. If she wanted to know where it was, she should ask him. I think she was taken aback but went with it.

Another night, Sam was putting away clean dishes from the dishwasher and came waltzing into the dining room, where I was busy writing a paper for my second master's program at the end of the table by the big window that overlooked the backyard. It was late, the house was quiet and the kids asleep when he suddenly appeared in the doorway with a ten-inch carving knife in his right hand. He stood there staring at me, quietly slapping the blunt, wide end of the blade into the open palm of his left hand in a controlled, angry way. His eyes bored into me, filled with rage and hatred. Startled, I looked up from my computer, taking in the scene. Sam was a tall man, over six feet tall, 250 pounds, with the broad shoulders of a football player, so this was a truly menacing sight. I sat there silently looking at him, my eyes locked on him as I quickly located my cell phone on the table with my peripheral vision, just in case I needed to grab for it. I had no idea what was wrong or what could possibly have gotten him this angry. He started to speak softly, but with an edgy tone.

"You're such a bitch!" he growled at me. "The world would be such a different place, a better place, if you were dead. Or, better yet, had never been born." Then after a beat, he continued, "Not a single soul would miss you. You're nothing." Then he walked back into the kitchen.

I held my breath, in near panic, and heard him slamming cabinet doors and drawers, heard the dishes and silverware clanging inside. I grabbed my cell phone, dialed 911 and put it down on the table without pushing send, while a hundred thoughts raced through my head. I knew we had been fighting a lot lately with the divorce mediation ongoing and trying to keep things "normal" for the kids. He'd been working crazy hours during the week and was playing guitar with this new band and gigging every single weekend, sometimes two or more nights, getting home at four in the morning. He was under stress, and so was I with lesson plans and the needs of my mother always pressing on me, and graduate school, but he had never spoken to me like that before.

There was that one time, years ago, when he got very angry over something, something I didn't remember now. He was full of rage, and when he couldn't control himself anymore, he shoved me, pushing me across the room and into a wall with such force that as I hit the wall, a shelf full of glass knick-knacks fell on top of me, shattering into thousands of tiny shards, making tiny cuts and scratches in my arms that looked like a constellation. Trying to stand up afterward, I cut the palm of my right hand on the glass. That left a two-inch scar that has since faded.

Sitting in measured silence, I listened intently to his every movement in the kitchen while unconsciously fingering the scar on my right palm with my left thumb. He was slamming doors and starting to murmur under his breath about me.

"I wish you were dead. The world would be so much better if you were dead. I wish you got cancer. Or AIDS. Or would get into a fatal accident. Life would be better …" He repeated this to himself, but so I could hear, over and over. How could he say such terrible things? Tears were welling up in my eyes as I was gripping the sides of the heavy dining room table for support.

Should I call the police? How long would the police take to come? Would they believe me if I told them the story? Would I be alive when they got to the house? If he heard me call 911, would that enrage him more?

Just then, he walked into the garage. I waited in silence for a minute to listen to the noises of the house and get a grip on myself. What should I do? He had never behaved quite like this before. Sure, we had fought. What married couple who was getting divorced didn't fight? But he had never spoken to me like this, threatened me like this before. Should I lock the garage door and call the police? If he was stuck in the garage, he couldn't hurt me. They'd surely believe me, wouldn't they? Panic filled me. I couldn't move.

Taking a deep breath to steel my courage, I was frozen where I sat. In a moment, before I could get up to do anything, he walked back into the dining room and instead of holding the carving knife, he was holding a toy of Ethan's that hadn't seen the light of day in years. He spoke to me in an eerie, soft voice full of nostalgia for when Ethan was a younger boy. I was reeling. Suddenly, his energy was calm and peaceful, and he walked away with the toy, sat on the couch, and put on the television in the den. I didn't know what to think.

The next day at our appointment, sitting at the conference table, I told the mediator about this incident. Sam didn't deny it. What happened next, takes on the image of a movie scene in my mind. The mediator told us that he represents us both in this divorce and had something to say to each of us. He turned his chair and whole body toward me and in a very level and even voice full of concern said, "You should have not hesitated to call 911 to protect yourself. There is no way to predict what someone will do when they are full of rage. His angry and violent words coupled with the wielding of the carving knife are very threatening. I'm sorry that happened to you." He made me promise that I would if it anything like that ever happened again, I would call 911 immediately. I promised him I would and instantly regretted that I hadn't.

Then he turned his whole body and chair toward Sam and in the voice of a scolding principal, he admonished Sam for his behavior. He said, "Your behavior was unacceptable and illegal, and you were one hundred percent wrong. If Marci had called the police, you would have been arrested, spent the night in jail and you would have lost custody of the kids right then and there. This was serious business. She could have just dialed 911 and hit send on her cellphone while you were threatening her, and the police would have been dispatched when the 911 operator heard the conversation and traced the address." Sam looked caught out like the bully in a school yard being chastised by his teacher. If I had done that, we would have had a very different outcome.

Using my parents' divorce and my friends' parents' divorces as cautionary tales, I knew that we could take it all apart, dismantle what we worked so hard to build, without destroying each other and without destroying our children, which is ultimately what we were able to do. I did everything I could to keep the divorce from blowing up into a big, catastrophic mess. Sometimes that meant ignoring Sam and his volatile comments, which at times was very hard to do.

I had confided in a friend at school who was a security guard and former military, all about Sam's threats and scary, near-violent behavior. He was going through a divorce as well and we commiserated with one another like we were swapping war stories. I felt that with the kids home I was safe from a repeat performance of the knife threating event, but in that parking lot after tense negotiations, who knows? Gerald felt protective of me and was worried about what Sam might do or say to me after our mediation sessions. He and his brother, also former military, volunteered to be my bodyguards. I wore a wire into each session to record what was said inside the mediator's office and in the parking lot and Gerald and his brother sat in their dark car in the parking lot across from entrance door to the law firm in black trench coats holding plastic wrapped baseball bats. They were monitoring us and were ready for anything. If Sam threatened me or had taken his hands out of his coat pockets, they would have been on him like fiery dogs from hell. Luckily, this never came to pass, but I felt safer and more confident to fight for myself and my kids in the divorce negotiations because I was protected. I have since lost touch with Gerald. I rewrote his resume for him, and he changed jobs. I never saw him again. People come into our lives for specific reasons. We both helped one another change our lives.

Sam and I got our divorce in about six months' time for a grand total of $5,000, sold our dream house, and dismantled our life together.

I remember seeing the Cameron Diaz and Kate Winslet 2006 movie *The Holiday*, in which a supporting character, who was a retired screenwriter, told Winslet's character that she should be the leading lady in her own life. This was pivotal for me. I knew what it was like to feel like an extra in my own life. Art affects life. My life and concept of myself, like those of Winslet's character, were transformed by this revelation. That was a profound lesson. Be the leading lady in your own life.

After all these years of feeling like an extra in the movie of my life, I finally, in 2006, figured out that I need to be my own leading lady. The difficult part was making it happen.

CHAPTER 29
THE MOTHER LION

I committed myself to dismantling our toxic family life in a manner that was focused almost entirely on the well-being of my children. It's cliched to say that motherhood is the toughest job you'll ever love, but it's true. For me, it is also true that being an excellent mother is most important to me and what I am the proudest of in my life. Ever since I was a tiny, young girl, I knew that I wanted to be a mommy. My parents were very nurturing when I was a small child, and I always felt loved. I had a loving extended family who doted on me and made me feel important, loved, and cherished.

Despite the fact that some of those relationships and what I got from them changed significantly when I reached adolescence, the foundation of love was there, at least enough to teach me how to love and give me the tools I would need to be an excellent mother. Of all the things I know I do well, being a mother is the aspect of my life in which I am the most confident. I am a great mommy.

Above all else I had to protect these little humans I birthed into the world.

When my children were born in March 1998 and March 2001, I was immediately in love with them. This is not true; I actually fell in love with them in July 1997 and July 2000 when I found out that I was pregnant with them and they were growing in my womb. I talked to them, sang to them, played them music while they swam around inside me. Once they were born, I nursed them, massaged them, read to them daily, and saw that every one of their needs was met. When they faced illness, I made sure they got the medical treatment they needed and nursed them back to health, with matzoh ball soup and stories, while cozying them and making sure they always felt loved and cherished.

As they grew, learning about the world around them, I eagerly taught them and guided them, focusing on their educations—academic, physical, artistic, creative, and emotional. I created my own hybrid of attachment parenting and mindful parenting—before I knew those were actual terms—that worked for me and for them. From graduate school, I learned about the constructivist teaching style, and this, too, influenced the kind of mother I would be. My style is an amalgamation of all three concepts: Attachment parenting, mindful parenting and constructivism.

As important as it is for parents to set expectations and limits for children to learn and adapt to their world, it is also vital that children learn their feelings are valid and important and deserving of respect. I did my level best to make sure my children always knew where I stood on things, that they always felt loved, always could share their real thoughts and feelings with me without judgment; that I would help them solve any problem they had and help them feel respected and capable.

I love being a mom. I mean, I really, really love being a mom.

The hardest thing about being a mom, or dad, is the letting-go part. I always urged my children to try to handle their problems on their own, knowing I would always be there to bail them out if need be. We would talk through a problem and, verbally or on paper, create a list of ways to solve the problem and feel better about whatever the situation. Then I let them handle it. Only a few times did they need me to step in with teachers or once with a coach to help make the situation right again. Most of the time, they were able to handle the situation on their own—with teachers, with classmates, with friends. It taught them independence, self-efficacy, and resilience. Those are key skills we all use every day.

We, moms, are too hard on ourselves. Never is what we are doing enough. If we stay home, we worry about making enough money to support the family and what kind of role model we are for our children. If we work part or full time, we worry that we aren't spending enough time with our kids or are too tired, stressed, or busy to be fully present in the time we spend together. There is no way to do it all—at least not simultaneously. Those articles that float cross our Facebook newsfeed, telling us moms that we can have it all are responsible for a lot of unnecessary anxiety and burnout. With a supportive partner, one who is fully immersed in the running of the household and the raising of the children, we might come close to having it all, but even with the most engaged partner in the world, moms are still the ones who seem to be the household managers, overseeing everything that goes on in the house from buying milk to cleaning the bathrooms, and with the kids as well, everything from immunizations to permission slips.

Mindful parenting, being present with my kids, is my goal. It just requires that with most of the time I spend with my kids I am awake to each moment and experience and am fully present.

Always the unnecessarily guilty working mother, I eagerly volunteered to be Cub Scout den mother, Boy Scout parent leader, Girl Scout leader, dance mom or team mom for almost all of my kids' clubs and activities. I needed to be involved to be a good advocate for my kids and because I like being involved in things and always wanted them to feel supported and appreciated. I'm a great organizer and although I'm a bit of a cautious introvert with some extroverted tendencies, when it comes to my kids, I'm out there in front with a loud voice and an open heart. I crave connection with people and these roles gave me an instant social circle.

It's going to sound silly, but as a mom I am very much like Lorelai Gilmore of hit television series *The Gilmore Girls* (2000-2007). Lorelai is independent and level-headed, and she works hard to create a fun household filled with music, books, and friends so that she is able to end the dysfunction from her family of origin. She raised Rory with love, respect, democracy, fun, laughter, and generosity. They faced the world side by side, sharing all the ups and downs of life. Lorelai is a great role model of a self-sufficient woman who makes a happy life through the sheer force of her own will, work ethic, and huge and generous heart. There were problems along the way—extremely tight finances, heartbreak, illness, death, and disappointment—but through communication and sharing, she and her daughter weathered even the most difficult of storms.

Simone, Jill, and I are obsessed with this show, and it is always on in our homes. We know all the episodes by heart and speak to each other about the characters as if they are real people. We have a running text message conversation about plot holes and inconsistencies that is so much fun to share. The show gives us a sense of comfort and peace, as we feel folded up and hugged within the town of Stars Hollow, Connecticut.

CHAPTER 30
FOR THE FIRST TIME

*"The only person who is going to give you
security and the life you want is you."*

—Unknown

We sold our "marital residence," the kids and I moved into a rental house in our school district in the neighborhood surrounding the elementary school, and I set up a cozy house to make them feel secure and safe. We stayed in the same town to keep the kids' lives intact. It was written into our divorce agreement that we had to stay in our town or forfeit physical custody of the kids. We really wanted consistency for the kids.

Sam moved in with his parents in the next county, for a time, until he bought a house on the other side of our town a few months later. At first, it was brutal. We had created our own shared custody schedule with equal parenting time. It was fair on paper, but in practice we found out that it ignored the human variables like how our kids felt and what their range of emotions were, what their school/homework needs were, school related activities, time with their friends.

Sharing custody was torturous. The kids were going back and forth between our houses, and they hated it. Ethan was nine and dealt with it better than Simone. He has always been a diplomat, eager to keep the peace in any situation. Simone was three years younger, and at age six, she didn't ever want to leave her mother. So many evenings she cried hysterically when Sam came to pick them up.

One Friday evening, we were sitting at my dining room table doing homework when he, according to the parenting, schedule arrived to pick them up. Their bags were backed ahead of time and Ethan easily got ready to go and opened the door to let his father in when he rang my doorbell, but Simone refused to leave. She was in the middle of doing homework and drawing with me and burst into tears at the prospect of leaving me to go with her father. I tried to reason with Sam.

"Sam, can't you see she's upset? She's in the middle of her homework," I said sitting beside her as she sat at the table with her face in her hands crying, her blonde pigtails shaking.

"It's time to go now. It's 6 o'clock. Let's go, Simone," Sam replied forcefully, not making eye contact with me but moving toward me. Simone did not get up, she sidled a little closer to me at the table, as I wrapped my protective and reassuring arm around her.

"Just give her another hour here with me and I promise I will bring her to you," I implored him hoping he'd let our daughter have some time to deal with her emotions, let me settle her down and get her to accept that she had to go with him. "This is a brand-new schedule for all of us," I said as I stood up between them as he was approaching. "I'm having trouble getting used to it and I'm a grown up. She's only six."

"The agreement says six o'clock on Friday, so I am taking her now," he shouted.

Then he skirted around me and scooped her up into his arms, threw her over his right shoulder and forcibly carried her kicking and screaming.

"Mommy! I want to stay with Mommy!" Simone repeatedly screamed as he carried her out of my house, into his car.

I chased after him into my front yard talking to Simone, trying to soothe her as she continued crying, "I want to stay with Mommy!" over and over and telling her it was going to be all right.

In a soothing voice, I told her "I will be home all weekend and I'm only ever a phone call away if you need me." And repeated, "I love you both to the moon and back." It was awful to be powerless as this happened.

My internal calculus ran through all my options. Pleading with him wasn't working. Trying to appeal to his fatherly compassion wasn't working, probably because there was none where she was concerned. He was so angry with me and I think he felt victimized by the divorce that he refused to give an inch now, even if it was to his daughter's benefit. I felt that if I called the police because he was being scary and aggressive in asserting his own parenting time, they'd say that it was his right to take her, according to the parenting agreement, and she'd have to go anyway. So, I let him drive off with them.

Sobbing and shaking with fury and helplessness I went back inside. I couldn't comprehend how he couldn't see that she needed more flexibility and gentleness. She was only six, for crying out tears, but he was too angry at me and hated me too much by then to even appear flexible, even if it was what our tiny, daughter needed. Sure, she stopped crying eventually but it was more out of exhaustion and helplessness, not acceptance or comfort. He, of course, didn't see it that way. He saw her acquiescence as proof that he was right, that she was crying crocodile tears.

Eventually, she got used to it to a degree, we all did, but she always had more trouble than Ethan with the back and forth. Over time, as Sam's anger waned, he eased up, allowing a bit more flexibility with regard to our children's changing needs and if one or the other, or both, were having a hard time or something, we could alter the hand-off time a bit. And if they were sick, they were all mine. He wanted nothing to do with sick kids and knew that then especially they would want me. It's a natural instinct when you have a loving and nurturing mother to want her when you're sick and need extra TLC. I'm very good at nurturing and nursing someone I love back to health. Years later, when Ethan had H1N1, Swine flu, I spent more than a week making him matzoh ball soup, jello and making sure he had plenty of fluids and plenty of entertainment. I set up my laptop on a small folding table and we streamed many of my favorite teen movies from the 1980s – *Ferris Bueller's Day Off*, *The Breakfast Club*, and *War Games*. He recovered and felt loved and nurtured.

Alone, as a single mother in my own home, I was adrift again. I had no choice but to cope. At least I had peace in the new home I created out of the sheer force of my will. I was very proud of myself for making this all happen and knew this was a marathon, not a sprint, and somehow, at some point in the future we would all be OK.

I had no idea how we would get there, but I knew that we would eventually.

My weekly therapy session goals were to help me develop the tools I needed to put my kids' needs first while trying to rebuild my life. I didn't become a mommy to only do it part time, and during the time the kids were at Sam's, I was lost and depressed. I cried much of the time wandering into their empty rooms caressing their things, lying on their beds smelling them on their pillows. I missed them so much it was physically painful and sometimes I couldn't even stand up.

Ultimately, I was happier and more at peace in my own place than I ever was with him or anywhere else for that matter. I realized that even if I was alone and celibate forever, this was the best choice for me. I was starting a new beginning, and I could remake myself however I wished. I could do what made me happy, whatever *that* was. Some nights, I was heartbroken and lost. Other times, although I missed them, I felt stronger and focused on hobbies, like painting and reading, fostering connections with friends and working on myself.

I had thrown myself into diet and exercise during my divorce. I think it was a coping mechanism. I took maniacal control of what I ate and how often I exercised. It was a game I played with myself. How few calories could I consume and still eat enough? How many calories could I burn by incorporating exercise everywhere in my life? I did daily Pilates, swam, even did squats while brushing my teeth. The weight was falling off me, and I was so obsessed watching pounds disappear every day that I forced myself to vomit a few nights after I over-indulged with food. This scared me. I'd heard too much about the dangers of eating disorders to let this go lightly. I had stuck my fingers down my throat to vomit up the food that I had started to think of as the enemy. I had lost fifty-five pounds between July 2005 and December 2006, which was too quick, and I knew it. I had to stop this to avoid becoming bulimic.

Focusing on my health put me in better shape than ever in my life, and maybe that's what gave me the strength to handle all the curveballs life was throwing. In my own house, I had even more control over this and remade my life to support these new healthy habits. My inconsistent attempts at yoga and meditation helped me find a bit of calm and peace as well.

I threw myself into cooking spectacularly healthy meals on weekends for the three of us, as well as the occasional friend who dropped by. We played games after homework was done. We got very good at Guitar Hero and Scrabble. We continued to read three books or chapters every night and hosted parties and gatherings. About once a week, we went to the local diner for dinner because the diner made the greatest noodle salad and my kids loved it. We always brought a travel-size game of Scrabble and instead of sitting at the diner trying to extract conversation out of them like I was doing dental surgery, we played the game. The kids balked at first but got used to it and learned to play well. We generally went on weeknights when the diner wasn't crowded so the management didn't mind.

I wanted to build a home full of love and fun, a place that was safe for us and would be our haven. For the first time, all these decisions were mine, and I was in control. It was *our* home. *My* place. *My* home. I was safe and secure with my kids and all was improving in our world.

For the first time in my life, I felt that I could truly relax. I no longer had to wonder when the next shoe would drop. I didn't have to skirt around someone else's wishes or moods. I no longer felt like an airplane circling the runway waiting for permission to land. This was my place. This was my safe space, my home. It was monumental.

Our living room was missing art, color and personality. I bought two of the largest canvases I could find that were approximately five feet wide by three feet tall. Simone, Ethan and I spread out a large sheet to use a tarp on the grass in our backyard and using their kid safe paints, we splatter painted our canvases with all the colors of the rainbow, in a style reminiscent of Jackson Pollack. It was a very liberating activity for us as we each threw, squirted, swirled, tossed and spilled paint creating a beautiful, colorful and harmonious design.

Once they dried, we hung them on the white wall of our living room. This art we had created together became a symbol for our happy, peaceful, colorful lives together and when we moved a year later, we hung them in that new living room. I eventually repurposed the canvases into other paintings for other rooms as our lives changed.

A few months later, Sam asked me to talk privately outside after he brought the kids back home to me. I had no idea what he wanted to say, but his energy was not angry or hostile. He stood there on my gravel driveway as the sun set behind my yellow and red maple trees and said, "Thank you for knowing that we were so miserable and for being gutsy enough to divorce me." I stood there in shock, looking at him silently as he continued, "I realize now that it has been a few months, that we were both much more miserable than I realized."

I think I stammered, 'You're welcome," with a look of dismay on my face.

"I would never have had the intestinal fortitude to do what you did and if it had been left up to me, we would have just drifted along in unhappiness forever. You did us both a favor."

All I can say is that I was utterly shocked, and to this day I cannot believe that he said any of this, but he did.

Soon, Sam started talking to me about his dates. He had posted a profile on an online dating site and was meeting and dating women. He told me about his dates. At first, I thought that although this was weird, it was a rare opportunity to help him select a woman who would potentially be in my children's lives. I was cautiously excited. There was a woman he had been dating for a month, and she was already jealous of the time he spent with the kids. I advised him to ditch her because that would never get better, and I could envision her not treating the kids well if they did stay together. He agreed, but it was awkward between us. After a time, this proved to be more difficult. I could only see this was a lose-lose scenario for me and I bowed out of giving him dating advice.

A new normal was slowly being established for all of us. The kids calmed down, and they were more comfortable. Sam and I started to share custody better. We still fought regularly, but the fights were over money and spending time with the kids and sometimes got quite venomous. We each loved them so much we wanted as much time with them as possible.

Just after I finished my second master's degree, I was offered two great, part-time job opportunities which I happily took because they were flexible and gave me the extra money I needed to afford my new life. The University of Phoenix, from where I had just graduated, offered me a job as adjunct professor teaching online English classes to business majors. And a local company, started by colleagues of mine in the district where I teach, offered me a job teaching online graduate education classes to teachers. Both jobs were one hundred percent in my wheelhouse of expertise, and I could do both of them, as the classes I taught met online and asynchronously, around my time at home with my children and at night after they went to bed. I was ecstatic. Several years later, I discovered an online company called *Teachers Pay Teachers* and began to sell my own lesson plans, unit plans and projects that I designed for my classes in all three jobs and made a decent amount of money every month. All of these opportunities helped make ends meet and provide myself and my children with some of the extras we all wanted. Sometimes, when we do well at our chosen profession and pursue excellence, opportunities present themselves. I was very busy, but I felt blessed.

That next March, in 2008, for the kids' tenth and seventh birthdays, I hosted a birthday dinner with my mother and stepfather. Trying my best to do what was best for my kids, I asked Sam to come by afterward for cake with our kids. This went smoothly at first, although I was very nervous that it would not go well. Neither Sam nor my mother was good at holding in opinions. When we had purchased our dream house several years earlier, we borrowed about $75,000 from my mother between the purchase of the new house and the sale of the previous one. Upon our divorce, I paid my share back; Sam still owed my mother his half. In my living room in front of all of us, in a not-nice way, my mother asked Sam for his half. Sam took the bait and started to scream at my mother. She screamed back. The peaceful energy of my home was replaced with toxic awfulness. The quiet party for the kids' birthday had spontaneously combusted, and the kids hid in one of the bedrooms, crying.

Lightning flashed before me. This was *my* house and I didn't have to let this continue. For the first time I was in control, and I threw them both out of my house. I yelled over them, grabbed their coats, pushed my ex-husband and my mother out of my house and locked the door. If they couldn't behave calmly in my house—my *sanctuary*—they weren't welcome. My stepfather silently skulked out the door a couple of minutes later. After Mom and Sam screamed at each other from my front lawn, they all left.

Peace was restored. I had taken control, and as I look back, it stands as my first battle in the long war against my own private dragons.

CHAPTER 31
HUNTING FOR A HOUSE AND MYSELF

In 2008, during the winter of my first year being single and living in a rental house, I wanted to buy my own house and settle permanently. I had my half of the proceeds from the sale of the marital residence and before I spent it on the miscellaneous things that life tosses as us, I wanted to buy a house. I looked at over thirty homes in the eastern half of our town searching for the right property. I looked at so many houses that I was afraid that they would start to blend, so I created a system of notetaking and picture-taking that would let me compare the houses and remember their features. I saw a lot of nice homes that I could picture us living in, but I wanted a house that was structured in a way that would allow me to rent out a portion of it to help defray the cost of the mortgage and make things easier for me. I wasn't sure that I would need the extra income but having that as an option was prudent and necessary.

In August of 2008, a year after my divorce, I bought my own house. All by myself. I had the right house. It is a six-bedroom Cape Cod style house with three bedrooms and a full bath on the main level, with a full, but half-finished basement for us and upstairs were three more bedrooms and a full bath that would work beautifully to rent out. The previous owner was an elderly widow who had raised eight children here and smoked like a chimney, so the house smelled of tobacco and nicotine and needed a great deal of cleaning and repainting to get rid of the smell. We gave the home the care it sorely needed. As we scrubbed the dirt and grime from the walls and removed the ancient dried wallpaper and disgusting old carpeting, I felt that we were reviving the house and in infusing it with our love, it would grow to love us and protect us as a family.

Sam and I mandated in our divorce that we both stay in our town and change as little about our kids' lives as possible to make the new family structure easier for them to handle. Just because our marriage didn't work, that didn't mean they had to suffer. I was proud of us for that. It was my idea actually as I had been reading everything about divorce and post-divorce childcare that I could get my hands on in my constant quest to do all of this better than my parents had.

I am so very proud of myself for being able to buy this house and create a home here.

I've been in this home for almost twelve years now and it's the place I have lived for the longest duration of time, other than the house I grew up in. It has become my sanctuary, my locus of peace and control and safety. It is here, within these walls, that I have raised my children and just as importantly, where I have raised myself and figured out who I am, what I am about and what I want my life to be. In this house, I became whole. At some point in the future, it will make sense to downsize and sell this house, but even the thought about that right now makes me anxious and my chest tighten.

In our new, permanent home, we could be even more at peace and in control of the tone of our daily lives. I hired a nanny who would come at 6:15 in the mornings so I could leave for work. She would wake the kids up, feed them breakfast, usher them through their morning routines, and get them on the school bus. Kelly managed the mornings at home so I could focus on my teaching job and know that my most precious babies would be well taken care of and happy. This lovely young woman lived a mile from us and became a member of family for a long time. When the time came for her wedding, Simone and I attended her bridal shower, and I was blessed to be able to attend her wedding to the love of her life.

After a few months, it became obvious to me that I needed financial help to be able to pay my mortgage on this house as I was drowning in bills and even though I made a decent salary teaching and working my two part-time adjunct professor jobs, and sold my original teaching materials on line, I needed to rent out the upstairs.

Denise and I had met through a mutual friend I had known since high school and had become friendly. She was in the painful process of breaking up with her abusive, long-term boyfriend and was looking for a place to rent while getting her life in order. She had met my kids, and seemed friendly, if not distraught, so I offered her the upstairs rooms in my house so she could get out of her bad situation. We agreed on a rent of $1,500 a month, and she would get the top floor—three rooms and a full bath—for herself. We would share the kitchen, laundry, and backyard. It seemed like the perfect setup. She would regain control of her life and I would get the financial help I sorely needed.

Denise didn't tell me she had mental health issues, was prone to angry outbursts and had a hard time staying out of other people's business. She was renting a part of my house from me, and we were friends, but she felt that she could interject her own opinions about how I was raising my children and impose her own, very different views on parenting. She was noisy and very disruptive.

Our peaceful sanctuary was being ruined.

Denise never paid the full amount we had agreed on because there was always some crisis in her life. She paid me late, and she paid me only $800 or $1,000 instead of the full $1500. I knew that she was struggling to finish her college degree so that she would be able to get a better job and change careers, so I got suckered into accepting her smaller rent payment as I thought I was helping her build herself a better life. I resented her for taking advantage of my generosity and empathy because I felt that she knew that she was taking advantage of me. This was not cool. Over time, while I tried to maintain a happy, peaceful home for my kids, it was getting harder and harder to do so with Denise in the house. Within six months, I knew that letting Denise move in was a big mistake, but what could I do? I bought this lovely house, on a quarter-acre in a quiet, tree-lined neighborhood and settled my kids who were adjusting and doing very well, getting used to our new normal. I was counting on her rent money to help me with the mortgage payment and didn't know how I would make it financially without that help.

I wanted peace in my life. I sat in my therapist's office overwhelmed, crying and explaining how I felt stuck and couldn't see my way out. I was stuck financially. Barbara looked at me square in the eye and said, "There is always a solution. Step back and look at all the possible solutions to this problem, no matter how unattractive they are."

I looked at her like she was crazy. I had no options. She quietly said, "Yes, you do. You just don't see them as options because they are not attractive options."

I just sat on her red, velvet couch and stared at her while my brain ran through all the possible solutions. I verbally ticked them off with her. "I could do nothing and live this way, which is a definite no. I could get her to move out, which I could do any time since we had no lease, but then how would I pay the mortgage and my bills? I already burned through the money I took as an advance on my pension." Barbara nodded and prodded me to keep going. "I could get another job, but with what time? Or I could stop paying my mortgage and the rest of my bills and eventually file bankruptcy." It didn't occur to me to ask my family for help. I was stubbornly self-reliant and didn't even see that as an option.

Barbara suggested that I could ask Denise to leave and find another tenant to take her place who would be more agreeable and reliable. I agreed to research that, but already was against it because letting in another variable like another tenant risked that I would be back here again in the future.

It was right then that I had my epiphany. My sanity, mental health and peace, and that of my kids, was worth whatever I had to do to secure it. If filing bankruptcy and losing my house was the price to pay for our freedom, then so be it. What I realized was that to rid my life of Denise's drama and toxic energy and to claim freedom from that for myself and my kids, I had to be willing to risk losing my house. It might not come to that, but if I couldn't figure out how to make up for the money she contributed, it might. The bigger picture here was that there was a solution I could live with. I learned an important lesson.

There is always a way out—even if I had to go through something hard to get there.

I could regain control over my life instead of giving that power away to someone else. I would ask her to leave and try to make ends meet as best as I could, and if that meant that I fell behind on my mortgage payments and eventually lost my house, then I would deal with that. Even declaring bankruptcy was better than Denise living with us.

I asked her to move out. She was shocked and upset, and we fought. She tried to make me feel guilty for throwing her out, saying she hadn't saved enough money to get her own place and had nowhere to go. I was unmoved. She refused to leave. We didn't have a lease, and nothing was in writing. We had only a verbal rental agreement, so I was free to ask her to leave anytime. I agreed to give her two months rent-free to she could save up a security deposit and kept reminding her of her dwindling time.

Eventually, she left. She just didn't come back one day. She didn't return her key or leave a forwarding address or take most of her stuff with her. A month went by without contact. I changed the locks on the doors to the house because I didn't want to be surprised by her returning, and I left her text messages and emails about contacting me to get her stuff. I heard nothing from her. I had no idea where she was. I just had to figure out what to do with all her stuff if she didn't come back and get it.

One afternoon, quite alarmingly, a policeman knocked at my door. I opened the door, and I could see over his shoulder that Denise was standing in the street with another officer between their two police cars. The policeman at my door asked me if I was the homeowner. I said yes. He asked me if I knew this woman behind him. I looked over his shoulder to the street and I said yes, her name is Denise and she used to rent a room from me, but she moved out over a month ago and I had been unable to find her.

The policeman told me that she had said she still lived here, and I was holding her stuff ransom and keeping it from her. I said that this was not true. She used to live here, I said, and I asked her to leave a while back and she did. We didn't have a lease; I changed the locks on the house and left her messages telling her to call me about getting her stuff. The police officer told me that I had to allow her to make an appointment with me to get her stuff, which I was very willing to do and had tried to do. Then he said that no matter what happened in the next few minutes, I should stay inside. I was happy to comply not wanting to get involved with her again or get in the way of two policemen. I watched the unfolding scene through my front living room bay window. She screamed and shouted at the two police officers, who were obviously trying to calm her down and get her to leave with them. Eventually, they all drove away: one police car leading, then her car, and the other police car following. Wow! I didn't see that coming. Somehow, she thought that she would bring the police to my house and get me in trouble for something? What was she thinking?

A few days later, I received an email from her about setting up a time to come get her stuff. I asked Sarah, a local friend of mine, to come over and hang out while Denise was coming to move the rest of her stuff out of my house. I wanted a witness so that she didn't try to pull any shenanigans. That afternoon was awkward, but quick.

Denise arrived with two moving men, who were professional and huge. They were very helpful man and I credit them with expediting the whole moving operation and getting her gone in record time. Whoever they were, I hope they are living happy lives.

That night, I walked around the newly empty second floor of my house of the first time in a long time. I had all this open space, and I was excited to figure out what to do with it. I was certain that, come what may, I was never going to take in a boarder again! I repainted everything a neutral white and cleaned up the three bedrooms and the bathroom. I cleansed the air with oregano essential oil in my cool-air mister to get rid of her toxic mojo, and peace was restored.

The Unlikely Pilgrimage of Harold Frye, by Rachel Joyce, was a charming novel I read during the turbulent period when

I was trying to get Denise to move out. Harold was such an innocent soul, someone who had lost his way and was misjudged by his long-suffering wife. Trying desperately to make a connection with his friend, Queenie, before she succumbed to cancer, he made an odd, rambling journey similar to the pilgrimage of the classic *Canterbury Tales*. At each of Harold's stops along the way, he met kind people who were inspired by his journey, which he thought would mythically, magically cure his friend; they each helped him in subtle and significant ways. This story touched my soul and renewed my faith in kindness and the indomitable human spirit.

My friends supported me and helped me stay sane. Tim, Kerrie, Justin, my Boy Scout family, my co-workers, they all will have my love forever for helping me restore balance in my life. Whether they knew it or not, each of them helped in individual and significant ways.

CHAPTER 32
LET'S GO TO DISNEY

My relationship with my father and Kay for many years was pleasant and caring, but superficial and somewhat distant. I had come into their nuclear family late. It was well established with the four of them ensconced in their house in Great Neck. I felt loved but as though I was kept at arm's length. My perception for a long time was that I felt like my father's stepdaughter. More accurately, I felt that my dad considered Beth and Jill's needs and well-being before he considered mine. They were together as a family because Beth and Jill were so much younger than I was. I was off in college when they were in middle school. I was in graduate school and working when they were in high school, and I was married and having babies when they were in college. I think that this age difference also accounted for some of my disconnect with my dad and his new family, even the whole extended family of my stepmother's from which I was a removed, but sometimes, a present part. I looked forward to holidays spent together and summer weekends at houses in Mahopac, Old Greenwich, Fire Island, Stanford and the lake house in Litchfield. Although my children and I have always been part of the family, until 2011, I still felt an unexplainable disconnect.

We didn't talk as regularly as my father would have wanted and most of the time; he wound up calling me and wanted me to call him more. I loved him and wanted to talk more but didn't get to it. I made excuses: I was a single mother, I worked one full-time job and two part-time jobs, I had two young children at home and faced constant stress coming at me from my mother and intermittently from Sam.

The truth is, though, I didn't call much because I felt interrogated by his questions and after having missed out on too many family trips and outings, and years spent feeling like an afterthought, I was emotionally battered and tired of waging war for anyone's attention. I kept them at bay in some sort of lame way of insulating myself. In my experience, when I tried to explain how and why my feelings were hurt by people who were under the impression that they were guiltless for hurting my feelings, I wound up defending myself and my right to my feelings. I was really freaking done with that. I didn't have to explain myself to people who weren't interested in understanding.

Sometime in the winter of 2011, while we talked on the phone, my father asked me why our relationship was shallow and distant, why I didn't call often. At this point, my tall pile of grievances with them was fresh, raw, and easily accessible, but I didn't know if I wanted to go into it. I remember some aspects of this call plain as day. I was sitting on the light blue glider rocker that I used to nurse my babies, in what was now in the dining room of my very own peaceful house, trying to decide if I was going to risk being put on the defensive again while tearing down my insulation to tell him explicitly what was wrong, why my feelings were so badly hurt, and why my children felt put off, too. I quickly realized that an opportunity like this, one where he was willing and open to listen, might not come again, and I owed it to myself to try. Kay got on the phone extension and I let them hear it all. I made a detailed list from A to Z while they listened on two phone extensions from their house in Florida. I said that these things needed to be addressed if they were serious about having a deeper, more involved relationship with us, or they could stay as they were.

When I was done, they said that they heard me and needed to process all that I had said. They hung up so they could figure out how they felt and how they wanted to respond. They would call me back the next night with their decisions. All night, I tried not to stew over the fact that my father needed to think about whether he wanted a more authentic, close relationship with his only biological daughter. This sucked.

Little did I know, it would not be the last time I waited for a parent of mine to decide if a relationship with me was desired. That sucked, too.

The next night they called back as promised and said that they were sorry for making me (and the kids) feel the way we did, and they wanted to work toward having a better relationship with us. I, of course, had to let them try, and try to be open and receptive myself, and to call them more often, too. They said that to inaugurate this new start, they wanted to take just the kids and me to Disney World over our April break from school. I said that we'd love to go, and I was genuinely excited. When I got off the phone with them, I told Ethan and Simone about the trip and ten-year-old Simone, in her usual cut-to-the-heart-of-it way, said, "They are trying to bribe us." And Ethan, in his practical manner, said, "So what? We are going to Disney!"

We had a great trip. We stayed on the property at Disney World at Fort Wilderness in a cute little log cabin. There was room for the five of us, a bathroom, and a kitchen. We ate breakfast at the cabin and tackled almost all the parks in about a week. The day we went to Epcot, we met up with my cousin, Emma, on my mother's side of the family, who worked there, and her toddler son. We walked around, had lunch, and had a great time. She got us a discount at the restaurant in "Japan," and we pretended that it was one of the kid's birthdays, that had just been in March. We were serenaded by the staff, and the kids got a free dessert. We played that game a lot that week.

Being a natural-born planner and organizer, Kay was great with the way she planned our attack of the parks. We cut our wait time using Fast Passes, the iPhone app with the line estimates, and the maps to maximize the number of rides we could go on and minimize the time waiting for anything. It was great and we had a wonderful, if exhausting, time.

The second day we were in the Magic Kingdom, it poured. I don't mean it was a heavy rain. I mean it was a monsoon, with driving winds and pounding rain that filled up Main Street faster than it could drain. The water was up to my thighs, and the only way we could have been wetter would have been to have been standing in the ocean up to our necks. Many of the rides were shut down because of the wind, and there was a mass exodus as everyone emptied the park. All the shuttles to the different resorts on the property were full, and we had to wait a while, getting wetter and wetter. My iPhone was inside a vinyl zippered pouch inside my zippered vinyl tote bag, and still it got waterlogged and ruined. I remember feeling very frustrated that my phone was unusable but liberated at the same time. Even then, I was developing a screen dependency.

I think it is safe to say that we all had a great time. We walked about 500,000 steps, ate well, laughed, met characters, rode many rides, and were exhausted by the end of the week, but we had a blast and had a lot of special bonding and talking time. I think it was the first time we, as adults, really started to see each other. Our relationships were set firmly on a new path with that trip; it wouldn't always be perfect, but nothing ever is. At least, it was improving and it felt better for us all. Dad and Kay cemented a new, closer relationship with Ethan and Simone.

Since then, I think my father and I have grown much closer and now enjoy a pretty wonderful relationship. I still get bugged by them sometimes (and I'm sure they get bugged by me). There are still moments with too many questions, occasionally a misinterpretation of something that is said trips us up, but for the most part I have come to know them both as people who love me and my kids, who will be there for us on the phone or in person when we need them. When I had my myomectomy and tubal ligation in 2013, they drove me to the hospital and back home afterward. They fussed over me and hired a home health care aid, who knew the family, to come take care of me. They are always a call or text away for advice on anything and everything, and I know that they love us with all their heart.

Recently, when I was trying to track down the cause and solutions to all my annoying, life-altering perimenopause symptoms, new gynecological diagnoses, and I started to consider a hysterectomy, Kay called me specifically to tell me how worried she was for me. She insisted that I go to the gynecological surgeon, who had performed her hysterectomy quite a few years earlier, and get a second opinion. She felt so strongly about my getting an appointment with her doctor that even though the doctor was not on my insurance plan, she and my dad offered to pay the $500 consultation fee. I went, and this lovely and thorough doctor agreed with my current doctor about the diagnosis and the recommended treatment. And through Kay's fussing, I felt loved and cared for, and with the two medical opinions in agreement, I felt more confident in my choice of treatment. When I had my hysterectomy, they were there with their hearts full of love and support.

Back in 1996, we all went on a family trip to St. John in the U.S. Virgin Islands and another trip to Key Largo, Florida, in 1997. Kay's whole side of the family took several trips together during these winters because they are all incredibly close and inextricably linked. Sam and I were included. Beth and Jill were the same age as Aunt Jane and Uncle Derek's kids, their first cousins, Rayna and Jason, and were very close with them. I always felt slightly separate from them. This was not my family of origin. I felt that I didn't know them all that well, and even though they were all uncompromisingly nice to me and welcoming, I held myself away. I was illogically angry at my father for not telling me about this family for a few years in my teens, which put me at a disadvantage because they all knew about me for a lot longer than I had known about them. It was hard for me to let my guard down, but during that St. John's trip, I felt myself relax and open up to them bit by bit. That was the beginning of starting to feel like this was my family, too. That I could be a part of this crazy, very weird, loving, extended family.

They continue to be major players and touchstones in my life, my kids' lives and now my husband's life as well, as they have all welcomed him with open arms. We spend Thanksgiving, Passover, Rosh Hashanah, and Yom Kippur together every year. Every holiday is shared with great, intellectual conversation, delicious food, familial warmth, love, and laughter. We also have the Goshen, Connecticut, house, the family compound, where we have all descended for fun-filled, relaxing weekends over every summer since 1994.

I love them all a great deal, and now, I feel like they have always been my family. I wouldn't change that for anything.

Now, with the wonders of communication tools on our ubiquitous iPhones, Dad, Kay, Jill, Beth, Michael, and I are all on a family What's App group chat. It's ongoing almost every day as we share bits and pieces of everything that is going on in our lives. It's an easy and convenient way to stay present, in each other's lives with news, photos, and videos as best as we can, spread over the globe.

After Thanksgiving 2019, my father was at my house, picked up the first one hundred pages of one of the early drafts of this memoir and as he read the pages tears streamed down his aging, but sweet face. He was so very sorry and so very upset that his actions during my adolescence hurt me so much. He only did what he knew to do and could only act on the hand he was dealt. I may not have known it then, but I do now. As a parent who has also gone through a divorce, I know that we can only do what we can to protect our kids. We do our best. I know that he was doing his best. Although his actions hurt me and often confused the adolescent me, the adult me knows that none of this was malicious or purposeful. He's human and always loved his only daughter with all his heart. We had quite a few very heart-felt, tear inducing conversations after that and I know we are closer as a result of making peace with all of those deep, dark, hurt feelings.

CHAPTER 33
FINDING MYSELF THROUGH THE END OF A PAINTBRUSH

"Decorating golden rule: Live with what you love."

—Unknown

At my therapist's insistence, as a way of continuing to heal from my divorce and navigate my way through the minefield of my life, I started to think about the things I used to do when I had a better sense of who I was. What hobbies and interests turned me on and lit me up from the inside? I needed to find the things that made me feel like me and grow comfortable with the version of myself that I wanted to be. It's important to find those things and to not let those things go.

I love reading and would always continue to read good literature and seek literary connections and inspiration. As an English teacher, this is in my blood. There are few things I get more excited about than cuddling up to read books, finding recurring themes in them. One of my favorite things is when characters in novels or protagonists in memoirs read and analyze the very novels that I love. Literary discussion in books within other books. For instance, throughout Azar Nafisi's captivating memoir *Reading Lolita in Tehran*, she draws connections between her favorite novels, such as *The Great Gatsby*, *Lolita* (obviously), and *Daisy Miller*, and how she and her students experienced reading those novels from inside the fundamentalist Islamic regime of Iran. These are novels I have loved, and to read about how they affected Nafisi, how they gave her hope, distracted her from danger, and gave the younger generation a different view of life than would have been possible without them energizes me and turns me on.

I decided to take one of my upstairs rooms and create a reading room—a library. I bought some ceiling-to-floor bookcases and moved all my books in there, bought a big, white, puffy couch to cozy myself up to read in peace and quiet. I found a beautiful purple-and-lilac patterned area rug for the floor and found gorgeous satin ruffled pillows. The room was beautiful, clean, and ready for peaceful reading, which would transport me to new places and times within the pages of fabulous books.

After some time and being alone with my thoughts, I remembered that I used to love painting and had postponed trying it again because setting up the kitchen table to paint and having to put it all away again to serve dinner or give my kids space to do their homework was such a pain in the ass. So I didn't paint for far too long. I decided to make one of the rooms a painting studio or a yoga studio. I love yoga and back then, I was pretty into my daily yoga practice. That would be intriguing. The room in the back of the house had great light, and I could put out my yoga mats and get some cool floor pillows. It could be lovely. The possibilities were limited only by my imagination and budget. I had trouble deciding which room to build. I needed some time to feel it out.

Stillness and quiet are necessary for mental health. I'd been hearing this, or something like this, for years and had dismissed it. But being forced by life circumstances to spend a lot of time alone over a few years after my divorce, I realized that I had spent much of my life avoiding being alone and quiet listening to my own self. I sat in my living room and listened to my house, the wind outside, the human noise of my neighbors. I walked hundreds of miles on the beach, drank cases of red wine, burned millions of calories at the gym, and cried tens of gallons of tears. I read Thich Nhat Hahn's wisdom about mindfulness and healing, but I still couldn't find happiness or peace.

I thought about crawling into bed, pulling the covers over my head and hibernating, but that felt like giving up, and I'm too stubborn to give up. I refused to believe that my life was destined to be flat, lonely, and disappointing.

There had to be more to life. I could be mom, a daughter, a teacher, a sister, a friend, but where was Marci?

I had to figure out where she was so I could get to know her again. If I ever knew her at all. I wandered around my house trying to figure out how to make myself happy. I was lost. How does one go about finding one's self and happiness?

Sometimes, when we reach an epiphany, the moment is so palpable that it almost feels like the Universe is shaking us awake. In the spring of 2012, I had this moment. Sitting out back on my patio, I was sipping a glass of wine and reflecting on my day, and as the sun started to set and throw deep orange and pink across the late afternoon sky, I realized that I wanted to paint again. I wanted to recreate on canvas that brilliant, outrageous sunset. I have always been an artist. I took fine-art classes in drawing, painting, and photography in college and made a meager living as a photographer before

I became an English teacher, but it had been a *long* time since I had seriously picked up a paintbrush.

With one of the upstairs bedrooms, I set up a home art studio, which was like setting up my first baby's nursery—full of hope and excitement. I picked out the cheapest area rug I could find, no matter how ugly. It is speckled maroon arcs of color blocked with large areas of tan and black. It's hideous, but I wanted to protect the beautiful hardwood floors without being all that mindful about what spilled on the carpet. I had repainted all the walls a neutral white right after Denise left, so now I was focusing on storage for art supplies and art furniture, I bought two large drafting tables that tilt up to be used as easels with colorful, cushy swivel chairs. One set for Simone (who is also an artist) and one set for me. We painted a gigantic color wheel on one of the diagonal cape window walls and a gray scale on another.

Simone was so excited to have an art studio of our own—so was I—and thrilled that I was encouraging (and helping) her paint on the walls. We created a useful, practical place to let our creative juices flow. We excitedly assembled the drafting tables and chairs when they arrived, and we organized all the art supplies we would need to get started. We were so excited to use our new space that we were up there most evenings after dinner and homework were done, with music on, painting our hearts out. I was concerned that Ethan would feel left out since there was no clear space for him in this new art studio. He understood that he wasn't an artist, and he had other interests. I let him sit at my drafting table whenever he did want to create something artistic, which didn't happen often.

I started to spend most of my alone time in my studio, painting. The goal was to learn how to paint again, and as I focused on blending colors and representing images on canvases, I slowly found myself. At first, I felt stiff, awkward, trying too hard to impress myself. It was stilted. My first creations were less than inspiring but encouraging enough to keep me going. It was cathartic and moving.

I felt creative energy bursting through me. I was finding purpose in artistic creation.

Painting, once again, was becoming a passion that excited me every day. I savored my turbulent, wild bursts of inspiration at all hours of the day and night. It became the gift of escape as it has reinforced the value of mindfulness, being fully present in the moment, allowing me to find my inner peace and make sense out of the jumble of questions in my over-thinking brain. It helped me find the distance necessary to clear the clouds away. It gave me time to think about other things, some off time for my brain.

Creating something new out of our own vision of the world to communicate how we feel, what we think, who we are or are becoming is one of the amazing parts of being human. We are all born with some drive, desire, or need to create. As children, we are close to our imaginations, which is the primary vehicle through which we learn about the world, so we are compelled to create connections to explore our worlds. As children, we hadn't yet learned the hateful art of self-deprecation and self-criticism, so we were freer to express ourselves unabashedly. Sometimes, as adults, we find it hard to connect with that ancient, necessary part of ourselves.

Painting reawakened my passion and is still teaching me patience. If I rush the painting process, the painting and all the colors turn to mud. Allowing each step to evolve organically is the only way to achieve the desired results. It's a valuable lesson and one that I'm continually learning. Where I once was intimidated, I learned to not be afraid of a blank canvas. If I didn't like the way a painting was coming out, I could paint over it and start again. There was no limit to the new beginnings I could create. I was free to experiment with color, shape, design; free to discover new techniques and instruments to paint with.

The only limits were imposed by my imagination.

Starting a new painting is exciting and full of promise. Many artists have shared this awe in creating a new world on a canvas. Norman Rockwell once said, "Every painting [was] a new adventure…[it's like] always looking ahead to something new and exciting." Seeing a new painting take on shape and depth is birthing something that never existed before.

While focusing on blending colors and composition, what I didn't plan on or realize was that I was allowing myself to process and reflect on my life, choices, and feelings. I learned to appreciate my mistakes and myself in all my imperfections. Just like a painting can be restarted when it doesn't turn out as planned, so could my life, my course. I could take another path.

Another invaluable lesson, maybe even the best lesson I realized through painting, is that it can be a pleasant surprise when a painting doesn't turn out as planned—it can actually be better. Predictability is stagnation. The unexpected is exciting and offers new challenges. Sure, my life hadn't, so far, turned out as planned, but maybe that meant it was going to be better than I ever imagined. I had hope and the ambition to surpass all my previous expectations. Learning to appreciate the unanticipated and serendipitous reminded me that I was flexible and loved spontaneity.

Life's little surprises were what made it fun and joyous.

Beauty could be found where it was least expected. Within a few months of rebirthing myself as an artist, I sold my first commission and had a collection of landscapes and abstracts.

I launched my artist's website and started a second career as an online art gallery owner. I'm happier than I ever thought possible. And when I stopped looking for love outside of myself because I was focused on my own life and art, I found love and meaning within. Being alone, sitting still, paying attention to our inner voices, being introspective and reflective about our choices, actions, and feelings, and searching for the things that feed our souls will give us a profoundly new sense of ourselves—dare I even say a healthier, stronger, and more accepting sense of ourselves. It's the time of stillness, solitude, and serenity that allows us to process our thoughts and feelings about our lives. So much noise screams through each of our days, though our connections with family and friends, work associates, schoolmates, through social media, and interaction through our ever-present cellphones that our own thoughts can easily become lost in the cacophony and swirl of contemporary life. It is no wonder so many of us feel lost, adrift, dissatisfied.

We each owe it to ourselves to listen carefully to the Universe and our own yearnings to find that which inspires us. We must look for the beauty in ourselves, and in the world in which we live. When we are still and quiet, focusing inward into our own breath and heart, listening carefully, only then can we hear our own truth.

Everything can be a creative act. Even teaching is a creative act. When I'm blocked or one creative avenue stops talking to me, I lose the sense of a painting, or characters in the story get hazy, I turn to another form of art. I sing for a while or I write something different or paint a new picture or encourage students to read a new book, play a new instrument, paint new pictures or edit student writing. Everything sort of folds in on itself and is inter-related, everything speaks to something else. Some of the most prolific artists are those who have taken different creative avenues to open themselves up.

One of the things I learned from painting was patience. I wrote about how painting too quickly can muddy the picture. It works the same in writing. If I try to rush an idea or a character or an experience, what I wind up with is a bunch of mush. So, I take a step back. I regroup, take a shower, go have a drink, have sex, go out with some friends, cook a meal, go out to eat, or have a nap. There are a million things you can do to recharge your creativity, to coax it out of its hiding places, but the one thing that you shouldn't ever do is give up.

I may have taken a hiatus from creativity now and then, especially when life got crazy busy, overly dramatic, and difficult, but I always came back to it.

Creativity is always there for me, calling me back to the temple of the divine to create something new and beautiful.

The sheer act of expressing myself in words or in color or in song is enough to make me joyous and gleeful. I feel harmonious and one with the world that we live on and are a part of.

I encourage you to do this for yourself. Find something inspirational, and don't judge, over-analyze, or overthink. Just jump in with both feet and have a good time. Find that long lost kid inside of you. And like my mother did with the finger paints when I was a little girl, stick both hands in and don't be afraid to make a mess.

Recently, someone asked me how I tap into my creativity and find the spark that creates something new. It is a process that is simultaneously complicated and simple. My art studio, where my paintings are born, is always flooded with music and light, and the shelf to my right is always stocked with a delicious selection of high-end dark chocolates. I can find inspiration in a song, photograph, story, a conversation— almost anything can trigger something in me that I'm driven to express. But chocolate is king. Chocolate is my Greek muse (or Mexican, actually).

Whether our self-expression is in the form of writing, music, visual arts like drawing or painting, tattoos and body art, culinary arts, physical activities like dance, or anything else for that matter, what inspires ideas to burst forth from our souls? How can we unblock our creativity?

After surveying (and probably annoying) more than a few creative people, I have compiled a list of strategies and practices that we can use to tap into our creativity, regardless of how we express ourselves and let loose the passions of our souls.

1. Create conducive environments that give us the space and freedom to drop our inhibitions.

2. Find like-minded, open-minded people with whom to collaborate and with whom to bounce ideas around.

3. Observe the randomness of life and appreciate serendipity—our ability to notice the world around us and translate that into something else is uniquely human.

4. Appeal to the Universe or spiritual muses for inspiration (just as the ancient Greeks did).

5. Ingest delicious and evocative foods that literally feed the body and soul.

6. Use alcohol or mind-altering drugs, which can loosen inhibitions and quiet negative self-talk. (These are not recommended in excess.)

7. Peruse the internet, print media, and social media for inspiring ideas and photographs, as many times the work of others is a catalyst for our own work.

Pinterest, Instagram, Flickr, Facebook, Snap Chat, TikTok, YouTube, etc ...

8. Exercise or dance—either solo or socially—the movement of our bodies can increase circulation, which unblocks our chi enough for creative juices to flow.

9. Listen to music to create a mood and release emotions and to encourage movement or calm.

10. Watch a movie or video or read or listen a book, an article, or a poem to recharge, help memories resurface and focus closely on images and senses.

11. Self-reflect on feelings and responses to situations and relationships in your life.

12. Laugh—the release and relaxation of shared laughter is invaluable—and sarcasm is a sign of intelligence and creativity (just ask Seth MacFarlane).

13. Walk or hike in nature while breathing deeply and taking in the beauty of the natural world—all that exists in harmony around us is often very helpful.

14. Fall in love and/or have sex. The energy, resurgence of youthful enthusiasm and physical passion have fueled centuries of beautiful art.

15. Spend time with small children—their unbridled energy and exuberance and lack of critical self-judgment can be very refreshing as they inspire us with their wonder and excitement.

16. Think deeply and with focus—whether it's just staying positive about the creative task, trying to look at things from a fresh, new angle can help us home in on what we are trying to communicate.

17. Daydream—allowing ourselves quiet time to let our minds drift off into randomness can often lead us to new, unexpected places.

18. Walk away. Leaving a creative project and giving ourselves time can give us the distance we need to release pressure, change our perspective, and recharge our energies.

19. Meditation relaxes and refocuses the body and mind and can awaken ideas and inspiration.

Who knows, maybe even reading this list inspired creativity. Wouldn't that be serendipitous?

CHAPTER 34
CATFISHED

*"The problem with love these days is that society
has taught the human race to stare at people
with their eyes rather than their souls."*

—Christopher Poindexter.

After I had gained a little distance from my divorce, I decided to put my newfound sense of self and patience to the test and begin dating. Ready to try again, I created an online dating profile, which was hard to do in my forties. Because I wanted to maximize my reach, I created profiles on several sites: JDate, Plenty of Fish, and Match.com. Scratching my head, I tried to figure out what to say. What facts about myself were important? How could I appear to be as attractive as possible? I used my skills from my PR days and painted a clear picture of who I was and hoping for the best I pressed enter. My profile was live. Now all there was to do was wait and see who responded.

The last time I had seriously dated, I was in my twenties. This was a whole new ballgame now. That got me thinking:

What did I want in a man? In my twenties, my stepmother suggested that I create a list of characteristics that I wanted in a man, the preferences and the deal-breakers. It was a fun exercise then and eventually led me to my ex-husband, but now I was in my forties and my twenty-year-old list was woefully out of date. It was time for a new list.

One night, after my kids were tucked quietly in their beds, I sat at my computer and started thinking about what I wanted, what I needed, and what were my deal-breakers. I pictured myself being deliriously happy with some new man and described him. Here is my list. I think it's pretty comprehensive:

What I want in a man…

- Taller than me

- Comparable age - mid-40's to early 50's

- Educated with at least a college degree, if not a graduate degree

- A good job that earns him enough money to live comfortably & responsibly

- No kids under the age of 8 (my kids should be the youngest kids)

- Has time for a relationship in his life, willing to make time to see each other

- Good, quirky sense of humor and appreciates my silly side.

- Generous with his time, energy, kindness

- Lives somewhat nearby to make building a relationship and being in each other's lives possible

- Has been in a long-term relationship or married previously

- Positive attitude toward life

- Doesn't get inappropriately or overly angry easily, takes things in stride

- Patient, flexible, and kind

- Good listener and really cares to hear what I have to say

- Likes and needs physical declarations of affection—hugs, kissing, cuddly, PDA

- Easy to talk to, easily communicates his emotions, thoughts, dreams

- Wants to share who he is and eager to learn about me

- Willingness to travel and explore new places

- Active and desires to do activities that we both enjoy

- Physically healthy and reasonably fit

- Healthy appetite for sex and desire to explore racy and kinky activities

- Strong hands with willingness to give and receive massages

- A spiritual side, but not overly religious

- A relationship with his family and/or has nice friends

- Supportive of me and my pursuits—music, painting, writing.

- Cleans up after himself and keeps a reasonably clean home

- Cooks decently well and eats well

- Has his own hobbies, creative outlets and interests that give him pleasure, balance and pride?

- Doesn't have a large dog

- Doesn't smoke

- Doesn't drink excessively

- Sincerely interested in building something meaningful with me and sharing our lives together

I received a lot interest from a wide variety of men, which buoyed my self-esteem, but little else. They were not who I was looking for. I kept thinking of Star Wars...*these are not the droids you're looking for.* Of the men who messaged me, the best of that initial lot was from Stuart, on JDate. It was direct, honest, assertive, and sexy. Stuart proclaimed to have most of the qualities I was looking for and a thousand-watt smile to boot. I messaged him flirtatiously. He replied. Before long, we were in a fluid conversation that made our meeting that next Friday night a foregone conclusion.

We met at a bar in Huntington and sat together in the far corner of the dimly lit leather-and-chrome bar. The heat between us was evident from a mile away, and we both had trouble keeping our hands to ourselves. Stuart was a lawyer from a town fifteen miles from where I lived; he worked in Manhattan, was almost divorced, and had twin daughters who were a couple of years younger than my daughter. I was smitten. Over the next couple of months, we met in all sorts of restaurants, bars, and hotels between our two homes and began a very passionate relationship. Stuart's passion for curvy women—ample breasts and booty—made me appreciate my own body like I never had before. Where I had been critical of certain aspects of my figure, he made me feel more comfortable and sexier.

He took me out of my comfort zone and made me feel alive for the first time in a very long time.

Soon after getting involved with Stuart, I started to catch on to some odd things he would say that seemed to contradict what he had told me about himself—some things were simply not adding up. He had told me that he was living with his ex-wife until they could sell the marital residence, that neither of them could afford to move out until this happened, but they weren't sharing the same bedroom anymore. At first, he told me that they were very adversarial with one another and had a hard time agreeing on anything and fought almost every day. But then he told a story in which he and his soon-to-be-ex-wife were sitting on *their* bed talking with their daughters about school. My curiosity had been aroused. I thought they didn't get along. I thought they were adversarial. If I was going to have conversation with my ex-husband about our kids' school, it would not be sitting on my bed. (Not even when we were still living together while disassembling our marital life would I have had a conversation with him sitting on the marital bed we were no longer sharing. I had decamped to the guest room as soon as I declared I wanted out.)

There was more. We were sitting at a restaurant one night, and he was telling a story about something his kid said that was really funny, and he used the pronoun *he*. I distinctly heard it. If he had twin daughters, why would he say *he*? There were lots of little nuanced comments or slips that made me think something else was going on here. Something was up here, but I didn't say anything to Stuart because I liked him so much and was afraid that whatever was going on might end our relationship. I ignored my intuition. Then he let slip that he and his soon-to-be-ex-wife went to a town planning board meeting together to apply for a variance for a fence for their house, that was why he had to cancel a date with me. He was explaining that they needed to make some improvements on the property to get it ready to put up for sale as the divorce progressed.

At this, I decided to listen to my intuition and do a little research. I googled him, and there was nothing about him on the web. How could someone have no digital footprint at all? I looked at his law firm's website, and there was no mention of him on their Meet Our Lawyers page. I even called their offices to try to leave him a message and was told that no one by that name worked there at all. Now I was on a quest. A mission.

Planning board minutes are a matter of public record, and I easily found them on the town's website. I read through the transcript of the date in question and found out some very juicy and infuriating information. The only Stuart to apply for a fence variance on the date of that meeting had a different last name than the one he had given me. Plus, a wife's name was included in the meeting minutes. And an address in dif-ferent town than the one in which he said he lived. *Hmmm.*

I then googled *that* name instead and found a Facebook page that showed he was still happily married to his wife, and they had twin daughters *and* an older son *and* another younger daughter. Further examination determined that he wasn't a lawyer at all, but an IT guy for a different legal practice. I called that practice, and in three seconds I was connected to his work voicemail. I didn't leave a message.

Naturally, I googled his wife and found out that she was a local dermatologist who practiced under her maiden name. On her website was a picture of her family—Stuart, smiling with his arm around her, and all around them, with beautiful glowing complexions, were their *four* happy children. Wow!

I had been catfished!

I called him immediately and told him that I never wanted to see him again, he needed to delete my number. It was over. I told him of my research and findings. He didn't apologize.

His only concern was whether I was going to tell his wife. He was afraid I would ruin his family. He didn't seem to get the fact that if his life got ruined it would be entirely his fault. I didn't want any part of what would surely work out to be like a *Jerry Springer* episode, so I told him that if I never heard from him again, I would not tell his wife. She would never know any of this from me.

Two weeks later was the date that he had previously told me he was going to have a garage sale at his house. Supposedly, it was going to be a moving sale to clear out kids' toys, household items, etc. I decided to go and thought that it would be a perfect way to torture and scare the shit out of him. The planning board notes included his actual home address, so that sunny Saturday afternoon, I drove over there. I took a deep breath and as casually as I could muster, I walked up to their gigantic and elegant center hall colonial and wandered around their circular driveway and yard with the other potential customers looking at what was for sale. I attempted to blend in with other garage sale shoppers.

After a few minutes, Stuart noticed me milling around amid a chatty group of browsers as we looked at items displayed along his curving, asphalt driveway. Through my sunglasses I could see a look of panic dawn across his face. Stuart walked over and addressed the whole group at once, trying to sound casual, but I knew it was forced casualness. Our eyes met, and he genuinely looked terrified. He had no idea what I was up to and—I'm sorry to say this indelicately— I thought he would shit his pants.

I walked away from the group and began to talk to one of his twin daughters, who was helping out with the garage sale, about a game that was for sale. She was a friendly, personable young girl, and she answered my questions. She obviously had no idea who I was, and she seemed like a very pleasant, friendly girl. I hoped that she would never learn what a scumbag her father was and that what he taught her about how a woman should be treated came from better examples.

Stuart walked over to us protectively, of himself not his daughter, obviously checking on what we were talking about. He saw and heard nothing but a conversation about a child's game. After a short while, I'd had enough of this charade, so I excused myself and left. I could feel his eyes following me to my car as he was obviously dying to know why I had come.

I knew that my visit had thrown him into a tizzy, and I loved that I was able to torture him just a bit. I'm not lucky I met him, but he is lucky that it was me whom he met. I believe that there are things his children should never have to know about him, and I had no intention of telling his little secret to his family; another woman, and I'm sure there have been and will be other women, might make another choice.

The most important part of a relationship is honesty, and therefore it is incumbent upon us all to enter into each relationship as honestly as possible. Online dating is fraught with dishonest people, so we must be prepared and skeptical. We must set firm boundaries and ask a million questions. Somehow people, men and women, don't understand that falsely advertising oneself in an online profile is never going to yield a healthy relationship. But as I learned, that is not always what people are looking for, even if they say it is.

It is important, as I learned, to be brutally honest with oneself about our feelings, observations, and expectations and to be open with the people we are dating about them, too. Had I asked Stuart about my suspicions earlier on, I might not have been so emotionally wounded by his betrayal, having confronted it earlier. I learned that I deserve more than I was asking for and that I needed to be smarter. Hopefully, you are smarter than I was then. Being catfished was not fun, but it makes for a great dinner party anecdote.

The one very huge positive thing I did get from my relationship with Stuart was a newfound sense of my own sexuality and sensuality. I felt better about myself and my body than I had ever felt, especially after years of rejection by Sam.

I was healthier and stronger as I continued to get to know and carry myself as a desirable woman.

My dear friend, Kerrie, and I grew much closer during this period of my life and hers. She is a former student of mine who was in my tenth-grade English class, and even then, when we met and I was in my forties and she was fifteen or sixteen, we knew that we were meant to be friends. Somehow, it felt like we already knew each other in a very other worldly and organic way. Kerrie is a highly intelligent, highly sensitive soul. Part scientist. Part mystic. Part creator. One hundred percent explorer and writer and thinker. We had maintained contact through social media and occasional lunches, but after she graduated college we started to hang out on weekends, especially when my kids were at their dad's house. I was seeing some men on and off and I had a ton of available time, so she would come over, and we'd open a bottle of wine and make some dinner. We would talk about everything and anything, watch movies, work on our projects side by side. We even taught each other to read tarot cards and spent many hours reading each other's fortunes. I don't think we knew enough about what we were doing to actually have any accuracy with this—if there is such thing as accuracy with tarot cards—and I'm sure we saw what we wanted to see many times. Maybe all the times.

To this day, Kerrie is a soul mate, a confidant, a writing partner, an early reader of this book and someone who I share my secrets and fears, and I know she knows that she can share hers with me. I love her like a dear friend, like another daughter, and will always be her biggest cheerleader.

At one time, in 2013, when I was heartbroken and lost after my mother died and dating was going particularly badly, she said, "You've got a great amount of independence and freedom to do what you want. If there's something you want to do, all you need to do is execute the action and it happens. You've got money and time to explore yourself and other things, if that's ever what you feel like doing, and you're not alone. Even if it feels that way. You've accumulated enough people in life to not have to be alone." She is wise beyond her years and always has been. I hope she finds the meaningful she life is working so hard to create.

CHAPTER 35
MAKING THE COMEDIENNE LAUGH

"There is nothing in the world so irresistibly contagious as laughter and good humor."

—Charles Dickens, <u>A Christmas Carol</u>

I n May 2010, I made Anne Meara laugh. Yes, the hugely famous Anne Meara of Stiller and Meara, Ben Stiller's mother. Hard to believe. Me, the over-thinker of the universe who thinks of good comebacks three hours after the conversation is over. I made Anne Meara laugh and got applause from Jerry Stiller.

You're curious now, huh?

I went with some friends to see *Love, Loss, and What I Wore*, by the Ephron sisters, Delia and Nora, off Broadway at the West Side Theater. The show was a series of monologues of five principal actresses whose topics included women's relationships and wardrobes and, at times, the interaction of the two. As any woman knows, our wardrobes are a time capsule of our lives. A long list of world famous, hugely talented actresses performed in the long run of this show: Rosie O'Donnell (from my own home town), Fran Drescher, Tyne Daly, Kristen Chenoweth, Rita Wilson, Jane Lynch, Rhea Perlman, Brooke Shields, Loretta Swit, Sally Struthers, Debi Mazar and Kelly Bishop (whom I love from *The Gilmore Girls*). And, of course, Anne Meara.

The play is about five female characters as they interact with each other and deliver pithy, hysterical monologues; the audience was loving it and hysterically laughing. We were relaxed and enjoying every second. We had front-row seats and I had the fortune to be sitting at Anne Meara's feet. Literally, at her feet. (If she stood up and had been wearing a short skirt, I could see straight up to heaven, so to speak.)

Anne Meara, as her character, was talking about shopping on the Miracle Mile in Manhasset, New York, looking for an outfit for a specific occasion, and did a whole bit about a store called the Forgotten Woman. I said out loud something the effect of "who could forget that store or what woman?" Anne Meara heard me and glanced down at me while continuing to act. I don't remember the text of what she said, but it was uproariously funny and sarcastic, and I kept coming out with one-liners, quips and comments to each bit of it.

As a young girl, I used to shop on the Miracle Mile with my mother, who *loved* the store The Forgotten Woman. It's a small world. I wasn't holding back in my usual way; I felt like I was free and in my element. Anne Meara repeatedly broke character to look at me and laugh. She was enjoying it, too. After a few minutes of me participating in her monologue from the front row, she completely broke the fourth wall and looked right at me and said, "Gee, you're very funny. You should write for television." The audience loved it and clapped. From the center section, about ten rows back, her husband, the famous Jerry Stiller, stood up and clapped for us both. It was probably mostly for his wife of fifty-six years, but I like to think that a little of it was for me.

I was in my element that day, fully present in my body, and easily accessing the humor center of my brain. It was flowing.

I was *The Marvelous Mrs. Maisel* kind of funny.

I should have waited in the theater to talk to them, or by the stage door. Maybe my life would have taken a different course from that moment on, or maybe I would have just had more juicy and funny details for this story. Was it a missed opportunity? Who knows?

There have been other times that I have been the center of attention, making others laugh. At the party after the Northport Chorale Winter concert in December 2018, all the singers and our spouses were gathered at the gorgeous home of one of our sopranos, and everyone was in a great mood, drinks were flowing, there was amazing food, music—the whole shebang. I was on that night, just like I was with Anne Meara, and having a great time, relaxed, the humor center of my brain firing on all cylinders. It happens but not predictably. I'm spontaneously funny when turned on by situations, people, or circumstances.

I'm frequently funny when I'm teaching—going with the flow of the class, talking about almost anything related to a high school English class—and the kids laugh and enjoy themselves while learning. I love puns, situational humor, and smart-ass jokes. I tell my students every year that my jokes are fast and smart, but usually terrible. I think that they are great and hysterical, but I'm famous for typical dad-jokes and puns, so they are groaners. As a teacher, I believe if you can make them laugh while they are learning, they will have fun and work their butts off. But, although spontaneity works for me, I haven't discovered how to be purposely funny in a planned-out way. It always seems forced and unnatural.

CHAPTER 36
DATING THE U. N.

"To find a prince, you gotta kiss some toads."

—Foxy Brown

Earlier in my life, in my twenties, I had always dated the same type of men, which proved to be so disappointing. There was the long, but ill-fated marriage to Sam and there was the big disappointment with Stuart. My new theory was to take my list of qualities and deal-breakers with me and enjoy getting to know different men of all types, races, and ethnicities, purposely dating out of type to see what they were doing with their lives, what they were like, and along the way learn of their interests, passions, music, books, philosophies, politics, movies. As I casually dated a wide variety of men, there was a slow but distinctive shift in my perspective. At first, I was packaging myself to be attractive to them. I always paid attention to my appearance and have always been reasonably attractive, but my main concern in so many of these early dates in my forties, much like it was in my twenties, was to be liked by the man.

Whether I like him, or myself with him, seemed almost beside the point. That's scary, isn't it? After twenty-plus years, my views of dating and my place within those scenarios hadn't changed much.

I was still aching for love and belonging and a safe place to land.

Over some time, as I went out with these very different men, I was offered glimpses into their lives—what they were like, how they lived, what excited them. I got to see them at their best or at least what was first or second date best for them. A few ill-mannered cretins said that in person I was too curvy for them, or too fat for them, or too tall, or too smart; what they said was rude, unflattering, and hurtful, but their words said more about them than me.

The too-smart comment was funny. The guy, who was a real estate agent, said that when talking to me he didn't know the meaning of many of the words I used in my ordinary speech. He asked me if I could dumb down the way I spoke while I was with him. I replied, "No, why don't you stand up taller?" His reply: "What? Am I too short, too?" It was my cue to leave.

One man agreed to meet me at the bar of a steakhouse. It was May 5, Cinco de Mayo, and I arrived on time and got a seat at the bar. I waited a while. When he was fifteen minutes late, I ordered a glass of Malbec and struck up a conversation with the friendly, grandfatherly bartender. I checked my texts and emails to see if my date contacted me. I found nothing. When it was obvious that I had been stood up, I ordered a small dinner for myself and another glass of wine. I enjoyed a lovely meal, watching television on the huge screen above the bar and chatting with the bartender. About an hour and a half later, I left and drove home.

My phone dinged with the arrival of a text message at 11 p.m. It was the man who stood me up. He apologized for not coming into the restaurant to meet me. He admitted to having shown up at the restaurant, and he sat in his car and watched me walk in. He was shocked at how much I reminded him of his dead wife, he said, and he was paralyzed with anxiety and couldn't get out of the car. He said I was so similar to his dead wife, except that I was much fatter. Then he said he could try to get past my curviness and asked if we could go out again. I said "no" in an unequivocal voice and deleted him from my contacts.

I met another man with whom I spent two great dates. We had a great time together. Then, after the second date, he called me at work one afternoon to ask to borrow $4,000 to pay off his credit card. *What?* I thought I had misheard him and asked him to repeat his question. He asked the same thing. "Can I borrow $4,000 to pay off my credit card?" I said that I didn't have $4,000 to pay off my own credit card. I was a single mother with two children and a mortgage, and I worked three jobs. No. He could not borrow $4,000. Delete.

A while later, I met another man online. We agreed to meet in a bar in Port Jefferson for a drink. We had a lively conversation about his hobby of restoring classic cars. I'm not very interested in cars, but his animation and passion were easy to catch on to. At one point, he rummaged through his pockets looking for his phone because he wanted to show me some pictures of his cars, but he couldn't find it. He asked me if I minded him going back to his car to get his phone. I made a joke that it was fine with me, as long as he came back. We both laughed. I sat and waited for him to return while sipping my wine. And waited some more. Five, then fifteen, minutes went by. Still he didn't return. I joked with the young, twenty-something bartender that I think he just bolted unless he parked in Patchogue, fifteen miles away. She laughed, but indeed, I had been left flat. She didn't charge me for my wine or his beer, which was very nice, and then I walked across the street and treated myself to a double chocolate ice cream cone.

While walking back to my car, I realized that in the conversation with the guy who ditched me, I had revealed the town I lived in and that I had recently begun collecting some artwork. Nothing really valuable, just some work by local artists that I love. Suddenly, I thought that maybe he had left early to rob my house.

I drove home in a sudden panic and felt the world caving in on me. How could I have been so careless and given him information? Could this be the guy's plan, to get information from dates, ditch them and then go rob their houses? When I arrived home, I dialed 911 and left the call unsent on my cell phone. Unlocking the door, I slowly entered my dark house, turning on all the lights as I walked, and everything seemed exactly as I had left it a few hours earlier. I took a huge cooking knife from the kitchen and walked through the rest of the house, turning on all the lights with my cellphone in one hand and the knife in the other.

Once I was satisfied that everything was safe and secure, I locked the door and set the alarm. Despite knowing in my head that I was safe, that night I slept with my cellphone, the kitchen knife, and my son's baseball bat next to my bed. This world can be a crazy, unpredictable place.

One can never be too careful.

After that, I started to screen more thoroughly and ask more questions up front. I was learning. The next man to get through my list of questions lived very close to me and was very forthcoming with how he felt about me—he thought I was sexy, brilliant, and funny. He said on the phone after our second date that he wanted to court me and make it his business to show me how much he cared. I was moved by these words and his directness. We had a few really fun nights together in the city and by his pool in his backyard.

Then one evening, while we were cozying up together on his couch and watching television at his house, he said that he thought we were moving too quickly, that he wanted to slow things down. I was confused. Wasn't this the guy who just a few weeks before told me he wanted to court me? I asked him what the confusion was, and he admitted that he didn't really know what it meant to "court" a woman. He had said it because he thought I'd like to hear it. What the hell? I asked him what he wanted from our relationship, and he was very frank. After a moment's pause, he said, "I just want to know that I can call you to come over whenever I want a blowjob." I think something in my head exploded. I heard a loud noise, which may have been my inner voice screaming her head off. I don't think I said anything. I silently stared at him. He was serious and not being snarky or playful at all. I just quietly picked up my purse and keys and calmly walked out the door. I never spoke to him again. He texted me a few hours later in genuine confusion about what happened. I declined to clarify for him. Another delete!

I came across a novel with two characters who found true love—a love that transcends physical body and a mortal life, love that renews one's soul and motivates one to grow and become the best version of oneself. That is what I was looking for in my life. I think we all are. These characters Will Traynor and Louisa Clark, the main protagonist's quirky style of dressing and naïve, yet sincerely authentic sensibility, reminded me of myself. *Me Before You*, by Jojo Moyes, gave me the hope that I would find love.

Slowly, I began to see myself through the eyes of the men who sat across from me on these dates. This was the first epiphany, or *aha* moment. I got to see what each of these men thought of me. And the most important revelation was that it was more important for *me* to like the version of me I got to be with each of these men than it was for them to like me.

Louisa Clark began to see herself and the life she could live through the eyes of her love, Will Traynor. He knew that she was smarter and better than she thought she was, and through his love and encouragement, she changed her life and really started to live as her fully authentic self.

During this time, I met some interesting men who taught me some things about myself as I dated the United Nations, as my therapist put it.

There were my weird dates with one German, a fifty-year-old man, who was a little harsh and abruptly honest, and ultimately unhealthy for me. We tried some interesting and adventurous things: art exhibits, museums, and varied restaurants together that satisfied my curiosity, but still left me alone and empty.

Then there was a date with an adorable Irishman, thirty-eight years old, who worked for a hospital, with whom I mercilessly flirted and talked about literature. Another date with a soulful Italian, forty-eight-year-old, father of two, who was an entrepreneur with whom I shared failed relationship anecdotes. Then there was a fifty-one-year-old Trinidadian writer who was sweet but too boring and conservative for me and could only talk about his ex-girlfriend's dog. For several weeks, I spend time a fifty-four-year-old British IT director, who captivated me with steaming hot sexual fantasies but proved to have no follow-through and was too geographically undesirable.

For a few months, there was a Greek fifty-two-year-old college professor with vague insinuations of a relationship that went unfulfilled and with whom I talked about education and fitness. We were hot and heavy for a short while until it became apparent that we wanted different things. He wasn't divorced yet, and although he wanted a relationship, he wasn't ready, so that fizzled out.

I was having fun and learning about myself. I met a forty-seven-year-old Bengali salesman, who talked of brain science and near-death experiences, which helped me develop my own cosmological view. I went out with a short forty-six-year-old who worked in the auto industry and got too attached way too quickly. He became cloying and began to resemble a stalker. I quickly had to put some distance between us. Then there was a forty-five-year-old Jewish corporate trainer who talked of art and sex and ultimately was looking for a mistress. He was very smart and sassy, and after the flirting ended, we had some very soulful conversations about parenting and raising children in the twenty-first century.

The last one of this blur of interesting men was a forty-eight-year-old Nigerian corrections officer who talked too much of work, gave me lessons in shooting an unloaded Glock, but was only looking for a FWB (friend with benefits). By this time, I had learned I am too great a catch to settle for that. Before we parted company forever, in one of our last phone conversations, he tried to get me to lend him $2,000. I laughed as we hung up the phone. Another beggar.

All in all, I met some interesting, but unavailable or disappointing men who offered me brief, sometimes fun and sometimes sexy encounters. We ate, drank, talked endlessly, kissed for hours, may have found temporary solace in each other's arms, and there was some pretty decent sex that kept the loneliness and ghosts at bay. But only temporarily.

What all these men had in common was that they each, in their own way, taught me about myself. They helped me refine the characteristics and qualities I desired in a future life partner, but more importantly, they helped me refine my opinion of myself. I learned to appreciate myself and expect to be respected by others. I deserved no less than that. I hoped to discover the new love my life. Instead of finding a soul mate in them, I found a soul mate in myself.

When I started really seeing the men I was dating and not idealizing them, I began to see the rest of the relationships in my life with improved clarity and a lot more honesty. This new level of honesty allowed me to really understand who I am in relation to all the others in my life; it allowed me to see myself for who I actually am.

Seeing others as they are was a gift, because I learned to turn this new mirror on myself, I got to know me in a whole new way.

For the first time, I began to truly see myself for the exceptional woman I am and to appreciate my talents and gifts. I learned that my intelligence is deep and varied; I can converse on a wide variety of subjects. I am fun, silly, adventurous, wild, loyal, and loving. I surrendered my questions and uncertainty to the universe and trusted that the answers would come when they are supposed to, when I was ready. I learned that I am the jackpot, and I had won big!

The thing that I finally learned was that I had my focus wrong for all those years. I think that most women do. We are raised, culturally indoctrinated, to think we must impress the guy with our good looks, sexiness, maybe other attributes like humor, intelligence, cooking ability, ability to earn an income. Whatever. But the idea is that we were supposed to impress him. Get him to like us. To do this, we inevitably change who we are, what we like, what we think is funny, etc. To attract him, we lose ourselves.

It was my grandmother's advice to me. She told me it was important as women to make ourselves like what our man likes. She told me that she never liked football or golf or *The Three Stooges*, but she pretended to like them because my grandfather liked them. She had pretended to like things for over fifty years, so her husband never knew that she didn't like them. In her generation, I think it was part of the game to get a husband. I was starting to see it all as a big lie.

In playing this get-a-husband game, by focusing on the question of whether he liked me, I distracted myself from the bigger question. Do I like him? Am I impressed by him? On a more personal note, can I be myself with him? Can I tell my stupid jokes, make silly voices to my cats, and cry in front of him without his bolting? Can I be completely me? One hundred percent my own adorably quirky self? Could I even be the me who hates football and forgets that most sports exist? Would I feel that I belong with him or just fit in with whatever he wants?

I began to see that while we pretend to be someone we are not in order to be the person we think the other person will love, we are really lying. Lying to them about who we are, the person they are in love with is a phantom and does not really exist. But more importantly, we are lying to ourselves about who we really are. We feel ashamed of who we really are because we are afraid. We are hiding our true selves away because, somehow, we feel that she, the real person we are, isn't good enough to be loved in return. So, it's a double betrayal that causes resentment and pain. There is nothing good about that. I wasn't going to do that anymore.

I was one hundred percent unabashedly and unapologetically me and was going to do my level best to always lead with that knowledge.

CHAPTER 37
THE FOUR-BY-FOUR
TO MY HEAD

"Mistakes are part of the dues one pays for a full life."

—Sophia Loren

After all this soul searching, a lot of journaling, conversations with my acupuncturist, and lots of sessions with my therapist, I began to figure some stuff out and I was high on life! With all my recent epiphanies, I thought I'd finally learned the secret to finding happiness.

Then I met Aaron online. We lived in the same town. He was a few years younger, had a master's degree in psychology, and worked in a local hospital. We talked for hours on the phone, quickly grew very comfortable talking to one another and both opened up easily about our pasts, and although he didn't meet all my criteria (remember the list), we decided to meet. We chose a local Italian restaurant to meet.

It was a Friday night, and the place was crowded. Wall to wall people. I walked past the bar that was very loud, crowds three people deep trying to get the bartenders' attention. A *maître'd* offered to help me find Aaron's table in the back, away from all the noise of the bar. I saw him. He looked just like his picture online, and as he stood up to greet me, I felt like we fell in love the moment our eyes locked. He smiled a smile that could light up Times Square, reached out a hand for mine and pulled me in toward him, and kissed me on the left cheek. He was warm, about a half a head taller than me and smelled great, like sandalwood and cinnamon.

Throughout the whole meal and a few too many drinks, he shyly smiled at me, held my hand across the table as we talked easily and openly for hours. We were comfortable with and wildly attracted to each other. He wasn't my usual physical type and had very trim facial hair, but I had long ago abandoned any real thoughts of type long ago. We quickly fell into pace with one another. Our working hours were compatible, and we spent a lot of time together.

Dating became serious right away, and we didn't want to see anyone else. He was a guitar player, and since I do a little singing now and then, we talked about starting a two-person musical ensemble. That was fun to dream about. We'd sing together to his guitar playing, which was a powerful aphrodisiac. Sex was raw, passionate, and powerful. He was not shy about what he liked and made me feel like the sexiest woman alive. This was fireworks for us both. The energy between us was palpable and magnetic.

As an educated, levelheaded woman, who, despite being a bit of a romantic, is very pragmatic and logical, I spent my entire dating life, before my marriage and after my divorce, being open but skeptical about dating. In my forties, I had just learned this great lesson about myself and my worth and told myself that this relationship was going to be different. I was so happy with Aaron and felt that I was being one hundred percent myself with him. I was me. I wasn't planning what I would say or measuring out how I was going to word something to gauge his reaction. I was just me. This was great. I thought he felt the same way.

I was dead wrong.

Sometimes, the universe steps in to show us we have no idea what we are talking about. The universe was testing me big time. Something significant was going on here. We both knew it. But we both knew different things. He saw me as the perfect prey. Someone to easily gaslight.

I was blindsided.

I thought that this was unlike anything I had ever experienced, but it was exactly like everything else I had experienced. Aaron felt like home to me because he was a charming narcissist, just like all the previous narcissists in my life. I was used to being charmed and gaslighted, so being charmed and gaslighted by him was very familiar and felt like home. I thought it was *bashert*, as my Jewish grandmother would say, but it was a disaster.

Let's face it, though. We live in the moment and try to be mindful of our happiness and joy. Instead of being cautious and taking my time to get to know him, I jumped in with both feet and swam in the phantom joy, love, and passion. Without using my brain and remembering my hard-won lessons, boundaries and pride in myself. I threw my own dating rules into the ocean. We were only together for about six intoxicating and toxic weeks before I came to my senses. He used his master's in psychology and his charming narcissism to get me to lend him thousands of dollars toward launching his first jazz fusion album, convinced me to ditch plans with friends, and tried to muscle in on Thanksgiving with my family and children by emotionally manipulating me and nearly convincing me that I was paranoid and anxious all the time. In actuality, I was anxious only around him, and not paranoid. I was anxious because he was growing more controlling and unpredictable by the day. He was paranoid of losing me but couldn't see past his own needs to grasp that. He wanted what he wanted and really wasn't all that interested in my perspective or my needs. I don't know how to explain how subtle it all was—the slow, slippery slope from charming, caring man to controlling, selfish liar. The subtlety is part of the trick—if you're reeled into dysfunction slowly, you don't recognize it as it happens and are less able to extricate yourself easily. With so many narcissists, this is the playbook: Once they have you, they have you.

Part of me was seeing through his bullshit but was being charmed back into the dark over and over. I was being manipulated. I always tried to keep the men I dated away from my kids, but for some reason, my kids met him briefly one day and hated him on sight. I was so far in the dark that I couldn't understand why. Because of this disaster, from then on, my kids insisted that I trust their intuition with respect to prospective dates. They were older now and their opinions mattered to me (and still do).

At this point in this thing with Aaron, my daughter and I got violently ill with food poisoning and were quarantined for days with such virulent disgustingness that forced me to throw all the bathroom rugs in the garbage, along with a set of bedsheets. I sent my son to stay with his father since he was not infected. We slept on and off, watched a lot of TV, hardly ate anything, and made very frequent trips to the bathroom. We took very good care of each other. Thank goodness for grocery delivery services because I was able to keep us stocked up in ginger ale and saltines.

During this week, Aaron had selfish needs that he couldn't see past. He called me and learned that we were sick, and instead of offering to help us in some way, he tried to get me to tend to his needs. He kept asking me to come over, not hearing me at all when I said we were terribly ill. When I refused to comply with his unreasonable demands, he screamed at me over the phone and called me a "selfish bitch." I hung up on him.

Then he showed up at my house, and I refused to answer the door. He kept knocking and shouting to get me to let him in, but my daughter and I were sick, and he crossed the line by screaming at me over the phone. I was done. My daughter was in her room, visibly upset by Aaron's off-the-hook behavior. I was in my bedroom ignoring him and talking on the phone with a friend, about what was going on. Kurt was calm and reassuring and he was trying to get me to just call the police to come deal with Aaron.

For more than a half-hour, Aaron wouldn't leave and kept knocking on my front door, shouting, and texting me. I thought we were safe inside our home, although he was freaking us out quite a bit. I should have called the police. I know this now. At the time, I didn't think we were in any danger, but a man that angry and that selfish could be capable of anything. The light had finally been turned on, and I suddenly saw him for the troll he was. That was that. I never saw him again. I blocked him quickly from every method of contact. This was one of the very few moments in our home when Simone felt unsafe and was very scared. Until recently, I didn't know how much this affected her and for my part in welcoming this creep into my life, our lives, I am very sorry.

Reflecting on this in therapy, I decided that this business with Aaron was a test of my newly constructed dating rules and my resolve to put myself first. The universe was teaching me that same lesson again. This time it was crystal clear.

I told my therapist that this was one last four-by-four to the head just to make sure that I learned the lesson and would never be gaslighted again.

During this period, I found a very important and unexpected friendship in Kurt, a former student, who helped me during the Aaron incident and also encouraged me to keep my standards high but to keep looking for love. I gave him the same kinds of pep talks about his life as we spent time on the phone or texting about life. Kurt was a student of mine his senior year in high school many years prior and was a pain in my ass at the time. He took nothing seriously except fooling around with his boys in class. I had had both of Kurt's older sisters and knew their family a bit, and I also knew that Kurt was a very smart young man with a huge amount of potential, but he didn't want to know anything about that at the time. He gave me grief no matter what I tried to say to him to motivate a turnaround.

After he started college, he sought me out at school to apologize to me for acting like an ass in class. He said that he finally heard what I had said to him eight months prior and he wanted to thank me for not giving up on him. I was very surprised by this confession and gratitude. This kind of thing does not usually happen. Kids might see the light later on, but their epiphany is private and not shared with their former teacher. Kurt was different. He's special, and we developed a genuine friendship. Every now and then, one of us will message the other to see what's going on to stay in touch. I think during this time in my life, he was my lifeline, along with a few of my primary friends.

The Alchemist, by Paulo Coelho, is an allegory for life that moved me from my first read, and it is a book I revisit at least once a year. I prefer listening to the audiobook version, which is performed by Jeremy Irons, whose majestic and haunting voice increases the mystical quality of the book. The main character's quest for his own personal truth is one that I relate to deeply. He travels on his quest for the treasure he seeks and along the way meets people who teach him things that he needs to learn to fulfill his quest and live according to his personal truth. This seems to be my life, and the lives of many others, as I navigate the relationships and challenges, seeking to learn about my inner life and my feelings and the world around me, which is why this is a universal allegory and so widely read and acclaimed.

CHAPTER 38
CHOOSING MY PERSON WISELY

"I don't have to chase extraordinary moments to find happiness – it's right in front of me if I'm paying attention and practicing gratitude."

—Brené Brown

My friend Michael and I first met in January 1987 and were fast friends from SUNY Geneseo through The Office (the name we gave to our friend group). We shared lots of the same friends. My first semester as a freshman, he had taken off to work and make money to pay for more college semesters, and while he was gone, I became friends with the group encompassing all of his friends. So, I was in sitting in one of the dorms with the Office group when Michael arrived on campus for the spring semester. We got along right away, and he asked me out a few hours later—the night we met. I was in a relationship with Mark (who had failed out for the first time and was home), so I declined. Happily, we remained friends, and although we got close to dating each other once, it didn't happen.

Time went on. We each got married, attended each other's weddings, and remained friends, but as the children were all born and we were raising our families, we drifted apart. With the help of a great group of college friends, and then social media, we were able to reconnect, stay in touch and remain loosely in each other's lives. We saw each other at Office gatherings every other year, for a time, and for a little while I was friends with his ex-wife, whom I knew from Geneseo as well. She and I got together with our children a few times, and she gave me a box of her son, Thomas's, baby clothes that Ethan wore when he was a baby. That friendship didn't last, as we had very little in common.

Years later, we had both gotten divorced and were dating other people and were never single at the same time. Despite the fact that we both lived on Long Island, we didn't see each other for quite a few years.

Being a natural researcher, always on a quest for answers and enlightenment, I had been reading *Elephant Journal* for a long while and found so many voices I recognized and ideas that lifted my spirits. Some months before, I decided to write a few pieces myself. I published them on *Elephant Journal* and shared them throughout my Facebook community.

Since Facebook allowed Michael and I to regain some of our friendship online and grow a little closer, we shared a lot about our lives, commiserating with each other along the way. He read all my *Elephant Journal* pieces, sent me encouraging words and was starting to feel more for me than just friendship. He secretly wanted to be in a relationship with me but didn't say anything specific yet. I was too dense to get his very subtle hints. We had a long conversation via Facebook Messenger, in early February 2014, in which Michael suggested that we go to the movies together. He was so unassuming and casual about it that I didn't know that he was suggesting we go on a date. I thought he was just saying we should hang out as friends. For some reason, it didn't ever happen. I don't know why. It's one of life's mysteries.

I published *Choosing Our People Wisely* on *Elephant Journal* on January 1, 2015, and Michael read it. The line that resonated with him was "Lost in the fog, I was an airplane endlessly circling an airport without permission to land. I wanted to be in my world, not hovering over it." It connected with him so much that he changed his Facebook cover photo to be an airport runway. If I was an airplane with nowhere to land, he wanted to be where I landed. (He's very romantic!) He wanted me to have a much larger role in his life, but for some reason he didn't say anything directly to me. Only much later, when we were falling in love, did he reveal the truth behind the airport runway cover photo. I had previously thought it has something to do with the videogames he liked to play.

I love Halloween and costume parties. In October 2015, I hosted my annual Halloween party. I was very newly dating Aaron at this time, and we decided to go as a zombie bride and groom. I had a great time slashing my wedding gown (from my wedding to Sam), throwing red paint at it and dragging it on the ground to get it dirty. Trashing that dress and converting it into a zombie bride costume was one of my most cathartic, creative projects. I invited Michael to the party, along with a lot of friends from the area—high school friends with spouses, friends from work, from choir, and from town. It was a great blend of people. Michael came to the party hoping to start moving our friendship much more into the relationship zone but was surprised and disheartened to see me with Aaron. By the week before Thanksgiving, the mess with Aaron was over.

That November, the night before Thanksgiving, I was lying in bed at 3 a.m. reading *Elephant Journal* on my phone, crying in despair and loneliness. There was so much that was great about my life. I had two great kids, we were all healthy,

I had a great job that I loved, I owned my own home. But I was lonely. I wanted real love in my life. I was angry at myself for falling into Aaron's trap and all too quickly abandoning my own rules.

I was at another crossroads.

My mother had died two years before, and I routinely talked aloud to her, asking for guidance and wisdom. I asked my mother for help—*help me find my true love.* Just then, I came upon an article about soulmates. It said that when you reach a certain age, you've probably already met your soulmate, and then it continued to list the qualities of this soulmate. The only person in my life who fit this description was Michael. I stopped crying, and before I could talk myself out of it—because what you dare to do at 3 a.m. you might not dare to do at noon—I sent Michael the article through Facebook Messenger. I asked him to read it and if he felt that this could be us, would he please let me take him to dinner to explore it?

Unbeknownst to me, Michael, who is more religious than I, went to bed that very night, praying for a woman exactly like me to come into his life, bring him love, and ease his loneliness. So, when he woke up on Thanksgiving morning to my Facebook message, he was ecstatically shocked! He thought that he never had a prayer answered so literally and so quickly in his life. He sent me a message right away saying he was definitely interested and felt the same way. We talked later that night after all the holiday and family stuff was over, and we talked for hours.

We went out on our first date in early December. I was nervous. Michael was picking me up at my house, and we were going to go to dinner and a movie. When he arrived, I asked him inside, we sat on the couch and chatted for a few minutes, and although we were friends for almost thirty years, it was awkward. I was nervous, and the air was charged with hopefulness and excitement. When we stood up to get our coats on to leave, he pulled me toward him, said, "I've waited a long time to do this," and then he kissed me. It was a forceful, passionate kiss.

It took my breath away.

Dinner was at an Italian place somewhere—I really have only vague memories about the meal because I was so caught up in our conversation, but I do know that I was nervous. After we'd been friends for so long, why would the fact that this was a date be a big deal at all? It didn't make sense to me. I knew him well; he's a genuinely kind and sweet man. Why would I be nervous? I had no idea, but I could tell that I was. We talked constantly, and I was annoyed by each of the interruptions from the wait staff because, although they were perfectly lovely and just doing their jobs, I didn't want our flow disturbed. We decided to go back to my house and watch a movie in my living room since our timing was off for the movie theater.

Somehow, we decided on *Stranger Than Fiction*, which I had already seen and loved. Maybe our date seemed stranger than fiction to me. I made us tea, and we settled in on my couch. During our conversation, Michael was talking about things we could do together in the spring and summer. For some reason, this kind of freaked me out. It was, after all, only our first date. Things were moving quickly, but you can't take it slowly with a man you've known for twenty-nine years, especially after you've directly stated you think that he is your soulmate. I'm a crazy person sometimes. We watched the movie holding hands and snuggling a bit on the couch. Then, afterward, he kissed me and went home.

Over the next few days we continued to talk, text, and message each other throughout the day and night, at all sorts of weird hours. Our conversations were warm and fluid, but I had cold feet. Part of me was freaking out. This was going to be a very serious relationship right from the very beginning, and the intensity of it threw me off. I hate to admit that, but it's true, and I told Michael this. Honesty was my new policy. If this relationship, or any, was going to work, I mean really work, then I had to be courageous and allow myself to be my one hundred percent honest, vulnerable self all the time.

Brené Brown says being vulnerable is brave, and I needed to be brave.

I told Michael that I was feeling weird, awkward, scared and although I wanted to be with him, I needed to take it much more slowly. This upset him. He was one hundred percent in. All in. I was, uncharacteristically, holding back. I think that so many relationships had gone wrong, completely wrong, disappointingly, devastatingly sour so many times that I was gun-shy. I didn't want to jump into this too hastily, not look around myself and see what was really going on. I needed time. Michael didn't take this well. I felt terrible, but the truth is the truth. I needed to slow down. He said he needed to step back and put his guard back up if I was gun-shy. I was afraid that things might stall before they fully started up.

A few weeks went by, and Christmas came and went. He declined my invitation to my New Year's Eve party. I felt like he should be there, but he said that if he couldn't come as my boyfriend, he didn't want to come. I get that. The party was pretty crappy anyway. I felt off, and I didn't know why.

On January 24th, 2016, my best friend, Tim, was turning fifty and I wanted to throw him a party. We were expecting more than twenty of Tim's closest friends, so of course we invited Michael. We had all been friends since the mid-1980s when we met at SUNY Geneseo. The week before the party, I called Michael to confirm that he was coming to Tim's party and he said that he would be there, of course.

It felt so wonderful to talk to him again. It had only been a couple of weeks since we had spoken, but something stirred differently in me.

That same day, Michael's daughter, Marie, whom I hadn't seen since she was nine, friend-requested me through Facebook. I accepted. She was divorced and had four children, but other than that I knew nothing about her. Acting as her father's PR agent, she messaged me that he is the best man she had ever known and that he would make the best boyfriend because he is so kind, loving and generous. Before long, she invited me to her oldest son's *Dr. Who*-themed eighth-birthday party, which was the last weekend in January. While I was messaging with her, I texted Michael and asked him if I should say yes since it was his grandson's birthday at his house. Michael lived with his son, Thomas, and with Marie and her four kids. I didn't want to accept the invitation if he would rather I didn't, but he loved the idea of my going.

During the six days prior to Tim's party, we spent the about five or six hours on the phone every single night, and we are not long-phone-conversation type people. He was working the night shift as foreman on his job, and although I should have been sleeping, I stayed up to talk to him and text with him. Those were the greatest conversations. He was at work on a low-key job with a lot of privacy and I was lying in the dark cozy in my bed. It was easy to be totally honest and lay all my vulnerabilities bare.

Each night, we learned that we had more and more in common. Despite very different upbringings and childhoods, quite a bit of the trauma was the same. We had many shared experiences, and because of this, we had a lot that connected us and quite a bit that seemed to knit us together. We talked about everything: our childhoods, school, our first marriages, dating in our forties, raising children, sex, politics, our view of the world. Conversation grew more intimate and more sensitive as the days passed, and my feelings for him deepened and grew more significant. By the time Friday night arrived, I knew I was in love with him.

Early Saturday morning the 24th of January, we had a snowstorm. It was not terrible, but the party I created with silver and teal balloons and catered food for twenty-four was curtailed. Because of the snow, everyone canceled. I was crushed because I wanted to make a fuss over Tim's fiftieth birthday. It wound up just Tim, Michael, and me. The three of us had a lovely time laughing and trying to eat and drink provisions for twenty. It was a very fun evening. I was sorry that no one else showed up for Tim, but we were there, and we love him. Tim went home around midnight, giving me his thumbs up and a wink, and Michael, who had also arrived early to help me go on last minute errands and set up, helped me clean up. Then, as we kissed, we moved toward my bedroom.

After years of physically and emotionally disappointing relationships, I needed to know that we had chemistry and physical connection. I was sure about intellectual and spiritual, but for a long successful relationship, this had to be in place, too. We went into my bedroom full of anxious expectation and confirmed we had physical chemistry. Big time! My reaction was, "Grandpa's got game!" We were so attracted to each other, and it was a truly beautiful thing: loving, passionate, and sensual. After we made love, I asked him to look at me (his eyes were closed), and I told him I love him. I wasn't nervous because it was absolutely right.

He smiled a smile that could melt the polar ice caps and told me he loved me, too.

And that was it for us both. We knew. We fell in love. Big Love! Huge hearts and flowers love! Neither of us had ever been happier. We had similar experiences akin to emotional abuse, failed marriages, two children, a love for movies and quirky "dad" jokes and puns. More importantly, though, life had taught us both to lead with kindness, empathy, and a good heart. We fit together perfectly, and where we might have anticipated problems, there were none.

On January 24, 2016, we officially stated in no uncertain terms that we loved each other—almost exactly twenty-nine years to the day after we first met, which was Saturday night before classes started for the spring semester of 1987 at SUNY Geneseo. We were inseparable. His kids and grandkids welcomed me from the outset, and after a while, my kids accepted and welcomed Michael. They knew I had had some unsuccessful relationships, and although they only met Stuart and Aaron, they were nervous about a new man. After all, Michael has been my friend, not theirs. They didn't really know him.

At the end of January, Michael's daughter, Marie, was hosting her son's eighth birthday party. I went the day before to help her set up even though I hadn't seen her since she was nine years old. I knew she needed the help, and this would give us the opportunity to get to know each other alone and I wanted to get to know her and her brother. She was and is lovely, kind, sweet, and affectionate, and she fiercely loves her father and her children. I fell in love with her as another daughter that day, and she said that she loved having a mother figure in her life who was a good listener, logical, compassionate, and kind. We bonded, big time.

At the party the next day, I got to meet all the kids and spend time with Thomas and see Michael in his own element. They all welcomed me with open arms, and I easily connected with them all. It was cute to see how the grandchildren figured out who I was. His middle grandson, also named Michael, walked over to me while I was playing Legos with his little brother, Logan, and asked, "Why are you here at this party?"

"I'm your papi's girlfriend," I replied.

"What?!" he asked, turning red in the face with embarrassment and giggles. "Papi has a girlfriend?"

That was a funny moment. Before long, they were all climbing all over me. We played games, sang songs, and read books. I was Marci, but also well on my way to being Mimi.

My own children were going to be a bit more of a tough sell. They had seen too much drama and heartache from the two men I dated whom they had met, and despite the fact that they only met two of them, they still saw too much. They were both protective of me, not wanting me to get hurt anymore, and were also protective of themselves because it's tough seeing mom with people you don't like and being powerless to do anything about it. Just because I knew what Michael and I had was drastically different from everything else before it, it didn't mean my kids knew that. I had to give them time.

I took Michael out for his fiftieth birthday a couple of weeks later in February. We went to my favorite Italian restaurant, Mannino's, and we ate very well. The conversation was easy and comfortable, and we both enjoyed every detail. He had a clam appetizer and veal marsala; I had their pear salad that I love and a lovely broiled grouper. Then came dessert, some rich French hot cocoa and great cookies. (Thank goodness for my journal entry or I would have never remembered what we ate—I can't remember what I ate last night.) When the check arrived, he was shocked that I was actually paying for dinner. In his past, he said that when others wanted to take him out for his birthday dinner, he was still expected to pay. After dinner, we parked up by the Nissequogue River to listen to romantic music and make out in the car like two lovestruck teenagers. I made a playlist for him, which was playing in the background the whole time. Ella Fitzgerald's *Always* came on, and I started singing it to him, softly, seductively while our faces were still inches apart. It was a beautiful and perfect moment. We both sang to each other. Pure romance. A screen play couldn't have been more well written than this moment.

Then an old man whose house we were parked in front of came out to ask why we were parked there. Michael said we were watching the submarine races, and the man looked a little embarrassed and went back inside his house. It was a funny way to end a perfect night.

In February 2016, we went to Florida to see my dad and stepmom. Michael said wanted to introduce himself to my father and allow him to "meet the man who loves his daughter and wants to take care of her forever." Those were his words and his reasoning for going to see my father on our vacation. He's such a mensch! It was a great trip. We all got along well. Michael and I were inseparable.

The *New York Times* published a feature in the Fashion and Style section called *The 36 Questions That Lead to Love*, by Daniel Jones. Michael and I wanted to see if these questions would deepen our connection. While at a Mexican restaurant in Florida, and all through that first vacation together, we continued to ask and answer all of the thirty-six questions, which morphed into much larger discussions of a very wide range of topics. We talked deeply, probing into our own hearts, and laughed until we cried. It was perfect. We had a great time, and I knew that I was in the right place and that I had a man who loves me for me.

At first, we saw each other only when my kids were with their father or had something else going on that didn't involve me. Then, slowly, Michael started to come over to our house for dinner or attend the kids' functions. He came with me and helped out at Ethan's Eagle Scout bake sale fundraiser. He helped me set up for the Eagle Scout ceremony and the small celebration afterward. He helped me chaperone Simone's trip into New York City to see Fall Out Boy with her friends. While they were in the concert, Michael and I saw a movie nearby and had dessert in a coffee shop across the street from Madison Square Garden. He helped us move Ethan into his dorm at UVM. The kids watched as he taught my father to use some features on his iPhone and helped my father fix the water heater in the basement of the house in Connecticut.

To my children, and my family, he was dependable, always around, the sweet guy on the sideline, never intrusive but always present, kind, helpful, and fun. He let them get to know him slowly, on their terms. On March 15, 2016, I wrote in my journal, "They are really holding back and only interacting with him on a very minimal level. Trying to dislike him, but they can't. He's just a nice man."

He didn't start to spend the night with me at my house when they were home until after we were on a very serious path, when it was obvious that he would be moving in soon anyway. When he stayed over and spent time here with us, we ate dinner as a family and had lively conversations. It was cozy, normal, and safe. Everyone was included and belonged.

We all fit together nicely.

By late spring, we decided to introduce all the kids to each other. We always spent First Seder of Passover with my dad's side of the family, but we realized how great it would be to make second Seder at home and have all ten of us together: all our children and grandchildren. I was excited for them all to meet, and I hoped the grandkids were on decent behavior and things went well so they all got along.

In my journal I wrote,

It's Sunday, April 24th—I got up early to put up the brisket in the slow cooker and started the rest of the meal. I made everything myself—matzoh ball soup, brisket, green beans with almonds. Simone made her garlic mashed potatoes. There were some cookies and chocolate for dessert. I cleaned the house and set the table. Around four in the afternoon, Marie and the four nuggets arrived. Thomas arrived shortly after. Michael and I introduced them all to Simone. Then Ethan came home from his job as a cater waiter dressed in his black tuxedo and he met everyone. The nuggets were well behaved and played in the basement with Simone's and Ethan's toys and on the trampoline in the back yard.

We had a lovely Seder. Everyone took part in the readings from the new Haggadah I found online. The food was great. Seder was ideal. Having all our kids together and being the ten of us was amazing. Michael and I were very happy. After the Seder, Melody found the afikomen. After dessert, Marie took the kids home. Thomas stayed and the five of us played Cards Against Humanity. We had a blast. Then all the kids went their separate ways and did their schoolwork. Mike and I went to bed and watched Orphan Black.

It couldn't have gone better. Everyone got along. Marie and Simone were like the sisters they always wanted to have. Thomas and Ethan were polite and comfortable. The nuggety grandkids were devilishly cute and precociously awesome. I had the big family I had always longed for, and I didn't have to give birth to two of them. Bonus!

A few days after the big family Seder, I got a text from Thomas. It suddenly seemed that I have another loving, communicative son. He asked me when I was coming over to the house where he lived with his sister, her kids and Michael, which was about a forty-five-minute drive from my house. This was our exchange.

"I'm probably not going to be there until Sunday. But am totally available to talk, FaceTime, text, whatever you want just about any time you want/need. I'm in your corner-always!!" I said.

"Okay. Thanks," Thomas replied.

"I love you! You know I'm around for you, even if I'm in Kings Park," I said.

"Love you, too. It's a strange feeling to have a mother figure in my corner like that, not gonna lie. Strange in a good way," he said.

"Well get used to it!" I replied, "I'm not going anywhere. You're my family now and I'm never letting you go!!"

I was really falling in love the stepmom and step-grandma thing. I love being included in all the group texts about family goings-on. During this late spring and summer, as Michael and I fell more deeply in love, we all, as a family, got to know one another better. Whenever I went to their house, I got cuddles and hellos from all the nuggets, and big hugs from Marie, who has taken to calling me Mama. I love that.

I wrote, "Michael and I were building the family we always yearned for and settled into the foundation of our deeply growing love."

I continued to write in my journal: "While I was telling him about feeling divided between my parents as a teenager and feeling homeless after their divorce was final, he told me that I'm always his first thought every day and last thought every night. That I will never be his afterthought and he kept telling me how much he loves me. He said some of the sweetest things that I've ever heard. This man really loves me. He really does. Exactly the way I need to be loved and I've never felt safer, more loved, cared for, protected, sought, defended, nurtured, than ever before in my entire life. I find such comfort being with Michael. He's so flexible, down to earth, easy, unflappable. Nothing bothers him. He just goes with the flow. Understands my kids. Understands me. Loves me so much and I feel so wonderful with him. Really safe to be me. Really safe. I want to marry this man and be by his side every day of my life. I know him. I know who he is, and I love him with all that I am and all of my heart. Michael told me that he always feels deeply loved by me and for that I am glad. I always feel loved by him."

My own words were the absolute truth about our feelings.

A couple months went by. We had been talking on and off about being together forever, getting married at some point, growing old together. I knew it was inevitable, but truthfully, we aren't getting younger. At this point, I was forty-eight and he was fifty. Since we had met in 1987, we had spent twenty-nine years not being together. There was no guarantee of how much time we have in life. After all, my mother was dead at sixty-nine.

I didn't want to waste another second, so I decided that I would propose to him. We had been watching the movie *Definitely, Maybe*, with Ryan Reynolds. It's a charming romantic comedy where Reynolds plays a divorcing dad who plays this romantic mystery game with his daughter, who is curious about how relationships work and fall apart. He told her about the women he dated after college. She had to listen and try figure out which one of them wound up being her mother. He changed all the names for the stories. It was very cute. By the end of the movie, we were goofing around and being silly, and Michael said that he proposed to two women in his life and if he was to get married again, he wanted to be the one who was proposed to. He was kidding, but I was inspired. I just needed my own plan. How was I going to do it? I researched it, of course. What did women do? A ring? A watch? An elaborate proposal or a simple one?

For a few days, we had been enjoying a silly ongoing conversation about advertising our love on screens all over the country. I thought, I can do that. I can make something to put on every screen in the United States—like the big screens in Times Square or at least on his phone. I planned it all out.

I spent a week making him a video slideshow proposal assembled out of photos of us together with text overlays of what I wanted to say to him. I set it to the song *Always*, by Ella Fitzgerald, which was the song I sang to him on his fiftieth birthday in February. It took me several hours to get the timing right, and then I uploaded it to YouTube. The plan was to take him out to dinner at The Athenian Greek Taverna, which is one of our favorite restaurants. After we ate, I was going to give him earbuds and text him the link to the video, but it was too crowded in the restaurant. He's an emotional crier like I am, so I rethought my plan and decided it would be better in private, maybe watching the late sunset on the river. After dinner, we drove to the Nissequogue river, where we had gone on his birthday, to watch the sunset. It was later than I thought, and we mostly missed the sunset and had bad cell service, so the video didn't load. Foiled again!

I abandoned that plan and decided to do it at home. We went home to my house and got into bed to watch a movie or get romantic, but instead of putting on a movie or music, I went to YouTube. Michael asked what I was looking for, and I told I made him something. He thought it was just a cutesy thing, which would make him cry nonetheless, but as he watched, he realized it was a proposal. We were cuddling on the bed as he watched and cried, and we kissed through tears, and he said, "Yes, of course I will marry you!" Then I presented him with the fancy Bulova watch he had been eyeing months ago. It was my engagement gift to him, figuring a ring would be strange. He was shocked that I remembered the exact watch he was looking at, but I pay attention. On the back of the watch, I had inscribed, "Since always. Until forever. My love for you transcends time." (I assumed we would get me a ring at some point, which we did—a lovely round sapphire-and-diamond engagement ring with matching wedding band.)

Now we were engaged and over the moon about it!

I had gotten his kids' blessings before asking him, so they knew and were thrilled. My daughter, Simone, was ecstatic and loves Mike. My son, Ethan, spends a lot of time at his father's and was thus removed a bit, likes him and was happy for us, too.

Everyone was happy for us. Some were taken aback with my non-traditional proposal, but to us, it was perfect. I've learned that I am quite a non-traditional woman with a lot of things. So, this fit me. I figured it was better to actively choose my life and ask for what I want than to passively sit around waiting to be chosen on someone else's schedule. I think it's a good example for our daughters as well. (And I started all this by asking him out the previous November.)

Michael and I started telling everyone else. His brother and sister-in-law were ecstatic. His mother was happy but guarded. I needed to tell my father and that side of the family—my stepsisters and stepmom. So, I called them in Connecticut and got my dad on the phone. I said that I had something important to tell him, and with only a slight pause, I blurted it out: "Michael and I are engaged!" My dad was thrilled. Big shouts and congratulations. Then the conversation took a turn. Here is how it went.

"How did Michael propose?" dad asked excitedly.

"He didn't," I proudly responded, "I proposed to him."

After a long silence, "Oh…really?" His judgmental silence was deafening.

"Yes, I proposed to him. It's 2016. I know what I want, so I asked him. He said yes!" I said defending myself.

Dad was skeptical and asked, "Is this a real engagement? Can I tell people?"

I was a little exasperated and couldn't understand why this was difficult for him to grasp. "Yes, it's real! You can tell everyone! We are telling everyone."

"Really, are you sure?" he asked again.

I was mildly annoyed but continued to explain. I said, "Dad, look at it this way. Isn't it a great thing you raised a daughter who knows her own mind and once she figured out what she wanted, she went out and got it for herself? Isn't it better that I asked for the love I want in my life instead of just passively waiting for it to happen?"

He paused, thinking about this and said, "Well, yeah. I guess so." I could tell he was still processing this … "Would Michael have asked you eventually?"

"Yes, of course. He was going to ask me next April, but I didn't want to wait that long," I replied. "We've known each other over twenty-nine years. There aren't going to be any big surprises. This is what we both want."

At this point, he acquiesced and said he was happy for us. My dad genuinely likes Michael, and over the last four years, has gotten to know him better and is very happy that I'm settled and happy. For his generation, my proposal was almost too non-traditional, but our happy marriage, in which his daughter is taken care of and loved, gives him less to worry about as he goes through the rest of his life.

Chapter 39
Off to Lalaland

2016 was a very busy and pivotal year. Ethan graduated high school, became an Eagle Scout, I fell in love and proposed to Michael, Simone was very busy in school, I was working my three jobs and we were about to see everything change – change for the better – but change, nonetheless. During this whirlwind year, with everything going on, I wrote this in my journal:

> *Ethan and I talked about physics, and he told me about his project and research. We ordered some of the supplies that he needs for this experiment and had some nice time together. At one point he actually said that he hadn't hugged me enough recently and then hugged me tightly. I was almost in tears. He's so tall now that he can rest his chin on the top of my head.*

After this crazy year, we needed a trip to recharge and celebrate and a chance to be just the three of us one more time before my wedding. I knew that my marriage to Michael was going to be a big shift for the three of us, and with Ethan's graduation and impending departure for college, we had even more change ahead. A trip would be the perfect thing. I gave Ethan the choice of any destination in the continental U.S., and he chose Los Angeles. The kids and I took a trip, by ourselves, in the beginning of August. We left on August 2nd, flew to LAX, and made our way to our hotel, The Westin Bonaventure. The hotel was great. It has lots of floors of restaurants, shopping, and cute seating areas. There are lots of movie memorabilia from famous movies they loved, which the kids found fascinating. Our room was bright and clean, not so big, but we managed. The shiny chrome hotel had lots of poke-stops as well, as this was during the height of the Pokémon Go phenomenon, so we collected Pokémon characters everywhere.

Our first morning in the hotel, Ethan woke up and didn't know where he was. Simone and I were still sleeping in our bed, and in the dark haze of his brain, he asked himself, "Who the hell are those people?" Then he realized where he was and that *those people* were his mom and sister. This became the running joke throughout the trip.

In the week we were there, we walked thousands of steps, explored many corners of L.A.: Venice Beach, Santa Monica Pier, La Brea Tar Pits and the outdoor installations of the Los Angeles Museum of Art, took a long bus tour of Hollywood, West Hollywood, Beverly Hills, etc. We did lots of typical touristy sightseeing and eating and seemed to always be searching for bathrooms, bottles of water, and places to charge our phones. We played Pokémon Go everywhere we went, bought souvenirs, enjoyed each other's company, and had a lot of laughs.

One of my favorite parts of the trip was the Paramount Studios tour during which I stood on the set of *Grace and Frankie*, gently touching the furniture and props on the set and imagining Jane Fonda and Lily Tomlin walking and acting in that exact spot. I've always loved them as feminist pioneers and actresses. Simone, who also loved the show, stole a rock for me from the outside porch section of the set. I had almost taken Jane Fonda's drug store sunglasses but put them down. I'm not the type to steal anything, and I didn't want the page, who was guiding the tour, to get in trouble. I had a script from the show in my hand and read a part of an episode from Season 3. Cool beans. I was starstruck by all of it, and Jane and Lily weren't event there.

We ate at some great restaurants, played cards, told jokes, enjoyed each other's company. Ethan started to see me in a different way, which was what I was hoping for. In the past, he had complained to me that he thought I talk to too many people and that I'm too chatty. But I like people and talking to them, and being friendly is my way of making my way in the world. So on the trip, I did what I always do and chatted people up—wait staff, concierge, servicepeople in the hotel, strangers we met at various sites, bus drivers, tourists, shop-keepers, etc., and he noticed (and said he noticed) how people react to me, how positively people react to me. I make them all smile and happy. And I make me happy.

That recognition by him was a pivotal moment, and I felt the warm glow of being proud of myself and him for being grown-up enough to notice and sensitive enough to acknowledge it.

Early in our trip, he was silently adding up all the money I spent and was shocked by it. I told him to stop. Things are expensive. Life is pricey, and being in Los Angeles was not cheap, but his constant counting it all and tallying it up was ruining my good time. I reassured him: "I have enough money for this. I budgeted the amount I was willing to spend, and it didn't come out of real-life money or college money. It was vacation money." Eventually, he stopped adding and just allowed himself to have fun.

Everyone drives everywhere in L.A. Los Angeles is *traffic*! I thought roads around New York City were crowded and jammed with cars, but New York traffic can't compare with the L.A. area. While we navigated around, Simone handled music from her phone, Ethan was the GPS navigator and handled directions as I drove. It was a great trip, worth every penny as we got to spend all this wonderful time together. I loved it. They loved it.

We bonded and enjoyed each other. What more could a mom ask for?

At the end of the trip, we were driving to the airport to come home and I said how proud I was of all of us for doing this—deciding to go, flying across the country, making our way around a strange city, and going and doing all sorts of great things. Without missing a beat, Ethan said, "Mom, you did all those things, you made those things happen. Not us." Holy big wow! Holy. Big. Wow. My son was blowing me away! I shared the credit. I wouldn't have done it alone. I'm glad I did it with them.

Every part of my body was smiling, most especially my heart.

CHAPTER 40
YOUR MOM IS A TEACHER?

"Above all else, I want you to know that you are loved and lovable. You will learn this from my words and actions...You will learn that you are worthy of love, belonging, and joy every time you see me practice self-compassion and embrace my own imperfections. We will laugh and sing and dance and create. We will always have permission to be ourselves with each other. No matter what, you will always belong here. As you begin your whole-hearted journey, the greatest gift that I can give you is to live and love with my whole heart and to dare greatly."

—Brené Brown

Throughout the eighteen years of parenting my kids between birth and driving them to college, I loved and cherished both their childhoods, which went by in a flash. When people say it was a blur and time goes by too quickly, they are right. It's a cliché only because it's true. How can I encapsulate their childhoods? It would take a volume of books to describe every event that happened in those eighteen years, if it is even possible to do so.

I'll use my son's own words to explain our family's influence on him. Ethan said he was

"*heavily influenced by [his] family's open-mindedness and values. A top priority in [his] family...[was] an emphasis on cultivating healthy relationships and integrity which has influenced how [he structures his] life and values. It has made [him] resilient and motivated to have a good work ethic. [He has been] inspired to think critically and to pursue [his] passion to the fullest.*"

There is nothing better than this. As parents, we hope that our kids will grow up and become the best versions of themselves that we see within them. It's rare that we get confirmation of that growth in such a concrete way.

Once, a former girlfriend of my son's told me that Ethan is a favorite among his friends because of his kindness and generosity of spirit, his quick humor, and his infectious laughter. She said that she has not ever met a kinder person than Ethan. I'm tearing up as I write this now, and when Annie said this to me, I was ugly crying all over the phone. Tears and snot everywhere. It doesn't take much to make me cry.

Simone and I are best friends as well as mother and daughter and share a great deal of our inner lives, not just our outer lives, but it wasn't always that way. For better or worse, she is a blonde version of me, but spunkier. She's learned things about herself and about life in her late teens that I didn't learn until my forties. We don't look that much alike, but our thought patterns, opinions, and many character traits are quite similar. She is generous of spirit, empathic and caring, creative and quirky, and has an endless capacity to love.

As I write this, Ethan is a senior in college. Simone is a sophomore, and all the science projects we worked on together, the reading we did every day exploring novels like *Hatchett*, *Twilight*, the Percy Jackson stories, and the entire catalog of *Calvin and Hobbes*, all the movies and television shows like *Eureka*, *Friends* and *Drake and Josh*, the analyses of problems solved that were the birth and fostering of their autonomy, the thousands of shared stories, experiences, memories, have fostered a close, caring, loving, highly interesting relationship between this mother and her beloved children. They are building beautiful lives for themselves following their curiosity and passion, and I could not be happier for them or prouder. Their work ethic and curiosity for their passions is unparalleled. They never shy away from tough experiences and are constantly evolving and growing. I like to think they got these qualities from me.

We three are very close (at least I think so), and I'm very lucky and honored that they come to me with sensitive problems in their lives because they know that I will treat their problems with respect and love and help them deal with whatever it is. Nothing is off the table: relationship problems like fights with boyfriend/girlfriends, arguments between friends, drinking and smoking in peer groups, stalkers, academics, jobs, essays to edit, etc... Except for a brief period late in their high school years, I was privy to it all. I was privileged to experience their adolescences with them. It took serious patience and concerted effort to cultivate this closeness, and I treasure it and them more than anything else on this planet. They are my *raison d'être*.

Mindful and constructivist parenting and raising respectful kids with the work ethic and frustration tolerance to succeed in life does require having high expectations, clearly delineated limits and boundaries, and consistent consequences for poor decision-making. Sometimes, it even takes some tough love, so they see the results of their faulty choices. It's not all daisies and rosebuds.

The single hardest thing, besides illnesses, that I have had to deal with as a parent is letting go. When they are babies, we parents are their entire world. We control everything that touches them—it's our job, but it's also the source of equal parts joy and neurosis. As they grow up and go to school, they start to meet people we don't know and experience things that we will only know about if we are active in their schools and if they decide to share. When they're teenagers, we try to be present in their lives to show them we love them and are involved. We give them boundaries, reinforce rules and structure to train them to be their own best advocates, to make healthy choices, and to be mindful of their health, safety, and surroundings even when being spontaneous and having fun with their friends. Go swimming with your clothes on but take off your $200 sneakers first. Go into the city to see Fall Out Boy but stay together and plan your route beforehand.

I was confident that my kids were ready to take the millions of lessons I imparted to them and go off to colleges several states away from home. The first to go was Ethan, naturally, since he is three years older and two years ahead of Simone in school. After the time consuming and emotionally harrowing college application process, when all was said and done, he decided on a university in Vermont. This is a beautiful campus set in between the Green Mountains and Lake Champlain. It is a place with a plethora of hiking, camping, and skiing areas—just what Ethan wanted. It was a perfect fit for him in every way.

In August 2016, we packed him up and drove him up there. All of us. In two separate cars. Sam and Ethan in one car, and Michael, Simone, and me in the other. Move-in day was hot but exciting. It was a little awkward, us all being there at the same time, but as his parents and stepparent-to-be and sibling, we all wanted to be a part of the unfolding of this chapter for him.

We all worked hard to get his stuff in his room, and I knew he had to unpack the way he wanted to, to make it his own. But I had this biological need, a deep longing, to make his bed. It may sound weird, but I had to do it the first time. Just to know, in some mom-emotional way, that he had a safe, comfortable place to put his head down that night.

A few weeks later, we went back up to Burlington to see him. This day, Ethan was showing us around campus and giving us the guided tour now that he was a native. Curious about his new life, I was asking him a million questions, and as we were walking down Main Street, adjacent to his residence hall, he stopped me, grabbed me by the shoulders and slowly spun me around. He said something I will never forget as long as I live. Ethan, while he was spinning me around, said, "Look at what I get to see every day, Mom." As I looked and really saw what he was showing me, I saw the gorgeous natural landscape of the Green Mountains on all three sides of us, majestically watching over the campus like mother nature's arms embracing us, and then straight ahead the stunning view of the wooded surroundings of Lake Champlain.

Ethan looked at me while I looked at the lake and said, "Thank you for allowing me to go here to experience this every day. I am in the right place. I love it here." Needless to say, I was crying and hugging my son. What a moment as a mom! Gratitude. Awareness.

Meaningful beyond words.

Simone is an artist—visual and textual. She, like her mother, has a lot of creative talent, a strong drive to succeed and make a beautiful and meaningful life for herself. Simone wound up at a small college in Massachusetts. The campus is gorgeous. I mean stunningly beautiful. Close your eyes and imagine what a college campus would look like in a movie—rolling green hills of tall grasses slowly dancing in the breeze, ponds and lakes surrounded by trees and vibrant foliage, paths cut through campus with wooden foot bridges over the ponds and lakes. And if that wasn't enough, the architecture of the buildings is varied and interesting, and there are four private college-owned beaches overlooking the Atlantic Ocean. Stunning.

This was her first-choice school, and she got accepted right away. We committed and sent in her deposit before Christmas during her senior year, so she was among the first to call dibs on her preferred dorm. Michael and I moved her in to the best room in the freshman dorm; she and her roommate shared a private bathroom. We were all full of excitement and, yes, I made her bed. I had to.

She is working hard on her coursework, balancing it all with a job that gives her a larger sense of purpose and responsibility and her own spending money. She is happy and is learning that she, like me, is a sensitive empath. As empaths, we experience an otherness, a distinct separation of ourselves from others because we see the world differently and feel so much of other people's emotions—even emotions that they don't know they are feeling. She will have to learn to balance her social needs with self-care, just like the rest of us.

Life is a journey, a delicate dance, and a mysterious one at that. We all make our way in our own way. College is about academics, but it's also about social life and figuring out who you are and your place in the world. Simone has learned a great deal about herself through her first several semesters in college and will continue to do so in her own time. She is learning that it's OK to take a different path when the path you're on doesn't serve you.

It's a testament to our resilience and fortitude as people that we can be self-aware enough to examine and figure out what in our life works and doesn't work, and then to be brave enough to change directions and fix it. Go in a new direction. Forge a different path. Seek meaning and inspiration, follow our passion.

What have I learned as a parent with my babies away at college? OK, so they're not babies; I get that. They will always be my babies in some emotional way. I've learned that even though they are far away and trying to do it on their own, they still need their mama. I'm a good source for advice on everything from academic problems to what to do after a fight with a friend or boyfriend/ girlfriend. I'm a good source of money when unexpected expenses crop up, or there is a spontaneous, once-in-a-lifetime trip they want to take. I can problem-solve how to get art supplies and materials from an off-campus vendor that doesn't do mail order when you don't have a car. And I'm great at finding an off-campus doctor to treat your bronchitis when the student health center doesn't play well with our health insurance. Plus, having an English teacher as a mother is wonderful when you have papers that need to be proofread and edited.

Letting them go off into the world to establish themselves as individuals is hard but trusting them to be good to themselves was easier than I expected. I am not worried that they will make poor decisions that will result in pain and hurt because they have great heads on their shoulders and good judgment and they know that I am a safety net, always a phone call or a text message away. I am concerned because the world can be a scary place full of harsh realities, but it's their world, too, and they have to learn how to navigate it and forge ahead under their own power and make their own dreams come true.

I know that in the years when they were under my roof full time, I imparted my wisdom, values, and ethics the best

I knew how to do. I protected them and nurtured them and then, from the sidelines, coached them to be their own advocates and to problem-solve on their own. They were ready for a bigger arena in which to test these skills. They are each on different paths, always knowing that I will always be their loudest cheerleader and advocate. I will always be their mother and always be their number one fan.

This whirlwind, the roller coaster of parenthood is daunting and scary, but also miraculous and meaningful. Being their mom has truly been the greatest joy of my entire life. And will continue to be for a very, *very* long time.

This notion of a parent as a guide and supporter doesn't end with my own children or stepchildren. It continues with my students. Each year, a new cast of 120 students enters my classroom and my heart. There are some who don't want to meet me halfway and accept what I'm offering, and they spend time in my class and learn what I teach them and move on. But some, the ones who gravitate to me, the ones with whom I develop a teacher-student friendship—for those kids, I become a safe zone, a school mom, a confidant, a mentor, a friend.

For almost twenty-five years now, I have taught high school English at a public high school on Long Island. I love my job. I get paid to read and discuss literature with adolescents who are trying to figure out who they are and how they fit into the world. We analyze characters, and through their struggles, we learn that no human experience is new, we all go through the same things over and over again. Only the subtle details change. Through this process, we learn emotional intelligence, empathy, and self-love. We learn to communicate how we think, see, and feel in speech and the written word.

Nothing is more beautiful than that. Nothing.

Becoming an English teacher at twenty-seven was the best career decision I ever made. I love this job, and it is a privilege to play a part in the lives of each one of the more than 3,000 students I have known (so far). Teachers are the backbone of society. Teachers make all other careers and all life choices possible. We teach children to think, to solve problems, to know where they came from and where they are going. We teach them how to express their thoughts and feelings and teach them that they are worthy, smart, capable, creative, wanted, accepted, appreciated, and loved.

People, who are not educators, think this is an easy job because they know what it was like for them to be in a classroom as a student, but that is an unfair comparison. Being a teacher is so much more than just planning and delivering a lesson, giving a lecture and a quiz, assigning a report card grade. If it were just those things, it still would be challenging, but the real challenge is to make the content interesting, relatable, and applicable to the ever changing lives of children and teens, while meeting state and national standards and meeting the learning needs of twenty-five to thirty individual students in each of your classrooms.

- We do all this while making students feel encouraged to be brave and safe and to risk being wrong in order to learn something.

- We do all this while connecting with them as people and maintaining boundaries and authority.

- We do all this while nurturing their feelings and validating their struggle.

- We do all this while also being a therapist, psychologist, confidant, counselor, coach, nurse, friend, disciplinarian, and sounding board.

It's a monumental and exhausting task and one that makes me thrive. This is a major source of my meaning.

This is what I was meant to do.

My students and I spend 180 days together each year, and sometimes I have them in class for more than one year. I have had many of their older and younger siblings in class and have gotten to know whole families. I become *school mom* for some, confidants for others, and friends with some once they graduate. Some of my favorite people are former students, and I'm blessed that we can continue to be a part of each other's lives.

Each day of each year, I am called upon to use all my life skills and hard-won knowledge about life, happiness, finding meaning, navigating family relationships, encouraging young people to work hard and seek the best in themselves and be a cheerleader of sorts and their champion as I encourage them to do it.

An example of this is a young woman, a high school senior and the younger sister of a former student who I was close with (and thanks to Facebook and Instagram am still in contact with) when she was a junior. She calls me Mom and will run down the hallway to hug me every single morning. She needs someone to talk to, someone with whom she feels safe. Another young woman has been with me for eleventh and now twelfth grade, has opened up to me about not fitting in at home. She doesn't feel emotionally safe or accepted by her parents and, understandably, this bothers her a great deal. She and I were talking about ideas for her college admissions essay, and she broke down in sobs as what we were talking about touched closely to something very painful to her. Instead of telling her to calm down and she would be OK, which would, in effect, tell her that I was uncomfortable with her emotions and tears, I held her and let her cry it out. I showed her I accepted her difficult emotions and was there as her witness and to share it with her.

When people express difficult emotions, it means they feel safe with me, or at least safe enough to risk their vulnerability. It is about them, not about me. I gave her a tissue and a hug, held her for a moment, and told her that she was safe and could cry it out. I was there holding space with her, listening to anything she wanted to say. Sure, she may have been looking for some advice, but more important, she was looking for someone to accept her and her difficult emotions, to express what she felt she couldn't express anywhere else. I gave her that safety and respect and love.

These are the moments that educators greet more often than anyone could guess. We live in difficult times of social strife, divisiveness, political clashes, eroding laws and national integrity, economic challenges, very real immigration fears as family unity is threatened by deportation or separation, sickness, death, and injuries. Each year, a greater percentage of students come from families touched by divorce, death, illness, military deployment, parental unemployment, immigration, and, oh yeah, the usual adolescent angst about body image, friend groups, and the ever-present struggle between fitting in and genuine belonging.

Many of the stories included here have been told in my classroom (with some details changed or glossed over to make them age-appropriate) as I share my authentic self with my students and let them know they are not alone on this human journey.

This job that I have, this calling, this privilege, this honor—I am able to step into the lives of these young people and shape who they might become over the next ten months or longer, or maybe their whole lives. In their own ways, they shape who I am and who I have become. They've touched my life in innumerable ways, and it's a blessing to my life to have them in mine. Students contact me all the time, years after they were in my class, years after they graduated, to ask me to edit a paper for them, for my advice on how to handle a problem, to share something exciting that just happened in their lives.

This semester, I received a message from a student who graduated about eight years ago, who just that weekend performed a comedic narrative at a bar in Manhattan (like a poetry slam for short narratives), and she wanted to tell me about it because she was inspired to do by an assignment in my class nine years prior. I ask my seniors and my creative-writing students to craft and perform, without notes, a three-minute narrative in front of the class. It has to be something that actually happened to them, so they know the story intimately. They can share almost any kind of event or experience within a framework. Many kids are nervous, but they all do it, and they are all glad they did once it's over. It's different from an academic presentation. They get to talk about themselves and, in many cases, receive validation, applause, and joy from their classmates and friends for being themselves. And who wouldn't want that?

I model this assignment on the performance narratives of *The Moth* (www.themoth.org), a storytelling group in many major cities in the United States; it functions like a poetry slam, but for spoken narratives. Regular people can show up with a prepared narrative that fits with that night's theme, get on the list, climb on stage and wow the audience. Sometimes there are celebrities and famous folk, sometimes it's a competition that has different rounds. It's always enjoyable. *The Moth* is on YouTube and has a free podcast that is easily found on iTunes. I sound like a commercial. It's an organization that I believe in because people want and need to be heard. And as a treat, I always write and perform my own *Moth*-styled narrative for them, so they get to hear about me as a regular but quirky human.

When I was going through my divorce and my whole entire life was turned upside down and I was worried about my children, worried about myself, worried about my livelihood, worried about every possible thing that I could control and couldn't control, I realized how deeply my job of teaching is an absolute blessing. It is an exercise in mindfulness. Being present, one hundred percent, in the present moment.

For the forty-one minutes of class, I have to put away all of the things that are bothering me and the problems of the day and focus exclusively on my students, the lesson plan, and their needs. I must focus on how to get from the first minute to the forty-first minute. And in their company, through the camaraderie, jokes, the lesson and their needs, I am able to lose some of the pain that I was going through and focus exclusively on my job. Teaching really is one of the most Buddhist professions that there is. It's a community of learners. It's sharing and mindfulness at its best because the only way to do the job is to put everything else aside and focus on the present moment.

There are many days where teaching is a joy; when the students are in a receptive mood, and there is some joking and talking along with lighthearted banter. When it comes time to do the work and focus, everybody is engaged and does their part to make the class great. There is great flow. There is great love. These days remind me why I do this job and why I so eagerly return to it every September. It's a joy.

Truthfully, obviously there are also many days when some students aren't in a receptive mood. For whatever their particular issues are that day or that year, they are not able to be fully present and engaged. Those students are a challenge. I try to light some sort of fire within them, turn them on to the material in some way, or at least get them to play the game of school and get through the day, the week, the semester.

Education has become too oriented to test scores and assessment benchmarks. We are stumbling down the wrong path. Despite this and the ever-present challenges, we work hard to bring the best we can to our students. This is still a job that I love and look forward to every day. Each morning, waking up at five and hauling myself out of bed is still an abhorrent chore, one that I will never get used to as a night owl, but I manage. Now, if we can only reduce the paperwork, that would be a blessing. Teachers are inundated by paper.

Teaching, like parenting, is messy, fun, difficult, rewarding, amazing, head-spinning, and more meaningful to me than almost anything I've ever done before. It's a close tie with motherhood. When I began this educational journey in 1995, I was unsure I would last ten years.

Now, I'm nearly a quarter-century in and not bored yet.

Recently, an old friend sent me an article about caring teachers who get emotionally burned out and thought I would find it interesting because, as she put it, I'm one of those kinds of teachers. The article made me think about teaching and my students. I have kids who come to me all the time with very serious problems. Kids message me from college, after they've graduated high school, to get my advice on handling crises in their lives; former students who are married and have kids of their own text me for advice on handing trauma in their lives.

With most my students, I never hear from them again once they graduate, and that is fine, too, but a small percentage are always coming back, and some have become lifelong friends.

It's all so human, real, and visceral. I feel that those are the real reasons I do this job, much more than the literature and the writing instruction. This job is more of a calling and a lifelong commitment to service in many ways.

CHAPTER 41

FRIENDS SHOW US
WHO WE ARE

*"A friend is someone who gives you
total freedom to be yourself."*

—Jim Morrison

I would never have thought I was someone for whom it was difficult to make friends. I've always had friends. There have been times when my friend group was larger than others. In high school in 1982, I had lots of friends. My primary friend group, the people I was the closest to, whom I spoke with daily and shared highly personal details, was quite small—maybe not more than three or four people—but I had a larger group of secondary or even tertiary friends. This makes sense. Those were people I knew through affiliations, clubs, classes, activities. We had things in common, we saw each other regularly because of some common external force, such as a weekly club meeting, a scheduled class, or a rehearsal. Once these external scheduling commitments were over, the friendships often dissolved. This also makes sense.

One of my best friends throughout my whole childhood and adolescence lived next door to me. She was two years older, but because of proximity we were always together. We were close, and it was through her that I learned of the birds and the bees. Dee told me everything. Every detail. My mother had very awkwardly talked to me about menstruation and held a tampon under a faucet so I could see it absorb water. At the time, I had no idea how this was related to a girl's period, and my mother made it clear that she didn't want me to ask questions, despite her telling me I could ask her anything. My friendship with Dee lasted until I went away to college and she got married and moved out of state. Now we are friends through social media and rarely actually talk, nor do we see each other. Lives get busy, families take priority, time marches on, but deep down I hope she knows I'll always love her.

My absolute BFF (best friend forever) in middle school and high school was Melanie. She was my soul sister and confidant even when I couldn't share secrets with anyone else. She and I were there for each other through our parents' bitter divorces, crushes on boys, our first everythings—boys, sex, drinking, lying, smoking tobacco and cannabis. We had a bond that we thought would last a lifetime. We graduated high school, went to separate colleges, and lost touch. I think there was a fight over something, but it has been so long that neither of us remembers what it was about. Just recently, we spoke on the phone for the first time in over thirty years. Neither of us remembered the sound of each other's voice, but we easily fell into deep conversation as we started to get to know each other as fifty-somethings. Who could have predicted it? We were friends from 1979 to 1986 and now again from 2019 until, I hope, the rest of our lives.

In college, my experience was largely the same: a small group primary friends and a larger group of secondary and tertiary friends. As a freshman at SUNY Geneseo in 1986, I quickly found a wonderful group of people, The Office, with whom I shared specific, desirable traits:

1. A desire for inclusivity and friendship with like-minded people, who were also looking for love and belonging.

2. A non-judgmental sensibility.

3. An affinity for deep conversations about ideas, literature, music, philosophy and art.

4. An aversion to shallow conversations about gossip, scandals, and salacious news.

5. A history of feeling excluded from close friendships and a perception of being judged.

Even within The Office, there were some people with whom I felt closer and others, naturally, with whom I did not. The magic with this group was our largely unspoken, although sometimes vocalized, commitment to our five commonalities and to the desire to reinforce and strengthen our mutual acceptance and sense of belonging with care or love. I know now how special this was. Even then, I was aware of how special this was. We joined activities, clubs, and groups of all sorts on campus according to our own interests that gave us other people with whom we developed friendships, but we always returned to our Office family. After we all graduated, over the course of several years because we weren't all the same age, we still kept in touch. I think our leader and chief organizer of our consistent communication was Kyle, who created a newsletter in the late 1980s that would be mailed to every Office member to inform us all about what was going on in each of our lives. Of course, we each had to write or call Kyle to tell him what was going on in our lives to be included in the text of the newsletter, but before social media, this was the way we stayed in each other's lives several times a year.

Additionally, Kyle and his wife, Hannah, who live on a several-acre piece of property in rural upstate New York, would open up their home and land for biannual weekend gatherings of all of us. We would all descend upon their home with tents, food, games, beverages, and tons of stories and a yearning to reconnect. This biannual weekend gathering happened consistently over the course of more than twenty years. Not everyone attended each one, but a great many were there for most of them. Over the years, our numbers increased as we brought along spouses and children, and they, too, became part of the Office family. We are still friends to this day more than thirty-three years later, and despite being more fractured over time, we are still in each other's hearts. Kyle stopped his newsletter, except for an annual holiday edition, when Facebook and other social media became ubiquitous. Now we are in each other's lives more because of the wonders of the internet. Some of us who live close to each other geographically keep in touch and get together frequently.

My best friend, Tim, with whom I have been friends with since 1986, lives less than ten miles from me, and we are a constant in each other's lives. We are a constant source of support and encouragement for each other. When Tim needed help bringing his fiancé here from Ghana, where it is illegal to be gay, it was my pleasure to help him with the financial documentation and legal paperwork necessary to bring him to New York to be with Tim. Then I had the honor of witnessing their marriage a few months later.

Tim had been the officiant at my second wedding, when I married Michael, who is also a member of the Office crew from Geneseo. In fact, Michael and Tim became friends in

1984 because they are two years older than me—a fact I never let them forget.

Tim and I also share our love for art and literature, as we are both artists and writers, but what is unique and the most invaluable about our friendship is that we are each other's bullshit meter. We are committed to keeping it real and calling each other on our nonsense. When one of us is blind to our fault in something that is upsetting us, we make sure to call attention to that and help the other one deal with what we had been ignoring. This might sound too "in your face" for some, but it's not for us. It's a gentle, but significant, nudge back into reality. Just knowing that someone knows me well enough to know when I'm lying to myself or ignoring something huge that I should be paying attention to is monumental.

What is also important and invaluable is that we are there with the in-your-face cheerleading when we are hard on ourselves.

When Tim's mother was very ill for over ten years and as Tim was her primary caregiver, he often felt trapped, lonely, frozen in time, or like he wasn't doing enough. I was there to remind him of all the wonderful things he was doing for her and for his family: all the ways in which he was a fabulous son to her. And the many, many times I felt unnecessary guilt over not being a good enough mom to my kids, or felt that I was failing during that long decade of being a single mother, he would remind me of all the things I was doing well and help me get off the pity party express.

One of the most touching things he has every said to me is that I have a "Ph.D. in love." He said that I am the most loving and emotionally generous person he has ever met. That's huge. I treasure our friendship every single day even if I don't tell him as often as I should. *Hey, Tim, if you're reading this, I love you!*

But what about other friends? How do adults, who are no longer in school, make friends? This is a tough question that many people ask. There are work friends, of course. People you talk to and get to know at your place of employment. These are often people with whom you have things in common—you all work in the same place, but you also will likely have interests, or a skill set in common, again because you work in the same place. Workplace conversation, in my experience, when it's not about the actual work that is going on or sometimes about our families and personal lives, occasionally revolves around superficial and hollow topics. Sometimes, it gets gossipy. Glancing back at the list of the commonalities of The Office, numbers three and four remind me how much I love those things. Work friendships, for me, are a blessing but also a challenge. I worry that if I share too much with someone that information might get around to others with whom I am not close and with whom I don't *want* to share that level of closeness. Or, if there is a falling out, then it becomes awkward when we see each other every day at work. I think it's best to keep those friendships at a balanced proximity and depth. I do know that what I just said contradicts three and four from the list, but that is another reason why workplace friendships should be exercised with caution. And yet, some of my colleagues where I teach are very important to me.

We provide camaraderie, solace, and friendly laughter for each other. This helps us remain sane while surrounded by teenagers year after year. Without them my daily life during the school year would be so bland and gray.

When I started dating my first husband, I became friends with all his friends and their girlfriends. I was in between phases in my life. I decided that the friends I had been spending time were like vampires and unhealthy for me. They did not transition well into daytime, happy friendships. I started to do things solo on my terms, and that led me, in a circuitous way, to starting with a clean slate when I met Sam.

Sam's friend group, with the addition of me, was four core couples. Each monogamous couple was educated and upwardly moving, forging our paths in new careers and working toward building an emotionally, physically, financially, and spiritually healthy future. We all got along well. They were all about numbers three and four on my list, and for the most part, all five on my list of desirables. We were in each other's weddings. We witnessed each other's children being born and were very much involved in each other's lives. But then the kids started to grow up and their activities took precedence, we saw each other less. Jobs necessitated geographical moves that drew us apart. Then, one by one, each of the four couples got divorced and the friend group was further fractured. Now I see only two of the ladies through Facebook, and we haven't seen each other in years.

Passing time has the power to change everything.

When my children were in public school, in groups like scouting or activities like dance and karate, it was natural to talk with the parents of their friends since we were there at the activities, too. For the collective fifteen years my children were in public school, some of my closest friends were the parents, predominantly moms, of my kids' classmates and activity friends. When the kids were small and it was customary for me to go along on play dates with them, it was necessary to talk with and get to know the parent of the kid with whom they were playing. My friend Lisa and I became friends because our sons became best friends in kindergarten.

Now that our sons are seniors in college, they remain friends, but Lisa and I rarely talk and have drifted apart. I miss her, but I have found this to be my norm. I don't know if others experience this, but since both of my kids are in college in different states and I no longer have them and their activities as the external force that brings us together; I have lost touch with my *mommy* friends and *parent* friends from those years. It seems sad on one hand, and sort of the natural flow of things on the other.

For close to ten years, my family was heavily involved in Ethan's Boy Scout troop, and we became part of a strong community of families. I really felt very supported and protected like I had a town full of sisters and brothers who had my back and my son's back—even if he didn't know it. I do and that is all that counts. I'm grateful for committee members, each assistant scoutmaster and scoutmaster for all they did on my son's behalf, for helping to make him the stand-up young man that he is, for instilling in him a commitment to excellence. Our scout family was truly a family in every sense of the word and gave to us the lifelong friendships that I will cherish forever even if we aren't in each other's lives every Tuesday because our sons have grown and moved on to build their own lives.

I suppose that by joining groups myself, I have made friends organically without the need of my children as the catalyst. This has some truth to it. I have become friendly with the people I met in the various art and writing groups I belong to, and those friendships, although still new for me, are proving to be quite significant and are more organic because of our shared interests and aren't catalyzed by my kids' friends or groups. Some of my favorite people were met through my-on-and-off eighteen-year involvement with the Northport Chorale. Those fine musicians and extraordinary people will always have a place in my heart.

This brings me to another phenomenon in my life. All this talk about friendship aside, I am often alone. Not lonely, but alone. I have an unusually active inner and creative life that has kept me sane throughout my turbulent experiences. It often keeps me occupied through journaling, writing, painting, reading and watching movies. I haven't ever been bored since I was five.

Carl Jung once said, "Loneliness does not come from having no people around you, but from being unable to communicate the things that seem important to you." There is a lot of truth to this. Loneliness doesn't have to feel bad; quite often, it feels peaceful and cozy, like my favorite sweater that I can pull close to me and snuggle inside.

The Buddhists have a lot to say about loneliness since much of Buddhist theory, as I understand it, is about letting go of attachment and being open to giving and receiving kindness and love. I recently read something Waylon Lewis said. "Loneliness is not a lack of something, but rather the aching fulfillment of our open, raw, caring nature … and in such open, empty moments, that the love that we seek is present, now." Loneliness is an emotion that, rather than signifying emptiness in our lives, actually is about a settling into the peace of our self-love and acceptance and all the creative flow we have coursing in our veins.

For most of my adult life, I've felt like I don't get invited places by other people, and sometimes I feel bad about it since I really do yearn for connection and community with others. Groups of secondary friends, which might even include my primary friends, get together socially and don't include me. I see friends on Facebook going to wineries, to shows, to pick pumpkins or blueberries, to movies, to restaurants, to see bands, and to each other's homes, and I am very rarely invited. I am a kind, gentle, emotionally available, interesting person. I am accepting and encouraging of people's uniqueness and quirkiness, as I am a bit quirky as well. I smile and make eye contact with people. I'm quick with a handshake or, better yet, a hug. I can count on two hands the number of times I have been invited to go out with a group of friends or to a party that they are throwing, so I have learned to be a good hostess. I have learned to graciously host gatherings and parties because that is the only way I will get to attend any.

If it sounds like I'm complaining or having a pity party, I don't mean to.

What I mean to say by writing this is that I don't know why this is so. My therapist seems to think it's because I have so many interests, projects, and goals that I am always busy with. Thus, I don't make room in my life for other things. Bigger than that, really, is that she thinks that others perceive me as not being interested in going with them to wherever they are going. So, they don't invite me because they think I'm too focused on my own activities. She thinks that people don't know what to do with that, feel dismissed by me, and don't invite me. I don't know if this is true. Is this the reason?

Lately, because of this theory of hers, I have been making an extra effort to talk to more people I see in the course of my daily life and striking up even superficial conversations about whatever is right there in front of me. Over time, I think it will yield more substantive friendships and more invitations or at least more organic connections. I thought I had been doing this my whole life, just like my grandmother had. When we were in Los Angeles in 2016, Ethan had even pointed it out and was impressed by it. Maybe I talk more with strangers than I do with secondary friends and acquaintances. I'm not sure.

When I was in elementary school, I was always the last one picked to be on a team. This was not great for my self-esteem. Honestly, though, did this have more to do with my lack of hand-eye coordination and klutziness, or was it something else? As an adult, I often find myself standing alone in a crowd. Everyone is talking to others. I am not. I'm find myself observing the crowd. Noticing body language, someone's infectious laughter, the rise and fall of the volume of voices, maybe even the content of extraneous conversations going on around me.

Maybe it's my own comfort or discomfort in different types of situations. I do know that I am more comfortable in small to medium groups rather than in large crowds. Large crowds call for shallow, small talk, and there is an overwhelming amount of emotion, energy and noise. Smaller groups, by nature of their size and energy, are more conducive to deep, real conversations. Maybe it's my need for honest dialogue and genuine sharing that keeps me more comfortable in smaller groups, and maybe I give off some sort of vibe to that effect.

Maybe I find the energy of crowds exhausting.

How does all this play out for me?

1. My personality is suited for smaller groups so I can fully engage the people I am talking with and really get into it with them.

2. I am a nurturer and a natural caregiver. I am genuinely interested in supporting and taking care of those I love. This includes friends and family, and also my students.

3. I am very practical and organized. I can see the big picture in a given situation and can break it down into manageable, digestible pieces.

4. I have zero tolerance for bullshit. (That's why I am good at calling other people on theirs and have learned to be pretty good at detecting my own. But I still need Michael's and Tim's views as well.)

5. Because I am both involved with other people and also have period of detachment, I have an active inner life—in my own brain, analyzing everything and looking for patterns—I often have clear insight into the motivations of others, whether they are healthy or toxic, or are good or not so good. For most of my life, I have been a great listener and can intuitively figure out what is bothering others and help them find a way to fix it or get themselves back on the right path. I know enough to navigate many situations, and I am smart enough to know when to seek a professional for advice and assistance, whether a therapist, medical doctor, dietitian, lawyer, or seamstress. Sometimes, asking the right question of the right people is all it takes. Well, and a willingness to let that insight in and make a change.

Taking a long look over my life, I see the choices I've made, the people I have fallen prey to and been used by, the talents I possess, and how I have been able to navigate myself out of harm's way into safety and health. What does all of this mean?

We need our friends—everyone has their own reasons. Friends offer us companionship, connection, belonging, love and care, support, laughter, and advice. Many of us—probably most of us—cannot imagine our lives without them.

Go call a friend. Send him a message. Call her on the phone. Make a date to get together. Make room in your heart and in your schedule to visit, share a beverage or a meal, open your heart and mind, give of your time, and make space in yourself for friends and your connections. Be open to new ones that bring you support, challenge, love, kindness, and laughter.

Chapter 42
SUNRISE, SUNSET; TRADITIONS THROUGH THE YEARS

"Sunrise, sunset
Sunrise, sunset swiftly fly the years
One season following another
Laden with happiness and tears."

— "Sunrise, Sunset," Fiddler on the Roof

I wasn't raised in a religious household. We were and are Jewish, but this is more of a shared set of customs, traditions, foods, and mindsets than it is a strong belief in a higher power. I went to Hebrew school but didn't get much out of it or complete the journey.

When I was in third grade, my parents started to send me to Hebrew school to learn the religious and spiritual customs and beliefs of the Jewish faith. We were not a very religious family. We didn't say prayers before we ate, we did not kiss the mezuzah on our door posts as we walked through them, we did not cleanse the house of leavened bread before Passover, we did not celebrate Shabbat each Friday or attend services at a local synagogue. We did, however, celebrate Passovers with full Seders, and we went with my grandparents to synagogue for Rosh Hashanah and Yom Kippur. We did celebrate Hanukkah with candles lit on our Hanukkiah each of the eight nights. Once or twice we attempted to build a *sukkah*. We were traditional Jews who kept some of the traditions alive, the most important of which are love, compassion, charity, education, and acceptance.

My father felt that it was important I learn more about Judaism and attend Hebrew School, but he couldn't afford the tuition at the reformed synagogue in our town, so instead he sent me to the orthodox synagogue in the next town. Most of the children in my class were from families that were more strictly religious than my own, and the rabbi was certainly of orthodox faith. From the start, I felt out of place.

This rabbi was very old-world with his beliefs about teaching girls. He taught the boys all they wanted to know about history, customs, the Torah, and Jewish law. With the girls, he taught us which prayers to say when and how often and hoped to impart a submissive attitude to us through dismissing our questions. He'd say, "It's not important if you can (insert skill here). It's only important that you listen to your father and then your husband and keep a clean house." I don't remember his exact words, but this was his meaning. I was appalled but knew better than to challenge him publicly. I kept my mouth shut. I don't even think I told my parents. The rabbi taught us all to memorize Hebrew so we could say the prayers, but he didn't teach the girls to read Hebrew, what the prayers meant or even why we should say them.

When I did ask, he ignored my questions and silently communicated the message that I was a waste of his time. This reinforced a subconscious feeling that I was not enough; I was less than. I learned very little there, but I did learn about anti-Semitism.

Purim is a spring holiday that celebrates the bravery of Queen Esther, who saved the Jewish people. My Hebrew school class was putting on a play. In March of 1977, when I was nine, I got to play Queen Esther herself. My mother sewed me a costume and made me a blue-and-gold shiny crown. I was very excited. This was something I could get into in Hebrew school—it was dramatic, and I got to be the heroine.

One afternoon, we were having a dress rehearsal for our Purim play outside in the front yard of the synagogue. The sun was out, it was a warm early spring day in the sunshine, and we were all happy and being silly like the kids that we were. Suddenly, there was a screeching of tires on the road in front of the synagogue. A car stopped as a horde of howling teenaged boys screamed, "You fucking kikes!" and threw large tomatoes at us. The mood had changed suddenly as fear, anxiety, and panic replaced the previously happy and silly scene. We were little kids and had no idea what had happened or what it meant. We did know what we heard and felt—tomatoes—and we knew we were scared.

I don't remember who explained it to us or what they said, but I know that it was the first time I learned of anti-Semitism and that people might hate me because I am Jewish.

It took me a long time to convincingly convey to my parents how dismissed and disrespected I felt at that school. At first, they didn't believe me when I told them how the rabbi treated the girls in the class. I don't know why they didn't. I never lied, was always a rule follower and orthodox Judaism has always had very strict, separate rules for males and females. Eventually, they moved me to the reformed synagogue in our town. There, I met with the kind rabbi, who looked like Tevye from *Fiddler on the Roof*, and he talked with me about my experience at the other synagogue. I was a shy child and don't remember how much information I gave him, but he did test my ability to read Hebrew and since I hadn't really been taught much and had paid less attention once I realized how misogynistic the orthodox rabbi was. I was very behind my peers. This new rabbi decided to put me in a third-grade class, even though I was in the sixth grade.

I was uncomfortable, feeling out of place and conspicuous, especially when I realized that even though these kids were three years younger than I was, I knew far less than them and should have been placed in an even younger class level. I hated every single second of being there and earned my lowest academic marks ever. I told my parents I hated it and always made a fuss about going. I never did my homework, which was not like me. I've always loved to learn, and school had always been something I loved. But this was torture, and I think that no one—not my parents, or the teachers, or the rabbi—was paying attention to me. It's obvious that a sixth grader in a third-grade class was not going to work for anyone, but it continued on this way for however long it took me to persuade my parents to let me stop going. Part of me regretted not becoming a Bat Mitzvah as most of my cousins did, but I shrugged it off and thought that maybe I'd do it as an adult. Then I dismissed it and stopped thinking about it.

My son, Ethan, went to Hebrew school late because we couldn't afford it at the time he was *supposed* to start, when he was in third grade and we were in the middle of our divorce. Ethan didn't really want to go, but he is a people pleaser and does like to learn, so eventually he went for a while because he knew how important it was to his father. Eventually, Ethan did become a Bar Mitzvah, after private lessons with a very kind, elder member of the synagogue congregation. It was not an over-the-top, extravagant event. We couldn't have afforded that, and Ethan is not the type of kid who liked that sort of attention and huge expense.

After the actual Bar Mitzvah ceremony, including his reading of the Torah, the religious portion of the coming-of-age ritual, we had a small gathering at the synagogue for everyone in attendance and the congregation for Shabbat. Then, later in the day, we had a luncheon for our immediate family. Sam and I shared in the joy of this mitzvah for our son and got along well that day. Sam's parents were there, as were some family friends of ours and Ethan's. My father and Kay did not come north from Florida for this because we thought we would eventually have a bigger party at some point, but we never did. Their not coming was a mistake, probably more mine than theirs, as they should have been there. My mother didn't come because it coincided with one of her black periods of depression and addiction. She missed her only grandson's Bar Mitzvah because of drugs.

Simone went to Hebrew school for a couple of weeks and demanded to stop, refusing to go further. She knew her mind and would not deviate. So, we gave up. It was much more important to Sam than it was to me, so that was that. I wasn't going to fight that battle despite always having the desire for traditional and cultural continuity. Being Jewish and celebrating holidays in the customary ways with my family and friends has always made me feel connected to the thousands of years of Jews before me. Many generations of Jews all doing the hora, singing the same prayers and songs, celebrating mitzvahs and sharing grief. They were connected and bound by traditions of family, hard work, love, and respect.

I've never had any great spiritual need for congregation and organized prayer, as I've nurtured my spiritual life on my own, but I do miss the sounds of the Hebrew and Yiddish languages, as I heard in shul and from my grandparents' generation. Grandma and her generation spoke Yiddish to each other, and when they wanted to keep secrets from us younger ones or when they got angry. It was the language of their youth from their home of origin, from the extended family back in Russia.

Reading books and watching movies like *The Chosen,
Yentl,* and *Fiddler of the Roof, Crossing Delancey,* and dancing
the hora at weddings, our holiday celebrations all bring me a
sense of connectedness with thousands of years of Jews. Maybe
that explains my connection with Passover. It's all about food,
family, and liturgy as we all pass down stories of ancient Jews
escaping the bondage of slavery in Egypt and establishing a
Jewish community of their own in the desert. The stories run
from the ancient to the young, thus reinforcing our strength
with each other and reaching forward through time to connect
with current events and modern culture.

We live in a potentially dangerous world now with author-
itarian governments on the rise and fear growing, and with
resurgent anti-Semitism in the United States and Europe. Shuls
have been bombed here and in Northern Europe. Jews have
been targeted once again, just for being Jews. White suprem-
acy is regaining a voice in United States, and uncertainty and
fear have increased in me. Since 2016, I've been aware of my
unease in hanging my Hanukkah holiday flag and putting
my Hanukkiah in my front window. I used to be comfortable
and did these things with abandon and unconscious freedom,
taking for granted our safety in the United States.

At the new production of *Fiddler on the Roof,* in Yiddish,
that Michael and I recently saw on Broadway, I found myself
thinking that we had a theater full of hundreds of Jews and
Jewish sympathizers and it would be a perfect scenario for
antisemitic violence. It was too horrible a thought to sit with,
so I pushed it away.

Seeing *Fiddler on the Roof* again reminded me of Jewish
traditions. I used to sing this score with my mom and grandmother. The themes were very present in our lives, in the lives
of many Jews. We are borne of stubborn Jewish stock, traditionally making the best of anything, dealing with whatever

happened, and never giving up. We healed, regrouped, started over. Jews have always been persecuted for thousands of years, been on the receiving end of hatred, fear and misunderstanding, only for being Jewish. I identify with the pride in survival. I identify with binding one's self together with family and friends, working hard, and taking pride in that work. And slowly, day after day and season after season, building a family, raising my children, and stubbornly fostering happiness and laughter and joy and love.

Indomitable. Resilient. Fierce. Strong.

CHAPTER 43
TOXIC CONNECTIONS AND SEARCHING FOR HOME

I have always craved connection. I've craved attention, connection, love, and belonging so desperately that I've often forgotten to take care of myself. I tried to take such great care of others that I overlooked things I shouldn't overlook. I'm an intelligent thinker, and sometimes I overthink things. It is also true that I have allowed myself to be easily swayed or manipulated by others and have sublimated my own feelings in favor of diplomacy, keeping the peace, or not rocking the boat. I have a history of pushing my feelings down not taking care of my inner child in trying to take care of others and letting them bully and repeatedly gaslight me. But ultimately, I had to take that power back and be mindful of what's around me and in my world.

Mindful of my place in the world, mindful of the nature, mindful of my children's love, mindful of my relationships with others.

I did it with my mother.
I did it with Danny.
I did it with Mark.
I did it with Sam.
I did it with Denise.
I did it with Stuart.
I did it with Aaron.

I was desperately afraid of being alone. My lonely inner child, who craved connection and love, was basically screaming in the dark. You can love someone and not treat that person well. Every abusive marriage starts out with the husband or wife saying, "But I love her so much, I would never hurt her," and yet the hurt is delivered. Love doesn't necessarily mean well-treated. Being who I am—an intelligent, creative, attractive, sexual woman who made it easy for others to seduce me into feeling like I had a connection with them because my hungry and desperate inner child was craving love—I fell for it every time.

I needed to stop that. I needed to take care of myself so my inner child isn't as hungry for attention and love. I needed to stop acting impetuously without thought. I learned to listen to my inner voices and be mindful on a daily basis. Mindful of the gifts that I have to give to the world and of the gifts the world can give to me. Find gratitude and build from there. Ultimately, I'm proud of my resilience, courage, and strength. No matter what happens, I will stay on my two feet and be fine. Better than fine, actually. I will be awesome. I've gone through fire to get where I am right now. I am not at all confrontational, but I am deeply stubborn, and the stubbornness has helped me forge my own path as I endeavored to make my life work for me and to be the best mother I could for my amazing children.

From the time I left for college to live in the temporary housing of a dorm, I felt homeless, like I was without a safe place to land. As part of my parents' divorce, they sold the house I grew up in and dissolved their shared life. In doing so, they also dissolved mine. The tether to my childhood home and to all I had known of my nuclear family had disintegrated into nothingness.

I was generously given a room in each of my step-parents' homes, where my own parents now lived, but these homes did not feel like mine, and despite being welcomed into these new families I felt like a guest, a visitor, an interloper. For eight years, between 1986 and 1994, I traveled so often between these houses, my dorm rooms, and temporary student apartments that I seemed to live in my car more than anywhere else. I craved a home—a peaceful place where I belonged and could rest my head and my heart.

This quest for a home of my own motivated more of my decisions as a young adult than I knew at the time. My parents were focused on rebuilding their lives in their new homes in their second marriages, and I felt alone and adrift, with a hole in my heart and no emotionally safe place to rest my head. Thus, I set out on an exhausting path to try to fill my heart.

My first college boyfriend introduced me to his parents, and instantly I fell in love with them. They were warm and emotionally effusive, and they welcomed me into their lives. Within a few hours, I was calling them Mom and Dad. In some ways, I found more love and solace in their home than with my own. Their home became an oasis of peace for me during a turbulent time. I put up with some pretty awful treatment by their son, who was abusing my trust and cheating on me, because I knew that leaving him meant that I also had to leave his family and I would no longer be welcome in their home. When we eventually broke up, which was inevitable, I grieved the loss of his parents and their home much more than I did the loss of him.

When I met my ex-husband's parents, the same scenario played out. I became extremely close with them and was welcomed with open arms into their family, creating memories and feeling loved. When he and I moved in together in 1994, the year before our wedding, for the first time in slightly more than eight years, I had a home of my own. We had created a peaceful oasis, a place where we would always be welcome because it was ours.

This was what I was waiting for—a home of my own.

When our relationship hit some rocky roads and I saw trouble on the horizon, I ignored far more than I should have, accepted so much less than I deserved, and suffered through our complete emotional disconnect, allowed myself to be bullied and disrespected, disregarded and gaslighted, choosing to sweep it all under the rug because that rug covered the floor in my own home. If I chose to deal with our issues, or end the relationship, I'd have to move that rug, give up my own home, and go back to my nomadic lifestyle, split between the homes of others. I saw these as the only two choices.

This was not a choice I was conscious of, nor was it something I was prepared to do. We married a year later, and we eventually bought our own home. Now I had the most permanent home I'd had in more than a decade and certainly more control over the goings-on in that home than I ever had before. I continued to sweep our marital problems under that same rug, which now covered the floor of my very own living room.

Throughout our journey as a couple, we would try to heal our wounds with real estate, with larger and more satisfying homes. Real estate cannot fix marriages any more than new cars or new babies can; our problems persisted and followed us. About eleven years into this turbulent marriage, I began to see that I had the power to create a home on my own, and the end of our marriage didn't mean I would be homeless.

I had a good career and enough money to support myself, and with some hard work, I created a home for myself and my children on my terms—one in which peacefulness, fun and love were the supporting pillars. And nothing would be swept under the rug.

We can all be in our own homes, no matter where we are, by holding true to our values and boundaries, by working hard to surround ourselves with peace, and by never settling for less than we deserve. Home is more than where you hang your hat. It is where you fill your heart with love and belonging and, hopefully, where you rest your head on your favorite pillow.

As I wrote in my 2015 article, *Saying Goodbye to Our Childhood Home*, "Our homes hold a special place in our hearts and minds. Never underestimate the power of place in our lives. Let's be grateful for the blessings of safety, sanctuary, family, and love. May they forever warm our bodies and hearts."

I can mark very clearly the moment I stopped letting Sam bully and dismiss me. I started this process of severing his control over my behavior when I divorced him, but at times while we raised our beloved children, as we shared custody, that I still felt him try to manipulate me and situations to meet his needs. He lied to my face. He changed the order of events or made up entire conversations to suit his desired narrative. One day he insisted I cried and begged him to take Ethan off my hands for a larger portion of the week because I couldn't handle him.

This was an absolute lie.

I would never have asked that or even thought it. Ethan was never a problem child and I was always a more than competent mother, but Sam had his own versions of the truth. (The truth, as I have always known it, does not have versions.) He bullied me into changing the days we celebrated holidays and sometimes reciprocated flexibly, but other times he'd blame me for always asking for changes to the schedule. It was petty and frustrating to deal with. But I finally broke the remaining bits of power he had over my emotions or behavior when I sued him in 2017 for the money he is legally obligated to pay toward our children's college educations, as per our divorce agreement.

When Ethan went away for college, Sam only paid for 50% of the actual tuition bill, leaving all the rest of the fees to be paid for by me. I had inherited a little money from my mother that I told my children that I would use to pay for my portions of their college educations so that they would graduate without student loans. This was something I really wanted to do for them, but it didn't absolve Sam from his legal obligations. By our divorce contract, we were each responsible for 50% of the total cost of attending a SUNY school and living on campus. In other words, 50% of the total cost of attending. Sam was cheap and figured he would pay less and force me to pay more. Instead, I sued him and won. He was now, as he had been before, legally obligated to pay for half of all their costs (based on SUNY rates) and I agreed to pay the rest. He was so intent upon screwing me over that he didn't care that he was really hurting his kids.

By suing him, I drew an indelible line in the sand that said, stop trying to screw with me or my children, you will no longer get away with it. For me, this was pivotal and life changing.

Ethan, Simone & me 2010   Ethan, Simone & me 2001   My mom & me 2011

My dad & me 2019   Our first dance 2017   Tim & me at my art show 2019

Tim, Michael & me 2017   Me serenading Michael at our wedding 2017

Our wonderful blended family 2018

Chapter 44

FINALLY, A SAFE PLACE TO LAND

By mid-September 2016, after we moved Ethan up to college, Michael moved in with Simone and me, and if possible, things kept getting better. The following summer, six months after our wedding, Thomas moved in with us, too, and then Marie and her children moved to Florida, to get far away from her abusive ex-husband, to move in with her fiancé, and be able to afford her life a little more easily.

After everyone was told about the engagement, Michael and I got to plan our wedding. We wanted a small wedding, but we did want to celebrate. After a small foray into local venues on the internet, I went to look at some places and found the perfect place. Insignia in Smithtown is an upscale, gorgeous restaurant with amazing food, and during certain times of the week, when the restaurant is closed to the public, they host fabulously classy weddings. Everything was perfect. They handled the food and beverages and had the setup of chairs for the ceremony and the tables and chairs for the party all down to a science. We had a cocktail hour with passed hors d'oeuvres in the big, wood-and-chrome bar area; photos outside and inside the atrium adjacent to the bar; a photo session in their wine cellar, which was actually on the second floor of the restaurant with a glass wall overlooking the dance floor.

All the rest of the details came from our friends and family. DJ services were a gift from a former student of mine, whom I grew close with over the years and was in the business. Our gorgeous and delicious wedding cake was made by a close family friend of Michael's who is an up-and-coming professional pastry chef and wedding cake designer. (She works for the bakery chain from the television show "Cake Boss".) Our photographer was a close friend of Marie's who has extraordinary talent. She took so many amazing pictures of our wedding that I will cherish forever. I designed the purple floral invitations and created centerpieces with floating candles in cylindrical vases of purple flowers and votive candles. Michael and I bought all our kids and his grandkids new clothes for the wedding; new charcoal gray suits for the guys and feminine gowns for the girls. It was so much fun going fancy-clothes shopping with everyone, trying on clothing and seeing our magical day come together.

We kept our guest list on the smallish size, which was a difficult thing to do. Deciding who to invite was challenging, but these things have a way of getting out of control and getting very expensive very quickly. We had about seventy-five people when all was said and done. We decided early on in our planning that we didn't want wedding gifts. We were combining two households and didn't want or need any more stuff. People are overburdened with too much stuff. Instead, we asked for donations to the Caron Institute to be made in my mother's name. Caron is a fabulous treatment center for addicts and their families that saved my cousin's life and could have saved my mother's life if she had allowed me to help her. Many of our friends and family donated making treatment and a start at a clean healthy life possible for quite a few people. Just as I had done myself after my mother's death. I was so upset about not having been able to have closure with her while she was still alive, and heart sick that a wonderful place like Caron exists and she refused to go.

The big question was who our officiant would be.

We are not particularly religious people, although we are spiritual. Michael is a little more traditional Christian in cosmology; I am traditionally Jewish, but not really religious, per se. And neither of us belonged to any congregations. We decided to ask our very best friend, Tim, to be our officiant. He had married other friends of his in New York City and got ordained online to do so legally just for us. About a month before the ceremony, in December 2016, we learned that his ordination was legal in New York City, but not out on Long Island. We had a problem.

Who would legally marry us?

A co-worker of mine at school told me about a lovely woman who was a licensed, professional wedding officiant on Long Island who had performed her wedding ceremony. Coincidentally or not, she lived in the same town that I live in—a sign from above? Who knows? Pastor April is one of the kindest, most loving souls I have ever met. Michael and I liked her at once, and she agreed to meet us at Insignia the morning of our wedding, before the guests arrived, to perform the actual legal marriage ceremony and sign our marriage license. Simone would be our witness, and it would all be legal before the actual wedding started. Then Tim would perform the emotional, symbolic ceremony. It was all going to be great.

I had a dream one night about our wedding in which we had a sand ceremony for us, our four kids and the four grand-children. My experience with decorative sand bottles from our craft fair days fed into this dream and came in handy. I found a stunning heart-shaped vessel with a rubber stopper top that rested on a curvy, wrought iron stand that would be perfect to create an original blend of different colors of sand that represented the unity and combination of our new, larger, louder family. Ten pretty mason jars of ten different colors of sand were assembled along with tiny funnels. During part of the ceremony, all ten of us would go up and take turns pouring our sand into the heart, and Michael and I would have an artistic representation of our wild family.

The only part of this that I would do differently if I could do it over again, which I would love to, is that I would get a different wedding dress. My original idea was to wear an artsy, flowy purple gown I found online on Pinterest. The designer was from Yemen, and the website link showed it was available for purchase. It would look great on me and be just the right thing. I ordered the dress and when it arrived it was nothing like the dress I actually ordered. It was a different dress entirely. I was crestfallen. Arguing with the manufacturer who was in China, even though I thought the manufacturer was in Yemen, proved to be futile. With the time difference and cost of return shipping, and their arguments and denials, we were both extremely aggravated. Eventually, I sold the *wrong* gown on Poshmark and all was fine.

By this point, I was getting married in six weeks and was the only member of our family who had nothing to wear. It was too late to order a wedding gown from a traditional bridal shop, even if I had decided to not wear purple and wear white. I ordered a deep purple gown from a reputable manufacturer in the United States, but when it arrived and I tried it on, Simone and I realized that it wouldn't photograph well. The purple was so dark that it seemed to suck in all the light from the room. No good. She, Marie, and Tim convinced me to order an off-white gown from the same online store, which would promise delivery in ten days. This gown came and a family friend, who is a couture wedding dress designer, did a few alterations and it was beautiful. As long as I stood up straight, the gown fit and was pretty. But it didn't move well, and the bust was so structured that it made me feel like I was wearing armor. I decided to have my purple touch by wearing a pair of beautiful purple suede, kitten-heeled pumps that were so comfortable I could wear them forever.

Finally, January 15, 2017, arrived. It was to be the happiest, most magical day of our lives. A hairdresser came over to our house to do Simone's and my hair, and we each did our own makeup. Michael, Simone, and I got dressed at home. Ethan was staying at his dad's house and was picking up two of his lifelong friends who were also coming to the wedding.

Things were going very smoothly. We were on schedule and excited. Then Michael went down to the basement in his brand-new purple wedding socks (the ones we drove around in the snow to find) to get the iron, only to discover that our cesspool flooded into the basement, filling the whole unfinished side of the basement and some of the finished side with its contents. This was a ten-plagues level of disgusting. Michael cautiously came upstairs to tell me, thinking I would freak out, but I just offhandedly said, "Let's worry about that tomorrow." He loved that! I was committed to our wonderful day and wasn't going to let anything get in the way of that. Basements and cesspools would be there tomorrow.

We had dropped off the centerpieces with a photograph of one fully assembled, two days before, so the staff at Insignia would have them to set up and all we had to do was show up. Pastor April was there on time, as promised. She performed a short but sweet wedding ceremony for Michael and me, during which we all cried, of course. Then she signed our marriage license, and Simone was our witness. It was lovely. It was all very emotional and quick. I tried hard not to cry and ruin my eye makeup.

Then, after we all posed for lots of photographs, came the real ceremony, which was perfect. Marie and Thomas walked Michael down the aisle, and then Ethan and Simone walked me down the aisle. My purple shoes, which had been so comfortable in the house, were brutal and painful at the wedding and kept falling off my feet. I nearly tripped over them walking toward my true love. Ethan and Simone steadied me as they always do.

Magnificent Tim created a beautiful ceremony for us. He is a gifted poet who crafts technicolor paintings with words and has a knack for simply explaining what I thought was indecipherable. Michael and I each wrote our own vows. I started months ahead of time and went through five drafts. Michael teared up during mine:

Michael, we have been friends forever and I have always known you to be a man of integrity, honor, love, compassion, strong convictions, crazy humor, and silliness. Within the safety of this long-standing bond of comfort and trust, our love blossomed. We both realized that, in each other, we could have everything we ever wanted. We need to love and be loved in exactly the same ways. You bring out the best in me and make me strive to be a better person. You accept me in all my silly weirdness, and love every part of me with a fierceness, tenderness, and protectiveness that takes my breath away. I am happier than I could have ever imagined and grateful for you every day. In giving me your heart, you have given me everything.

My favorite moments with you are our silly laughter and typical "dad jokes," the deep, introspective conversations in our time bubbles, the private, cozy times when we seem to be the only ones who exist in the world, spending time with our bigger, louder, loving family, falling asleep in our cocoon, feeling you reach for me in the middle of the night and hearing your sleepy "I love yous;" feeling loved, safe and cherished by you every single day. You are all the pieces that were missing from my puzzle.

Today, surrounded by the people who love us and whom we love, I choose you, Michael, to be my husband and to join my life with yours. I promise to choose you every day of our lives together, to love you with every word, action and every heart-beat, to laugh with you, to cry with you, to grow with you, to create with you, to explore with you, to honor the kindness in your soul, to cherish the compassion in your heart, to take care of you, to walk beside you, to respect and value you as a partner, knowing that we will continue to grow and perfectly complement each other until the end of time.

With these words and the all the love in my heart, I give you my hand and my heart, as I pledge to you my love, devotion, faith and honor. I join my life to yours and joyfully become your wife. Today. Since always. Until forever. I am yours.

We have different styles. Michael didn't write anything ahead of time, he just knew what he wanted to say. He told the story about our November 2016 "meet cute." How he prayed for a woman exactly like me to come into his life on precisely the same night I read the article about soulmates and messaged him. He broke down in tears while talking. It was incredibly moving and sweet. There wasn't a dry eye in the place. I wish we had videotaped the ceremony, but its memory is indelibly written in my mind.

While the soft melody of *Somewhere Over the Rainbow*, by Israel Kamakawiwo'ole, was playing, our family unifying sand ceremony went very well, just as I had dreamed, and I had an out-of-body experience watching us all doing it. It was charming. We blended four kids and four grandkids—for a total of ten people—into this new family. We each used our different color sand to create something beautiful and new. Our sand filled heart-shaped vessel stands next to a wedding picture in a gorgeous frame given to us by Aunt Maggie and Uncle Isaac, and it is a constant reminder of how blessed and loved we are.

The food was great, the music was energetic, our guests were loving and supportive, and we had the best time ever! The whole day went by in a flash! We had our first dance together to Ellie Goulding's *How Long Will I Love You*, which was so personally moving to us both. Knowing the long and circuitous paths we each traveled to get to this moment and feeling the deep, soulful love we share made this dance very special. I knew that this was a forever love, and dancing in each other's arms encircled by all the people we love most in the world was beyond moving.

We promised that we each will always take care of each other and keep each other safe. He is the most thoughtful, romantic man in the world. And he's all mine. Forever.

My brothers in law played guitar for me as I sang the Ingrid Michelson song *You and I* to Michael, and everyone else joined in on the chorus like a flash mob. Michael wasn't thrilled with the surprise of it but loved that I thought to sing to him, and once he realized it was a family affair, he joined in. We had a wonderful time, and in the end, we became husband and wife and a big family.

Choosing this man to be my husband was the best decision I could have ever made for myself!

Had Michael and I gotten together any earlier in our lives than we did, I don't think it would have worked as well. We both were babies when we met in 1987 and had very different personalities back then. We were young and inexperienced and really knew nothing about ourselves or love to have been able to make it work. Life has a keen way of teaching us what we need to learn whether we like it or not. Sometimes, lessons take a long time to learn, like they did with my experience with my mother. Sometimes we need to learn them over and over and over again until they stick, like what happened throughout my romantic life until late 2015.

Rarely, if ever, are life lessons learned quickly or painlessly. The only thing I can really say about that is I hope that when you finally learn each of these lessons that life has to teach you, you are proud of yourself for surviving, learning, growing, for having the patience, and for having kept trying.

Life isn't easy. I don't want to paint an overly, rosy picture that falsely depicts our life together. We face life head on, holding hands, sharing our hearts, passions, and ideas. Always knowing that we are forever in this crazy life together.

Each of us, our children included, comes with his or her own drama, and we deal with that as it comes. We don't have similar parenting styles. I'm much more hands-on, in their face, and Michael is more laid-back and casual, but I think that we complement each other. I spur him to action when needed, and he calms me down and gets me to take a step back at times when that is appropriate. It also helps that our kids are all adults and need different parenting than small kids. This would have been a totally different ball of wax if our kids were public-school age. I'm so glad we didn't have that to deal with. Whew! Dodged a bullet there.

I look forward to enjoying the rest of our lives and our children's and grandchildren's lives together. The adventure is just beginning.

EPILOGUE
TAKING THE LONG VIEW

*"You live life looking forward, you
understand life looking backward."*

—Soren Kierkegaard

When I look back and take stock of my life, I see it has been a roller coaster of experiences: my parents' separation, their bitter, six-year battle that twisted us all in knots, my mother's bipolarity, her torturous decade of addiction and subsequent death, my own divorce from a narcissistic man after a decade-long, minefield of a marriage, being a single mother and working very hard to manage my own inner life to break the multi-generational patterns and raise my own children better than I was raised, and several crazy relationships with aggressive, narcissistic, confused, and inappropriate people.

Each member of this parade marched through my life greedily taking my love and devotion and inadvertently teaching me to accept and expect less and less for myself.

By the time I ended this parade, I could barely fill a shot glass with my self-esteem, and I under-valued almost all of my (now favorite) characteristics. I let myself get emotionally invested in others' lives too easily, gave away my sense of inner peace, and allowed their opinions of me to mean more than my own. I had no boundaries, and as an empath, and an E/INFJ, I was easy prey for narcissists. I surprised myself and got off this sadistic merry go round in an attempt to find my way back to myself. I had to be a better role model for my children. I had to create a space where love could fill up my life, where I could be present every day and mindfully show up each day full.

Then I left my slow, clumsy canoe and climbed aboard my new motorboat and set out on a new course to finish my own education through my second master's degree, working multiple jobs to make ends meet, raising two amazing children to be extraordinary adults, becoming an artist and starting an art business, remarrying to the love of my life, blending our families, and now writing this memoir.

Before any of that good stuff could happen, I had to do the deep, hard work of examining myself and figuring out why I let myself fall victim to the whims of others and dedicated myself to their needs above all else. And more importantly, how could I make better choices in the future? How could I learn to say no to things I don't want to do? How could I create healthy boundaries in my life to protect what I hold dear? Why were dating and relationships so scary?

My theory is that when relationships (familial, friendship, or romantic) go bad, as so many did, when those we've trusted the most disappoint us, or hurt us, trash us, or betray us, it leaves a gaping hole in our hearts that seems nearly impossible to fix. Will these holes in our hearts be repaired? Will we learn to trust again? Will we get over the heartbreak and disappointment, and will we gain the courage to eventually let in someone new and risk vulnerability? Will we not let others intimidate us or belittle us and our rights to our own real and valuable feelings?

I was barely treading water in my life, increasingly losing my way. Crying almost nonstop. My profound question became this: How does one live one's life and stop treading water and find solid ground? I was lost. Adrift. I was missing someone. I was missing who I was. I was missing me. I could not see myself in the fog. I felt like a plane endlessly circling an airport without permission to land. I wanted to be *in* my world, not hovering *over* it. How could regain my clarity, sense of purpose, passion, and sense of direction, and rediscover myself?

My therapist, whom I have been faithfully seeing twice a month for many years and who has seen me in, through, and out of all of these relationships, is always the voice of reason and my constant cheerleader. She helps me sift through the shifting sand in my crazy head and make sense of it all, little by little. She helped me see that there is always a solution. There is always a way out. The choices might not be as desirable or easy as we would like, but they are there.

I think I've always been an intuitive person. Somehow, I can feel others' energy when they're angry or they're sad or they are happy. When I'm emotionally connected to a person and my happiness is wrapped up in my perception of them in our relationship, that clouds my ability to read them effectively because my own emotions get in the way. During the times when I have been emotionally desolate, I have turned that inwardly on myself, written endlessly in my journal so the empathy or intuition get coupled with my already active internal life. Over time, I'm able to see patterns in my behavior and analyze why I behave a certain way. With a little luck and a little bit of time, or a lot of time, I'm able to cognitively and logically get myself on a better path. Then, once things are calm, I can go back to being intuitive about things external to myself.

There have been many times in my life when I have felt clueless and alone or I have felt adrift and without direction, full of genuine confusion and genuine anxiety over an issue. That leads me to research and leads me to find professionals who can help me with those issues. I might seek a doctor, or a therapist, or an accountant, or an acupuncturist, or a massage therapist, or a stylist hairdresser, or a dietitian. Throughout my life, I have been aware that I needed to ask for help. I couldn't do *everything* on my own, even if I could do *many* things on my own. I sometimes still needed help, although it is, at times, difficult to ask for it. When I was a kid, I confided in teachers. Later, I confided in professors. I once had a psych professor give me therapy for free in her office hours when I was too distraught over family issues to focus on academics. I know when I have a problem and I don't procrastinate in finding a solution. I find a professional or a clinician and I seek the help.

Six memoirs written by six strong, brilliant women inspired me to write this memoir after years of procrastinating: Michelle Obama's *Becoming,* Tara Westover's *Educated,* Samantha Power's, *The Education of an Idealist,* Azar Nafisi's *Reading Lolita in Tehran,* Elizabeth Gilbert's *Eat, Pray, Love,* and Demi Moore's *Inside Out.* Each of these books shares the vibrant lives and courage of these women and their often heartbreaking and tumultuous experiences. Through their writing, I have come to realize that we all share experiences and truths as humans, as students of life, as vulnerable souls. These women all are vastly different from each other, and yet they've each burrowed directly to my heart. I have deeply felt what they had to say, which brought identification to my heart and tears to my eyes. Their candor in sharing the details of their lives encouraged me to tackle this memoir and made me realize that I, too, have something to say and share. I want to thank them for helping me find my own voice and for helping me learn to trust it.

I think it's important to immerse ourselves in whatever it is that we love. If you want to be a singer or a musician of any kind, immerse yourself in music. If you want to be a basketball player, immerse yourself in basketball strategies and dedicate your time to practice. Do you want to learn how to paint? Do you want to learn be a makeup artist? Do you want to learn how to write or dance? Do you want to learn how to skate? Do you want to earn your Ph.D.? Learning how to do anything is a marathon, not a sprint. Everything is a process, and everything must be learned over time. I think a lot of people have low frustration tolerance, a low attention span. They don't know how to be resilient, overcoming setbacks and challenges.

Focusing on long goals, and the smaller sub-goals along the way, as well as silencing our inner critics and ignoring judgmental others can go a long way toward creating a long view. As Brené Brown says, "if you are not in the arena also getting your arse kicked, I am not interested in your feedback."

In my past, I was easily bored and changed jobs often, but I was always looking for my passion and what gave me meaning. Being a curious, think-on-my-feet type of person, who is motivated to learn, solve problems, and overcome challenges, makes teaching the perfect fit for me. I may teach the same literature and assign the same types of writing assignments year after year, but the kids who sit in my classroom are different from those who came before, and therefore the whole experience is different, too. Each year in subtle ways and not-so-subtle ways, I'm also different, so the experience changes: every year and every day. All my previous jobs bored me to death in less than a year, but with teaching, it's been twenty-five years and I'm not bored yet.

Young people today—some of them, anyway—are missing work ethic and frustration tolerance. Because of the ubiquity of screens, videos, games and Googling, everything they want is instantaneously at their disposal. If you order something on Amazon, it can be at your house within hours. I think that we, as a society, have lost the idea that you must work for something. That things that are worthwhile, things that bring meaning into your life take a long time to achieve. If you get them too easily, you don't appreciate them.

Athletes, musicians, and artists get this concept because of the time and commitment it takes to excel at their passion. That may be one of the strategic reasons that athleticism, musicianship, and art are so important to schoolchildren of all ages—kindergarten through seniors, through college and beyond. Those endeavors reinforce the idea that you have to work hard for something over a long period to achieve some measure of success.

Throughout this journey of excavating my journals dating to 1983 and reliving my memories and experiences through an older and perhaps wiser set of eyes, I am struck by the shadows of behavioral patterns, of action borne of the pain and loneliness the younger me faced. She did this with more than her share of suffering and disillusionment, but also with a tenacity and courage that she didn't know she possessed. That *I* didn't know she possessed.

I feel dreadful for the pain, loneliness, and anguish of my younger self. She was lost. She thought she was powerless in her own life and felt unnoticed and forgotten, left behind as her parents focused on their own lives and rebuilt them. I had so much trouble moving on and dealing with my emptiness and fruitlessly went on so many dates looking for boyfriends, looking for love, connection, and a feeling of closeness.

I was looking for love outside myself because I learned to feel good about myself when others were happy with me, when I did nice things for them and took care of them. Smiling all the time, forcing myself to be happy became the way I coped. Maybe for a time I was addicted to the rush and the high of connection and sex, but I couldn't avoid the emptiness. Sex was sex, not love. Timing was off, and timing is everything. If anyone tells you it's not, they're lying. Inside felt unworthy and afraid of not finding connection with others, being excluded from love and belonging. The only place I confessed all my feelings, experiences, and judgments was in my journal. Nowhere else.

And while I feel bad for her and her pain and suffering, I also know, from the other side of the timeline, that she learned that her strength, resolve, compassion, and perseverance would get her through the toughest battles. That even if she had no one to count on but herself, she would prevail. She was strong enough to prevail.

My story is that of a not-so-ordinary ordinary woman from Long Island who faced her own personal dragons with courage and tenacity and in so doing became her own hero. She used the tools she bore deep in her psyche and combined them with intellectual discoveries, faithful advice, devoted companionship, and an extraordinary gift of hope to create a healthy, happy life. No ordinary accomplishment. And yet, it's a universal story, too.

We all either have those qualities or can cultivate them.

The heroes/heroines in fiction—short stories and novels—have struggled against external forces and their own personal demons to discover their authentic selves and build for themselves lives that made them happy and helped find meaning. As Paul Coelho shows us in *The Alchemist*, each person is continually on their own personal quest to live their own *personal truth*. I think finding one's own *personal truth* is something that happens throughout life and is constantly being refined and rediscovered.

Each experience we have and manage to survive shows us a new, refined, and stronger version of ourselves.

JOURNAL WITH ME

"The years go by. The time, it does fly. Every single second is a moment in time that passes. And it seems like nothing - but when you're looking back ... well, it amounts to everything."

—Ray Bradbury

I would like to invite you to do this personal journey to excavate your own path, dig out memories and phantoms from your own brains, and see how you can fit the pieces together and take the long view of your own life. In the companion journal book *Permission to Land: Personal Transformation Through Writing*, I provide you with inspiring writing prompts to trigger memories and give you the space in which to create your own written log of your life. It is a genuinely cathartic experience that will set you free from the demons that haunt you, at least in some respect and to some degree. It might just lighten your load, and who wouldn't want a lighter load to carry?

Let's write away the demons and write the memories into bloom. Let's write the joy, laughter, and the love. Let's set it all free into the universe, where it can call mingle and part the heavens. And in so doing, you will lighten your heart and free it from worry and the burden of carrying all those memories around. By sharing your life, or portions of it, you can allow your friends and family to get to know you on a deeper level, on a really human level, and not just as the way they currently see you now, whatever that is. We are all much deeper and much more hidden then we probably would be comfortable admitting and this process can open us up to ourselves as well.

Or, if you're not ready to share with others, you will simply fortify your relationship with yourself. What a gift that can be!

What else will you get out of it? Catharsis. Growth. Healing. A deeper sense of understanding of yourself. Please consider taking the journey. Encourage others to take this personal journey along with you. I'll meet you on the other side or walk with you hand-in-hand as you get there.

Purchase a book and register at https://marcibrockmann. com to receive your free downloadable copy of *Permission to Land: Personal Transformation Through Writing.*

CITATIONS

Alexander, E. *(2012)*. *Proof of Heaven: A Neurosurgeon's Journey into the Afterlife.* Simon and Schuster. United States.

Allen, R. & A. Stillman. *(1957)*. *Chances Are.* (Song). Columbia. United States.

Awdry, R.W. *(2015)*. *Thomas the Tank.* Random House Books for Young Readers. United States.

Badham, J. (Director). (1983). *War Games.* (Motion Picture). United States. United Artists.

Bart, L. (1960). *Oliver.* (Play). West End. London, UK.

Bennett, H. (Producer). (1974-78). *The Six Million Dollar Man.* (Television Series). United States. Harve Bennett Productions, Silverton Productions, Universal Television.

Berlin, I. *(1925)*. *Always.* (Song). Verve. United States.

Bock, J. & S. Harnick. (1964). *Sunrise, Sunset.* (Song). Fiddler on the Roof. United States. Gannon, K. & W. Kent. (1943). *I'll be home for Christmas.* (Song). Decca Records. United States.

Bridwell, N. *(2010)*. *Clifford the Big Red Dog,* Cartwheel Books. United States.

Brockmann, M. (2015). *Saying Goodbye to Our Childhood Home.* www.elephantjournal.com.

Brooks, A. (Director). *Definitely, Maybe.* (2008). (Motion Picture). United States. Universal Pictures.

Brown, B. (2017). *Braving the Wilderness: The Quest for True Belonging and the Courage to Stand Alone.* Random House. United States.

Brown, B. (2018). *Dare to Lead: Brave Work. Tough Conversations. Whole Hearts.* Random House. United States.

Brown, B. (2015). *Daring Greatly: How the Courage to Be Vulnerable Transforms the Way We Live, Love, Parent, and Lead.* Avery. United States.

Brown, B. *(2017). Rising Strong as a Spiritual Practice.* Audible Audiobook. United States.

Brown, B. (2010). *The Gifts of Imperfection: Let Go of Who You Think You're Supposed to Be and Embrace Who You Are.* Hazelden Publishing. United States.

Brown, B. *The Power of Vulnerability: Teachings of Authenticity, Connection, and Courage.* (Audiobook). True Sounds Audio. United States.

Brown, B. (2013). *Why Your Critics aren't the Ones Who Count.* www.HabitsforWellBeing.com. United States.

Coehlo, P. (2006). *The Alchemist.* Harper One. United States.

Cosby, A. & J. Paglia. (Creators). (2006-12). *Eureka.* (Television Series). United States. NBC Universal Television.

Crane, D. & M. Kauffman. (Creators). (1994- 2004). *Friends.* (Television Series). United States. Bright/Kaufman/ Crane Productions.

Emerson, R. W. (2010). *Self-Reliance and Other Essays.* Nashville, TN: American Renaissance. United States.

Ephron, N & D. *(2008). Love, Loss, and What I Wore.* (Play). New York, United States.

Etheridge, M. (1988). *Chrome Plated Heart.* (Song). Island. United States.

Fitzgerald, F. S. *(1925). The Great Gatsby.* Charles Scribner's Sons. United States.

Fleming, V. & G. Cukor. (Directors). (1939). *Wizard of Oz.* (Motion Picture). United States. Columbia Pictures.

Forster, M. (Director). *(2006). Stranger Than Fiction.* (Motion Picture). United States. Columbia Pictures.

Gelbart, L. (Creator). (1972-83). *MASH.* (Television Series). United States. 20ᵗʰ Century Fox Television.

Gilbert, E. (2007). *Eat, Pray, Love: One Woman's Search for Everything Across Italy, India and Indonesia.* Riverhead Books. United States.

Grey, J. (2019). *Fiddler on the Roof (in Yiddish).* (Play). New York, United States.

Hahn, T.N. (2012). *The Pocket Thich Nhat Hanh.* Shambhala Pocket Classics.

Hammerstein II. O. (1943). *Oklahoma.* (Play). New York, United States.

Herman, J. (1964). *Hello Dolly.* (Play). New York, United States.

Holyfield, W. (Songwriter). (1980). *Can I Have This Dance.* (Song). Capitol. United States.

Hughes, J. (Director). (1985). *The Breakfast Club.* (Motion Picture). United States. Universal Pictures.

Hughes, J. (Director). (1986). *Ferris Bueller's Day Off.* (Motion Picture). United States. Paramount Pictures.

James, H. *(1878). Daisy Miller.* Harper and Brothers Books. United Kingdom.

Jewison, N. (Director). (1971). *Fiddler on the Roof.* (Motion Picture). United States. The Mirisch Production Company

Johnson, K. (Creator). (1976-78). *The Bionic Woman.* (Television Series). United States. Harve Bennett Productions, Silverton Productions, Universal Television.

Jones, D. *(2015). The 36 questions that lead to love.* New York Times. United States.

Joyce. R. *(2013). The Unlikely Pilgrimage of Harold Frye.* Random House Trade paperbacks. United Kingdom.

Kamakawiwo'ole. (1983). *Somewhere Over the Rainbow.* (Song). Mountain Apple Company, United States.

Kauffman, M. & H. J. Morris. (2015 -). *Grace and Frankie.* (Television Series). United States. Skydance Media. Skydance Television.

Kelley, D. E. (Creator). (1997-2002). *Ally McBeal.* (Television Series). United States. 20th Century Fox Television.

Lear, N. (Creator). (1971-79). *All in the Family.* (Television Series). United States. Tandem Productions.

Lear, N., D. Nicholl & M. Ross. (Creators). (1975-85). *The Jeffersons.* (Television Series). United States. Embassy Television.

Lee, H. *(1960). To Kill a Mockingbird.* J. B. Lippincott & Co. United States.

Lewis, W. (2009). The Buddhist View of Loneliness as a Good Thing. *Elephant Journal.* United States.

Lucas, G. (Director). (1977). *Star Wars: A New Hope.* (Motion Picture). United States. Lucas Films.

Luketic, R. (Director). *(2001). Legally Blonde.* (Motion Picture). United States. Metro-Goldwyn-Mayer.

Meyer, S. (2008). *The Host.* Little Brown & Company. United States.

Meyer, S. (2007). *Twilight* (series). Little Brown & Company for Young Readers. United States.

Meyers. N. (Director). *(2006).* The *Holiday.* (Motion Picture). United States. Columbia Pictures, Universal Pictures.

Michaelson, I. (2008). *You and I.* (Song). Cabin 24. United States.

Miller, A. *(1953). The Crucible.* Penguin Books. United States.

Miller, M. (2016). *The Divine Feminine.* (Album). REMember Music, Warner. United States.

MobileReference. (2008). *Moll Flanders*: by Daniel Defoe. Boston: MobileReference.com. United Kingdom.

Moore, D. (2019). *Inside Out: A Memoir.* Harper Audio. United States.

Morrison, J. (1971). *Riders on the Storm.* (Song). Elektra. United States.

Moyes, J. (2012). *Me Before You.* Penguin Audio. United Kingdom.

Nabakov, V. *(1959). Lolita.* Olympia Press. Paris, France.

Nafisi, A. (2008). *Reading Lolita in Tehran.* Random House Trade paperbacks. United States.

Newman, S. (2005). *Dr. Who.* (Television Series). UK and Canada. Sydney Film School.

Obama, M. (2019). *Becoming.* Random House Audio. United States.

Palmer, A. (2014). *The Art of Asking: or How I learned to Stop Worrying and Let People Help.* London, United Kingdom: Piatkus.

Pierson, F. (Director). (1976). *A Star is Born.* (Motion Picture). United States. Barwood Films

Potok, C. *(1987). The Chosen.* Fawcett. United States.

Power, S. (2019). *The Education of an Idealist.* Harper Audio. United States.

Raffi. *(1994). Bananaphone.* (Song). MCA Records Rounder. United States.

Roddam, F. (Director). (1998). *Moby Dick.* (Television Series). United States. American Zoetrope.

Silver, J.M. (Director). (1988). *Crossing Delancey.* (Motion Picture). United States. Warner Brothers.

Schneider, D. (Creator). (2004-07). *Drake and Josh.* (Television Series). United States. Nickelodeon Productions.

Schwartz, S. (1972). *Pippin.* (Play). New York, United States.

Shaiman, M. & S. Wittman. (2012). *Mr. & Mrs. Smith.* (Song). Columbia. United States.

Sherman-Palladino, A. (Creator). (2000-07). *The Gilmore Girls.* (Television Series). United States. Dorothy Parker Drank Here Productions, Warner Brothers.

Sherman-Palladino, A. (Creator). (2017-). *The Marvelous Mrs. Maisel.* (Television Series). United States. Amazon Studios.

Springer, J. (Host). (1991-). *Jerry Springer.* (Television Series). United States. Multimedia Entertainment, Inc.

Stewart, M. (1960). *Bye Bye Birdie.* (Play). New York, United States.

Streisand, B. (Director). *(1983).* Yentl. Ladbroke, (Motion Picture). United States. Barwood Films, United Artists.

Thoreau, H. D., & Carew, T. (1854). *Walden, or, Life in the woods.* Boston: Ticknor and Fields. United States.

Valastro, B. (Producer). (2009 -). *Cake Boss.* (Television Series). United States. High Noon Entertainment.

Walker, A. (1982). *The Color Purple*, Harcourt Brace Jovanovich. United States.

Watterson, B. *(2005).* The Complete Calvin and Hobbes. Andrews McMeel Publishing. United States.

Webber, A. L., C. Hart & R. Stilgoe. *(1986).* All I Ask of You. (Song). Phantom of the Opera. London, UK.

Webber, A. L., C. Hart & R. Stilgoe. (1986). *Phantom of the Opera.* (Play). London, UK.

Westover, T. (2018). *Educated,* Random House. United States.

Wyler, W. (Director). (1968). *Funny Girl.* (Motion Picture). United States. Columbia Pictures.

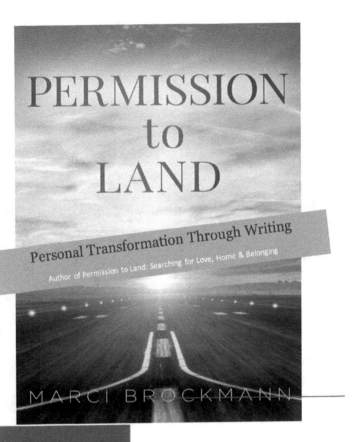

PERMISSION
to
LAND

Personal Transformation Through Writing

Author of Permission to Land: Searching for Love, Home & Belonging

MARCI BROCKMANN

MarciBrockmann.com

ORIGINAL PAINTINGS, CUSTOM PRINTS, SILKY SCARVES

Beautiful art for every décor!

Buy art from living artists
the dead ones don't need the money

www.MarciBrockmann.com.

Original paintings.   Custom prints.   Gorgeous scarves.

CPSIA information can be obtained
at www.ICGtesting.com
Printed in the USA
BVHW080828150720
583537BV00006B/12/J